"In his latest book, Paul Copan strides bold   en, fearlessly confronting some of the most diffi   is- tian Scriptures, and the faith built upon them   ls with these complex and sensitive issues so c   ...ᵤ same time, in such clear and approachable language. His uᵥ.ᵤᵤse of the biblical God is learned, courageous, and convincing."

—**Philip Jenkins**, Edwin Erle Sparks Professor of Humanities, Baylor University

"This is the book I wish I had written myself. It is simply the best book I have read that tackles the many difficulties that the Old Testament presents to thinking and sensitive Christians and that give such ammunition to the opponents of all religious faith. Paul Copan writes in such a simple, straightforward way, yet covers enormous issues comprehensively and with reassuring biblical detail and scholarly research. Use this book to stock your mind with gracious but factual answers in those awkward conversations. Better still, give it to those who are swayed by the shallow prejudice of popular atheism without reading the Bible for themselves. I strongly recommend this book. We have wanted and needed it for a long time."

—**Christopher J. H. Wright**, international director, Langham Partnership In- ternational; author of *Old Testament Ethics for the People of God*

"The New Atheists have attacked the morality of the Old Testament with a vengeance. In honesty, many Christians will confess that they struggle with what looks like a primitive and barbaric ethic. Paul Copan helps us truly understand the world of the Old Testament and how it relates to us today. I recommend this book for all who want to make sense of the Old Testament."

—**Tremper Longman III**, Robert H. Gundry Professor of Biblical Studies, Westmont College

"Lucid, lively, and very well informed, this book is the best defense of Old Testament ethics that I have read. A must-read for all preachers and Bible study leaders."

—**Gordon Wenham**, emeritus professor of Old Testament, University of Gloucestershire

"Paul Copan is the nation's leading apologist regarding problems with the biblical text, and *Is God a Moral Monster?* is vintage Copan. He takes on current New Atheist biblical critics and powerfully addresses virtually every criticism they have raised. I know of no other book like this one, and it should be required reading in college and seminary courses on biblical introduction."

—**J. P. Moreland**, distinguished professor of philosophy, Talbot School of Theology, and author of *The God Question*

"Most Christians today, myself included, are in dialogue with people we love who have been heavily swayed by the criticisms of Richard Dawkins, et al., against the morality of the Bible and its depiction of a horrific Yahweh God. What struck me in reading *Is God a Moral Monster?* is the degree to which we as Christians need to rethink in radical ways our reading and understanding of the sacred text if we are to have any persuasive reasoning in this ongoing exchange. Sometimes the real monster lies not so much in criticisms from 'without' as in our own holding to certain incorrect paradigms of thinking about the Bible. Aside from the apologetic importance of Professor Copan's work, of far greater value for Christians is the way in which his book forces us to reevaluate the very nature of the God we worship. Read this book. It will awaken your vision of God in wonderful ways!"

—**William J. Webb**, professor of New Testament, Heritage Theological Seminary, and author of *Slaves, Women, and Homosexuals*

"The most difficult questions that can be asked about Scripture include a list of ethical challenges to several Old Testament texts and teachings. These issues have been taken up with more fervor of late, owing to the growing popularity of radical atheism and skepticism. There's virtually no scholar I'd rather read on these subjects than Paul Copan. Building on his earlier research, Paul launches here into a treatment of a detailed list of such challenges, including the so-called genocidal conquest of Canaan. This handbook of responses to these and other tough ethical issues is able to both diminish the rhetoric as well as alleviate many concerns. I recommend this volume heartily."

—**Gary R. Habermas**, distinguished research professor, Liberty University and Seminary

"In a civil and reasoned manner, Paul Copan leads us through the wilderness of challenges to the God and the message of the Old Testament. By amassing and clearly expressing arguments with awareness of the ancient Near Eastern cultural context and of the Hebrew text of the Bible, the author presents a thorough treatment of key issues. This is essential and fascinating reading for anyone engaged in the 'New Atheism' debate."

—**Richard S. Hess**, Earl S. Kalland Professor of Old Testament and Semitic Languages, Denver Seminary

"Paul Copan has done an outstanding job of explaining some of the most confusing and puzzling issues that emerge from the pages of the Old Testament. He engages with a myriad of serious philosophical and moral challenges to the portrayal of God in the Old Testament, and he answers these challenges adroitly with clear and easy-to-understand explanations from the biblical texts themselves. This is a very readable book, and it will be a valuable resource for all Christians who desire to understand the Old Testament in today's context. I heartily recommend it!"

—**J. Daniel Hays**, professor of biblical studies, Ouachita Baptist University

Is God
a Moral
Monster?

Other Books by Paul Copan

Creation Out of Nothing: A Biblical, Philosophical, and Scientific Exploration (coauthored with William Lane Craig)

"How Do You Know You're Not Wrong?": Responding to Objections That Leave Christians Speechless

Loving Wisdom: Christian Philosophy of Religion

"That's Just Your Interpretation": Responding to Skeptics Who Challenge Your Faith

"True for You, but Not for Me": Deflating the Slogans That Leave Christians Speechless

When God Goes to Starbucks: A Guide to Everyday Apologetics

Will the Real Jesus Please Stand Up? A Debate between William Lane Craig and John Dominic Crossan (editor)

For other edited books as well as articles and essays by Paul Copan, go to www.paulcopan.com.

Is God
a Moral
Monster?

MAKING SENSE OF
THE OLD TESTAMENT GOD

Paul Copan

BakerBooks

a division of Baker Publishing Group
Grand Rapids, Michigan

© 2011 by Paul Copan

Published by Baker Books
a division of Baker Publishing Group
P.O. Box 6287, Grand Rapids, MI 49516-6287
www.bakerbooks.com

Printed in the United States of America

Library of Congress Cataloging-in-Publication Data
Copan, Paul.
    Is God a moral monster? : making sense of the Old Testament God / Paul Copan.
        p.   cm.
    Includes bibliographical references (p.   ).
    ISBN 978-0-8010-7275-8 (pbk.)
    1. Ethics in the Bible. 2. Bible. O.T.—Theology. 3. Apologetics. I. Title.
BS1199.E8C67 2011
239'.7—dc22   2010033473

18   19   20   14   13   12   11

To our excellent son Peter,
Who, to our delight, has grown in wisdom and stature
and in favor with God and men;
Full of good humor,
thoughtful conversation, and passion for God's kingdom—
A source of immense blessing from the Lord,
to our family and many others.

Contents

Introduction   11

Part 1   Neo-Atheism

1   Who Are the New Atheists?   15

2   The New Atheists and the Old Testament God   20

Part 2   God: Gracious Master or Moral Monster?

3   Great Appetite for Praise and Sacrifices? Divine Arrogance or Humility?   27

4   Monumental Rage and Kinglike Jealousy? Understanding the Covenant-Making God   34

5   Child Abuse and Bullying? God's Ways and the Binding of Isaac   42

Part 3   Life in the Ancient Near East and in Israel

6   God's Timeless Wisdom? Incremental Steps for Hardened Hearts   57

7   The Bible's Ubiquitous Weirdness? Kosher Foods, Kooky Laws? (I)   70

8   The Bible's Ubiquitous Weirdness? Kosher Foods, Kooky Laws? (II)   79

  9 Barbarisms, Crude Laws, and Other Imaginary Crimes?
      Punishments and Other Harsh Realities in Perspective   87

 10 Misogynistic? Women in Israel   101

 11 Bride-Price? Polygamy, Concubinage, and Other Such
      Questions   110

 12 Warrant for Trafficking in Humans as Farm Equipment? (I): Slavery
      in Israel   124

 13 Warrant for Trafficking in Humans as Farm Equipment? (II):
      Challenging Texts on Slavery   135

 14 Warrant for Trafficking in Humans as Farm Equipment? (III):
      Slavery in the New Testament   150

 15 Indiscriminate Massacre and Ethnic Cleansing? The Killing of the
      Canaanites (I)   158

 16 Indiscriminate Massacre and Ethnic Cleansing? The Killing of the
      Canaanites (II)   169

 17 Indiscriminate Massacre and Ethnic Cleansing? The Killing of the
      Canaanites (III)   186

 18 The Root of All Evil? Does Religion Cause Violence?   198

Part 4 Sharpening the Moral Focus

 19 Morality without a Lawgiving God? The Divine Foundation of
      Goodness   209

 20 We Have Moved beyond This God (Haven't We?): Jesus as the
      Fulfiller of the Old Testament   216

      Discussion/Study Questions   223

      Notes   235

Introduction

Tackling Old Testament ethics is a challenge. Besides a lot of territory to cover, the ancient Near East seems so strange and even otherworldly! We need a good bit of background discussion to help make better sense of this world and of certain Old Testament texts.

Old Testament ethics is one hot topic, and it creates all kinds of reactions—from bewilderment and confusion to anger and outpourings of hostility. I've sensed the need for an accessible, less-lengthy book on this topic. Though I've done scattered writing on Old Testament ethics in various books and articles, I wanted not only to expand on these themes but also to add a good deal of new material. In this case, I'm killing two birds with one stone—not only tackling a tough subject but also using the New Atheism movement as a springboard for discussion.

As this book is supposed to be reasonably popular-level,[1] I started out with the goal of keeping endnotes to a minimum, but to no avail. Given the nature of this topic, I didn't want to appear to make claims without some scholarly justification! Along these lines, let me add that my research carefully follows reputable scholars in Old Testament studies. A good number of them assume a high view of Scripture's authority, while others don't. This book's perspective represents a *broad general agreement* on the main issues I cover. The Old Testament world and literature have their share of murkiness and mystery. So while I might cite scholar X and scholar Y about this or that point in my book, an equally reputable scholar Z may quibble with them (and me!). I don't want to get sidetracked by detailing all the reasons, pro and con, taken by all sides concerning the various Old Testament ethics topics I discuss. My chief point is this: I am basing my work on thoughtful, credible scholarship that offers plausible, sober-minded explanations and angles that present helpful resolutions and responses to perplexing Old Testament ethics questions.

Another key issue is the relevance of the Old Testament in today's world. I'll mention at various points how the Old Testament applies (or doesn't apply) to Christians, although I can't go into a lot of detail. Unlike national Israel, God's people—the new and true Israel—are an interethnic church with a heavenly citizenship. This heavenly citizenship must be of earthly good, however. Christ's disciples are to live out God's kingdom values, being salt and light and doers of good. The Christian faith has this-worldly implications. If it doesn't, it's not Christian; rather, it's a detached Gnosticism that ignores culture and ultimately denies reality.

The people of God are no longer national, ethnic Israel, whose homeland is in the Middle East. As the New Testament makes clear, the interethnic Christian community is the true circumcision in Christ whose citizenship is heavenly and who stand in a new relation to the Mosaic law. The law is a part of our heritage and self-understanding, even if a good deal of it doesn't directly apply to the people of God.

Others have ably shown how the Old Testament should impact Christians: Christopher Wright, William Webb, John Goldingay, Gordon Wenham, Richard Hess, and others. So throughout the book I refer readers to their writings and insights.

I hope and pray that this book will address a vital need in the Christian community, which is often perplexed and sometimes immobilized by these difficult Old Testament texts. In order to facilitate the "digestion process" of this material, I've included in the back of the book a study guide for small group discussion in adult Sunday school classes, Bible study groups, and university campus groups.

I would like to thank Richard Hess, Richard Davidson, Tremper Longman, Jerome Walsh, Daniel Hays, and John Goldingay in particular for their comments. I'm grateful for their display of remarkable Christian charity as they've responded—sometimes at great length—to emails I've written over the past year or so.[2] Thanks to Barna Magyarosi for furnishing me with a copy of his dissertation on "holy war." Thanks too to my colleague Nathan Lane, who made helpful comments on the manuscript.

I'm grateful to my editor Bob Hosack at Baker for his friendship over the years. Thanks too to project editor Wendy Wetzel for her labors and graciousness in working with all of my unscheduled updates and corrections. As ever, many thanks to my wonderfully encouraging and supportive wife and children; they bring immense joy.

PART 1

Neo-Atheism

1

Who Are the New Atheists?

In February 2007, I was one of several plenary speakers at the Greer-Heard Forum, an annual conference held in New Orleans. This year the topic was "The Future of Atheism."[1] One featured speaker on the orthodox Christian side was British theologian Alister McGrath. The other far-from-orthodox speaker was Daniel Dennett, the naturalistic evolutionist and philosopher of mind from Tufts University.

This was the first opportunity I had to meet one of the "New Atheists." My wife and I enjoyed chatting with Dan at meals, and, as his room was right across the hall from ours, we interacted during our comings and goings over the weekend. Dan is a witty, engaging conversationalist with a pleasant life-of-the-party demeanor. His Santa-like face and beard only add to the conviviality.

As a "New Atheist," Dan is one of several God-deniers writing bestsellers these days. Some have called him one of the "four horsemen"—along with Richard Dawkins, Sam Harris, and Christopher Hitchens—of the Neo-atheistic apocalypse. What's so *new* about this New Atheism? Hasn't atheism been around from ancient times? Yes. For example, the pleasure-promoting Epicurus (341–270 BC) and his later admirer Lucretius (94–54 BC) were materialists; that is, they believed that matter is all there is. If deities exist, they're irrelevant. And when you die, that's it—over and out.

In more recent history, we've had "newer" atheists across the modern and contemporary philosophical landscape—from Karl Marx, Friedrich Nietzsche, Jean-Paul Sartre, and Bertrand Russell to Thomas Nagel, John Searle, Keith Parsons, Graham Oppy, and William Rowe. Atheism is certainly alive and kicking. As we'll see, the New Atheists add, shall we say, "spice" to the God discussion.

The New Face of Atheism

In the eyes of many, the Christian faith has an image problem. Many unchurched persons have been turned off to "Christianity"—though not necessarily to Jesus. They don't like politicized religion in America, along with what they see as ample Christian arrogance, hypocrisy, judgmentalism, and disconnectedness from the real world.[2] The perceptions of church outsiders are obviously not totally accurate, but they can often provide an illuminating corrective to help professing Christians to properly align themselves with Jesus their Master.

Due in large part to the September 11, 2001, terrorist attacks on the Pentagon and the Twin Towers, the New Atheists have capitalized on evil done "in the name of religion" to tar all things religious with the same brush. (Of course "religion" is notoriously difficult to define, but the New Atheists aren't into making nuanced distinctions here.) Neo-atheists are riding the crest of this new wave, capitalizing on the West's increasingly "post-Christian" status. This current tide of emboldened opposition to the Christian faith lumps Christianity into the same category as radical Islam. Neo-atheists are the new public, popular face of atheism—a topic no longer seemingly limited to ivory tower academics.

Not that the New Atheists have convinced everyone. According to the eminent sociologist Rodney Stark,[3] the New Atheists are making a big media splash and have had several bestsellers to their credit. Many have interpreted this as a sign that multitudes of Americans are ready to renounce God publicly. But for most people, saying they have no religion just means they have no church—not that they're irreligious. The number of atheists in America in recent history has remained fairly consistent. According to Gallup polls, 4 percent of Americans were atheists back in 2007—the same percentage as in 1944! Rumors of God's death have been greatly exaggerated. And when we look at the non-Western world, people are becoming Christians in record numbers. The Christian faith is the fastest-growing movement around, often accompanied by signs and wonders, as Penn State historian Philip Jenkins has ably documented.[4]

Whether from atheists or theists, we are seeing something of an all-around consensus about the Neo-atheists' arguments. *First, for all their emphasis on cool-headed, scientific rationality, they express themselves not just passionately but angrily.* Rodney Stark describes them as "angry and remarkably nasty atheists." Christian thinker Michael Novak, author of the thought-provoking book *No One Sees God*, comments about the Neo-atheists' writings that there's "an odd defensiveness about all these books—as though they were a sign not of victory but of desperation."[5]

Dennett tends to be more measured in his criticism of religion. He thinks the jury's still out on whether religion's benefits outweigh its deficits—unlike other New Atheists, who insist that religion without exception is downright *dangerous*. But even so, he doesn't always fairly engage the opposition by his selective quoting.[6] And he's bestowed the name "brights" on the atheistically minded—with a not-so-flattering implication for theists!

The New Atheists are right to point out that manifestations of ignorance, immorality, and hypocrisy characterize professing religious believers of all stripes. In Matthew 7:15–23, Jesus himself warned about morally bankrupt false prophets; they wear sheep's clothing to cover their wolflike interior. They do outwardly pious acts but are ultimately judged to be "evildoers" (NIV). This is tragic, though anticipated by Jesus and the lot of New Testament authors. And, of course, the discerning person will recognize that Jesus shouldn't be blamed because of the abuses of his professed followers.

Second, the Neo-atheists' arguments against God's existence are surprisingly flimsy, often resembling the simplistic village atheist far more than the credentialed academician. The Neo-atheists are often profoundly ignorant of what they criticize, and they typically receive the greatest laughs and cheers from the philosophically and theologically challenged. True, they effectively utilize a combination of emotion and verbal rhetoric, but they aren't known for logically carrying thoughts through from beginning to end. Their arguments against God's existence aren't intellectually rigorous—although they want to give that impression. Yes, they'll raise some important questions concerning, for example, the problem of evil, but again, their arguments are a collage of rhetorical barbs that don't really form a coherent argument. I've observed that while these men do have expertise in certain fields (biology and evolutionary theory in the case of Dawkins and Dennett), they turn out to be fairly disappointing when arguing against God's existence or Christian doctrine. And a quick check of Dawkins's documentation reveals a lot more time spent on Google than at Oxford University's Bodleian Library.[7]

Pulitzer Prize–winning journalist Chris Hedges is the author of *I Don't Believe in Atheists* and certainly no friend of conservative Christians. He chastises Sam Harris for his "facile attack on a form of religious belief we all hate" and "his childish simplicity and ignorance of world affairs." The Christian can rightly join Hedges and the New Atheists' disgust at "the chauvinism, intolerance, anti-intellectualism and self-righteousness of religious fundamentalists" without buying into their arguments.[8] Rodney Stark puts it this way: "To expect to learn anything about important theological problems from Richard Dawkins or Daniel Dennett is like expecting to learn about medieval history from someone who had only read *Robin Hood*."[9]

Yes, it's easy to attack a caricature with emotionalism and simplistic slogans. So with the New Atheists "going village" on us, this makes it hard to have a decent conversation. What has amazed me is that so many have been intellectually swindled by such fallacious argumentation and blustery rhetoric.

Don't just take it from me. The atheist philosopher of science Michael Ruse says that Dawkins's arguments are so bad that he's *embarrassed* to call himself an atheist.[10] Terry Eagleton, an English literature and cultural theory professor, severely criticizes "Ditchkins"—his composite name for Dawkins and Hitchens. He considers them to be both out of their depth and misrepresenters of the Christian faith: "they invariably come up with vulgar caricatures of religious faith that would make a first-year theology student wince. The more they detest religion, the more ill-informed their criticisms of it tend to be."[11]

In a book I coedited with fellow philosopher William Lane Craig, he wrote an essay titled "Dawkins's Delusion," which responds to Dawkins's book *The God Delusion*. Craig does his best to piece together Dawkins's argument against God's existence, which is really "embarrassingly weak." At the end of his essay, Craig writes:

> Several years ago my atheist colleague Quentin Smith unceremoniously crowned Stephen Hawking's argument against God in *A Brief History of Time* as "the worst atheistic argument in the history of Western thought."[12] With the advent of *The God Delusion* the time has come, I think, to relieve Hawking of this weighty crown and to recognize Richard Dawkins' accession to the throne.[13]

Third, the New Atheists aren't willing to own up to atrocities committed in the name of atheism by Stalin, Pol Pot, or Mao Zedong, yet they expect Christians to own up to all barbarous acts performed in Jesus's name. In one debate, Dennett refused to connect Stalin's brutality and inhumanity with his hard-core atheism. In fact, he claimed that Stalin was a kind of "religious" figure![14] In September 2009, I attended a debate between Hitchens and Dinesh D'Souza in Orlando. Hitchens refused to admit that Stalin killed "in the name of atheism." Somehow Stalin, who had once attended a Russian Orthodox seminary but later came to convincingly repudiate Christianity, was still "religious" after all. Yet Hitchens insisted that a religious residue still stayed with him. So atheism wasn't the culprit. Yet in another debate, Hitchens was pressed to make the seemingly rare confession: "It has to be said that some of my non-believing forbears seized the opportunity to behave the same way [as immoral religious persons], sure."[15]

I think the reason it's difficult, if not impossible, for these New Atheists to acknowledge immorality in the name of atheism is because it would take much wind out of their sails when criticizing religion. If we'd stop to ask, "Would Jesus approve of the Inquisition or persecuting Jews?" the question answers itself. As a counterillustration, what about serial murderer and cannibal Jeffrey Dahmer? Dahmer reasoned, "If it all happens naturalistically, what's the need for a God? Can't I set my own rules? Who owns me? I own myself."[16] He wondered, if there's no God and we all just came "from the slime," then "what's the point of trying to modify your behavior to keep it within acceptable ranges?"[17]

The reverse side of the coin is New Atheists' refusal (or great reluctance) to acknowledge the profound, well-documented positive influence of Christian faith in the world. This list of contributions includes preserving literature, advancing education, laying the foundations of modern science, cultivating art and music, promoting human rights and providing better working conditions for persons, and overthrowing slavery. These contributions are acknowledged by atheists and theists alike. For the New Atheists, religion poisons everything, and atheism poisons nothing!

We'll come back to this later. But for now I'm just registering my complaint.

One Unaddressed Area

Despite the strong intellectual response to New Atheism, one area left unaddressed is that of Old Testament ethics. In some ways, this topic is probably most deserving of our attention and clarification. The New Atheists commonly raise questions about strange and harsh Old Testament laws, a God of jealousy and anger, slavery, and the killing of the Canaanites—and that's just the beginning of the list. Not only this, but they're usually just as simplistic and uninformed here as in their general attacks on religion.

As I've done some writing in this area, I wanted to use the New Atheists' critiques as a springboard to clarify and iron out misunderstandings and misrepresentations. It's not an easy area to cover, as the ancient Near East is a world that often seems so bizarre to us. As we explore some of the main criticisms of Old Testament ethics (we can't cover them all here), hopefully we'll gain a new appreciation for what is going on in the Old Testament, especially when we compare it to other ancient Near East cultures.

Further Reading

Copan, Paul, and William Lane Craig. *Contending with Christianity's Critics: Answering New Atheists and Other Objectors*. Nashville: B & H Academic, 2009.

Ganssle, Greg. *A Reasonable God: Engaging the New Face of Atheism*. Waco: Baylor University Press, 2009.

McGrath, Alister. *The Dawkins Delusion*. Downers Grove, IL: InterVarsity, 2007.

Meister, Chad, and William Lane Craig, eds. *God Is Great, God Is Good: Why Believing in God Is Reasonable and Responsible*. Downers Grove, IL: InterVarsity, 2009.

2

The New Atheists
and the Old Testament God

As I write this book, the Neo-atheists are not quite as cutting edge as they once were. They're so 2006! Yet they dig up the dirt on many perennial Old Testament ethical challenges, and Bible believers shouldn't shove them under their holy rugs. As people of the Book, Christians should honestly reflect on such matters. Unfortunately, most pastors and Christian leaders are reluctant to tackle such subjects, and the results are fairly predictable. When uninformed Christians are challenged about these texts, they may be rattled in their faith.

The ancient heretic Marcion rejected the seemingly harsh Creator and God of the Israelites for a New Testament God of love—a heavenly Father. Likewise, the New Atheists aren't too impressed with Yahweh—one of the Hebrew names for God in the Old Testament.[1] Christopher Hitchens's book title expresses it: *God Is Not Great*. This is in contrast to the Muslim's call, *Allahu akbar*, "God is great(er)." Richard Dawkins calls God a "moral monster." As we read the New Atheists, we can compile quite a catalog of alleged offenses. Let's start with Dawkins and work our way down the list.

Dawkins deems God's commanding Abraham to sacrifice Isaac (see Gen. 22) to be "disgraceful" and tantamount to "child abuse and bullying." Moreover, this God breaks into a "monumental rage whenever his chosen people flirted with a rival god," resembling "nothing so much as sexual jealousy of the worst kind." Add to this the killing of the Canaanites—an "ethnic cleansing" in which "bloodthirsty massacres" were carried out with "xenophobic relish."

Joshua's destruction of Jericho is "morally indistinguishable from Hitler's invasion of Poland, or Saddam Hussein's massacres of the Kurds and the Marsh Arabs." This is just one example of why religion is, as Dawkins's 2006 BBC documentary phrases it, "the root of all evil."[2]

To make matters worse, Dawkins points out the "ubiquitous weirdness of the Bible." Many biblical characters engaged in morally scummy acts. Here's a sampling:

- A drunken Lot was seduced by his recently widowed daughters, who eventually bore his children (Gen. 19:31–36).
- Abraham gave a repeat performance of lying about his wife (Gen. 12:18–19; 20:1–13).
- Jephthah made a foolish vow that resulted in his daughter being sacrificed as a burnt offering (Judg. 11).
- David power-raped Bathsheba and engaged in murderous treachery toward her husband, Uriah—one of David's loyal "mighty men" (2 Sam. 11; 23:39).[3]

We can add more to the list. Dawkins's most notable description of Yahweh is this one:

> The God of the Old Testament is arguably the most unpleasant character in all fiction: jealous and proud of it; a petty, unjust, unforgiving control-freak; a vindictive, bloodthirsty ethnic cleanser; a misogynistic, homophobic, racist, infanticidal, genocidal, filicidal, pestilential, megalomaniacal, sadomasochistic, capriciously malevolent bully.[4]

Then there's Dan Dennett. He declares that the "Old Testament Jehovah" is simply a super-*man* who "could take sides in battles, and be both jealous and wrathful." He happens to be more forgiving and loving in the New Testament. Dennett adds, "Part of what makes Jehovah such a fascinating participant in stories of the Old Testament is His kinglike jealousy and pride, and His great appetite for praise and sacrifices. But we have moved beyond this God (haven't we?)." He thanks "heaven" that those thinking blasphemy or adultery deserves capital punishment are a "dwindling minority."[5]

Christopher Hitchens (who at the time of this writing is grappling with esophogeal cancer and for whom many of us are praying) voices similar complaints. Chapter 7 of *God Is Not Great* is titled "Revelation: The Nightmare of the Old Testament," noting God's "unalterable laws." The forgotten Canaanites were "pitilessly driven out of their homes to make room for the ungrateful and mutinous children of Israel." Moreover, the Old Testament contains "a warrant for trafficking in humans, for ethnic cleansing, for slavery, for bride-price, and for indiscriminate massacre, but we are not bound by any of it because it was put together by crude, uncultured human animals." And the Ten Commandments are "proof that religion is manmade." For one thing, you don't need God to tell you that murder is wrong; this information is available to all humans.[6]

Sam Harris similarly chimes in. His *Letter to a Christian Nation* deliberately sets out to "demolish the intellectual and moral pretensions of Christianity in its most committed forms." If the Bible is true, then we should be stoning people to death for heresy, adultery, homosexuality, worshiping graven images, and "other imaginary crimes." In fact, putting to death idolaters in our midst (see Deut. 13:6–15) reflects "God's timeless wisdom."[7]

In *The End of Faith*, Harris, referring to Deuteronomy 13:6–11, insists that the consistent Bible believer should stone his son or daughter if she comes home from a yoga class a devotee of Krishna. Harris wryly quips that one of the Old Testament's "barbarisms"—stoning children for heresy—"has fallen out of fashion in our country."[8]

Harris reminds Bible-believers that once we recognize that slaves are human beings who are equally capable of suffering and happiness, we'll understand that it is "patently evil to own them and treat them like farm equipment."

A few pages later, Harris claims we can be good without God. We do not need God or a Bible to tell us what's right and what's wrong. We can know objective moral truths without "the existence of a lawgiving God," and we can judge Hitler to be morally reprehensible "without reference to scripture."[9] Harris calls this "the myth of secular moral chaos"—that morality will crumble if people don't have a Bible or if they happen not to believe in God.

We've accumulated quite a working list of charges coming from the New Atheists:

- Canaanite "genocide"
- the binding of Isaac
- a jealous, egocentric deity
- ethnocentrism/racism
- chattel slavery
- bride-price
- women as inferior to men
- harsh laws in Israel
- the Mosaic law as perfect and permanently binding for all nations
- the irrelevance of God for morality

I don't want to give the impression that all of these questions are easily solved. The noted Christian Old Testament scholar Christopher Wright has written a direct, honest exploration of certain Old Testament difficulties, especially the Canaanite question, in *The God I Don't Understand*.[10] Will gaps in our understanding of these texts still exist? Will some of our questions remain unanswered? Yes and amen. But I believe that with patience, charity, and humility we can navigate these waters with greater skill, arriving at far more satisfactory answers than the New Atheists allow.

One big problem for *any* interpreter is this: we're dealing with an Old Testament text that is remote in both time and culture. In many cases, the New Atheists aren't all that patient in their attempts to understand a complex text, historical contexts, and the broader biblical canon. Yet this is what we need to do and what this book attempts to do at a popular level.

In each chapter, I'll be borrowing from the phrases of these Neo-atheists to frame the discussion. Hopefully, we can see these Old Testament ethical issues in their proper context. In doing so, we'll get a firmer grasp on what the Old Testament ethical issues really are and how we should assess them.

Further Reading

Novak, Michael. *No One Sees God*. New York: Doubleday, 2007.

Wright, Christopher J. H. *The God I Don't Understand: Reflections on Tough Questions of Faith*. Grand Rapids: Zondervan, 2008.

God: Gracious Master or Moral Monster?

3

Great Appetite for Praise and Sacrifices?

Divine Arrogance or Humility?

Humility is a misunderstood virtue. The country singer Mac Davis boldly sang that it was hard to be humble since he was perfect in every way. I grew up hearing lines such as "Humble—and proud of it!" or "Have you read my book, *Humility and How I Attained It?*" We immediately detect something wrong with this picture. Yet the New Atheists wonder how God—who is so, well, God-centered—can't also be accused of narcissism and vanity. According to Richard Dawkins, God is obsessed with "his own superiority over rival gods."[1] The God of the Bible seems to seek attention and crave praise—an altogether unflattering characteristic. He's out to "make a name for Himself" (2 Sam. 7:23). He delivers his people from Egypt "for the sake of His name" (Ps. 106:8).

So does God have an unhealthy self-preoccupation? Do our atheist friends have a point? Not on this one. On closer inspection, God turns out to be a humble, self-giving, other-centered Being.

Defining Our Terms

On one occasion Winston Churchill described a particular person this way: "He's a humble man—and for good reason!" Apparently that man had his limitations and needed to keep them in mind.

Before approaching most topics, it's good to clear the decks and first define our terms. What do we *really* mean by "pride" and "humility"? Pride, we know, is an inflated view of ourselves—a false advertising campaign promoting ourselves because we suspect that others won't accept who we really are.[2] Pride is actually a lie about our own identity or achievements. To be proud is to live in a world propped up with falsehoods about ourselves, taking credit where credit isn't due.

Yes, in a sense, we can "take pride" or be gratified in our work; Paul did so as an apostle (2 Cor. 10:17). Paul was proud of early Christians' progress in their faith and in their proper use of God-given abilities (2 Cor. 7:14; 9:3–4). In such cases, Paul recognized that God is the great Enabler. The God-dependent believer can "boast in the Lord" (2 Cor. 10:17) and in the cross of Christ (Gal. 6:14). This is no "pull yourself up by your own bootstraps" type of self-reliance; that would be a failure or refusal to acknowledge our proper place before God in light of his grace.

What then is humility? This involves having a realistic assessment of ourselves—our weaknesses *and* strengths. Plagiarism (a big problem in the academic world these days) is an attempt to take credit for someone else's work. Plagiarizers create an impression that's out of touch with reality. But think about this: for Yo-Yo Ma to claim that he "really can't play the cello all that well" or for Landon Donovan to say he "can't really play soccer" would be equally out of touch with reality—a *false* humility. (What's more, these kinds of statements are usually a backdoor attempt to get attention!) True humility doesn't deny abilities but rather acknowledges God as the source of these gifts, for which we can't take credit. What do we have that we didn't receive (1 Cor. 4:7)? To be humble is to know our proper place before God—with all of our strengths and weaknesses.

Well, then, *is* God proud? No, he has a realistic view of himself, not a false or exaggerated one. God, by definition, is the greatest conceivable being, which makes him worthy of worship. In fact, our word *worship* is a kind of contraction of the Old English word *weorthscipe*—or "worth-ship." So if an all-powerful but despicably evil being demanded our worship, we shouldn't give it to him. He wouldn't be worthy of worship.

God doesn't take more credit than he deserves. For example, he doesn't claim to make the choices that morally responsible humans must make, nor does he take credit for being the author of evil in the name of "sovereignty" (which some Christians tend to assign to him when they praise God *for* evil things). No, God doesn't "think more highly of himself than he ought to think" (Rom. 12:3). Rather, he thinks quite accurately about himself.

God's Image—Divine Pride or Gracious Gift?

Daniel Dennett's charge that God is just a super-*man* who has an appetite for praise seems to be justified by the idea that God makes humans in his image (Gen. 1:26–27). God is like a vain toy maker creating dolls that look just like him. Isn't God's act of creating humans in his image just another sign of his vanity?

Actually, to be made in God's image and to receive salvation (entrance into God's family) are expressions of God's kindness, not divine arrogance. When God created human beings, he uniquely equipped them for two roles, as the early chapters of Genesis suggest. The first is our *kingly* role: God endowed us to share in ruling the creation with him. The second is our *priestly* role of relating to ("walking with") God and orienting our lives around him. Being made in God's image as priest-kings brings with it the ability to relate to God, to think rationally, to make moral decisions, to express creativity, and (with God) to care for and wisely harness creation. This is privilege, not bondage!

Our being made in God's image is simply God's "spreading the wealth." God's rich goodness overflows to his creation, which lives, moves, and has its being in him. Though God created freely and without constraint, God is bursting with joy and love to share his goodness with his creatures. He allows us, his image-bearers, to share (in a very limited way) in his characteristics. God enables us to participate in the life of the divine community, the Trinity—a life that fills him with great joy and pleasure (see 2 Peter 1:4). God bestows on us the great compliment of endowing us with a privileged position and with important capacities—ones that reflect God's own wonderful nature.

The Biology of Religious Devotion?

The inventor Thomas Edison said that humans are "incurably religious." History certainly bears this out. But *why* have humans been so religiously inclined across the millennia and civilizations? Neo-atheists Dawkins and Dennett interpret the phenomenon this way: theology is biology. To Dawkins, God is a "delusion"; for Dennett, religious believers are under a kind of "spell" that needs to be broken. Like computers, Dawkins says, we come equipped with a remarkable predisposition to do (and believe) what we're told. So young minds full of mush are susceptible to mental infections or viruses ("memes"). Charismatic preachers and other adults spew out their superstitious bilge, and later generations latch on to it and eventually create churches and religious schools. Even if there isn't a "God gene," humans have a certain religious urge—an apparent hardwiring in the brain that draws us to supernatural myths.[3]

Some conclude, therefore, that God doesn't exist but is simply the product of predictable biological processes. One big problem with this statement: it is a whopping non sequitur. It just doesn't follow that if humans are somehow wired to be religious, God therefore doesn't exist. This is what's called "the genetic fallacy"—proving or disproving the truth of a view based on its origin. In this case, God's existence is a separate question from the source of religious beliefs. We need to sort out the *biology* of belief from the *rationality* of belief.

There's more to say here. We could turn the argument on its head: if God exists and has designed us to connect with him, then we're actually functioning properly when we're being directed toward belief in God. We can agree that natural/physical processes partly contribute to commitment to God. In that case, the basic argument of Dawkins and Dennett could actually support the idea that religious believers are functioning decently and in order.

On top of this, we're also left wondering why people would think up gods and spirits in the first place. Why would humans *voluntarily* sacrifice their lives for some intangible realm? Maybe it's because the physical domain doesn't contain the source of coherence, order, morality, meaning, and guidance for life. Humans, though embodied, are moral, spiritual beings; they're able to rise above the physical and biological to reflect on it and on their condition. This can result in the search for a world-transcending God.[4]

Attempts by these New Atheists to explain away theology as a useful fiction or, worse, a harmful delusion fall short of telling us why the religious impulse is so deeply imbedded. If God exists, however, we have an excellent reason as to why religious fervor should exist.

Worship: Getting in Touch with Reality

During his "Christian phase," singer Bob Dylan came out with the song "Gotta Serve Somebody." "It may be the devil or it may be the Lord," he sang, "but you're gonna have to serve somebody."[5] Jesus tells us that worship is directed to either God *or* a God-substitute of our making (that is, an idol). In the Sermon on the Mount, he asserts that we can't serve two masters at the same time; we can't love both God *and* wealth (Matt. 6:24). In Romans 6, Paul affirms that we'll either be slaves to obedience or to disobedience (v. 16).

As we've seen, we're naturally religious creatures. Ecclesiastes acknowledges that God has placed eternity in our hearts (3:11). We're designed to worship and serve. Now, if God truly exists, then worship turns out to be moral, spiritual creatures getting in touch with reality. Just as genuine humility is rooted in reality, so is worship. Why does God insist that we worship him? For the same reason that parents tell their young children to stay away from fire or speeding cars. God doesn't want humans to detach themselves from ultimate reality, which only ends up harming us.

God's calling for our worship isn't a manifestation of pride—of false, overinflated views of himself. The call to worship means inclusion in the life of God. Worship expresses an awareness of God's—and thus our—proper place in the order of things, and it also transforms us into what we were designed to be. In the end, God desires to be known as God, which is only appropriate and the ultimate good for creatures. On the other hand, for humans to desire universal, eternal fame would be reality-denying idolatry.[6]

Seeking Praise?

We get rather disgusted when a person is constantly fishing for compliments, don't we? Why then does God do this? Why all the praise seeking?

Actually, in the Bible, God isn't the one commanding us to praise him. Typically, fellow creatures are spontaneously calling on one another to do so—to recognize God's greatness and worth-ship. Praise naturally flows from—and completes—the creature's enjoyment of God. God is self-sufficient and content in and of himself. He doesn't need frail humans for some sort of ego boost. As Psalm 50:12 reminds us: "If I [God] were hungry I would not tell you, for the world is Mine, and all it contains."

C. S. Lewis had his own misconceptions about this notion of praise and wrote of the lesson he learned:

> But the most obvious fact about praise—whether of God or anything—strangely escaped me. I thought of it in terms of compliment, approval, or the giving of honor. I had never noticed that all enjoyment spontaneously overflows into praise. . . . The world rings with praise—lovers praising their mistresses, readers their favorite poet, walkers praising the countryside, players praising their game. . . . I think we delight to praise what we enjoy because the praise not merely expresses but completes the enjoyment; it is appointed consummation.[7]

Lewis realized that praise stems from doing what one can't help doing—giving utterance to what we regard as supremely valuable: "It is good to sing praises to our God." Why? "For it is pleasant and praise is becoming" (Ps. 147:1).

Another related point: when we creatures *truly* show love for God, it's not because of a crass desire for rewards or to avoid punishment. The sheer enjoyment of God's presence—the greatest good of humans—and his approval of us are reward enough. Once again, Lewis has offered a delightful picture:

> Money is not the natural reward of love; that is why we call a man mercenary if he marries a woman for the sake of her money. But marriage is the proper reward for a real lover, and he is not mercenary for desiring it. . . . Those who have attained everlasting life in the vision of God know very well that it is no mere bribe, but the very consummation of their earthly discipleship.[8]

The Humble, Self-Giving God

Many Christians have the false impression that something resembling divine humility appears occasionally in the Bible—for example, in the incarnation of

Christ—but that humility isn't an enduring divine quality. Upon closer inspection, God—yes, even in the Old Testament—is characteristically humble. The "high and exalted One" dwells "with the contrite and lowly of spirit" (Isa. 57:15). Psalm 113:5–6 affirms a God who stoops to look upon us. In God's interaction with Israel, we see an other-centered, patient endurance despite Israel's rebellion, grumbling, and idolatry.

The New Testament only *expands on* this theme of divine humility; it doesn't *invent* it. There, God's humility is made more apparent in three ways.

First, God is triune. Three distinct divine persons share an eternal, unbreakable unity of one being. (As an analogy, think of the mythological three-headed dog Cerberus—three centers of awareness having a canine nature but in one dog.) God is inherently loving and self-giving within the relationships of the divine family, the Trinity. In this divine inter- (and inner-) connection of mutuality, openness, and reciprocity there is no individualistic competition among the family members but only joy, self-giving love, and transparency. Rather than being some isolated self or solitary ego, God is supremely relational in his self-giving, other-oriented nature.

Second, God becomes human. Further evidence of divine humility is the incarnation of Christ. God becomes a Jew in the person of Jesus of Nazareth! Because humans are made in God's image, it's not a contradiction for God to become human; after all, what makes us human is derived from God's nature in the first place.

So the incarnate Christ describes himself as "gentle and humble in heart"—this in the very same context as his declaration of (1) uniquely knowing, relating to, and revealing the Father and (2) being the one who gives the weary rest for their souls (Matt. 11:27–29). Greatness and humility don't contradict each other. In fact, God's greatness is seen in his willingness to serve us: "I am among you as the one who serves" (Luke 22:27). Jesus comes not to be served but to "serve" and to "give His life a ransom for many" (Mark 10:45).

Third, God takes our place on a cross. A Muslim friend, Abdul, once expressed his difficulties with God becoming a human and dying on the cross. "It's such a humiliation!" he exclaimed. For the Muslim, God is so utterly transcendent and removed from us. Yet Philippians 2 marvelously displays the depths to which God is willing to go for our salvation: God the Son humbles (empties) himself, becoming a slave (*doulos*) who dies fully naked, for all to see—in great shame and humiliation (vv. 6–8). Jesus's crucifixion is a picture of both humility and greatness. God's humiliation turns out to be his own mark of distinction and moment of glory! Jesus, who was faithfully living out Israel's story as God had intended it, was actually enduring the curse of exile and alienation so that God's new community could receive blessing.

John's Gospel refers to Jesus being "lifted up" on the cross (12:32; cf. 3:14–15; 8:28). This is both *literal* and *figurative*. Being lifted up is both the physical act of being raised up onto a cross and the figurative reference to exaltation and honor from God, including the drawing of the nations to salvation (John 12:32). The moment of Christ's humiliating death is precisely when he is "glorified" (John 12:23–24; 13:31–32). God's great moment of glory is in the experience of the greatest humiliation and shame—when he takes the form of a slave and suffers death on a cross for our sakes.

This is how low God is willing to go for our salvation! This act of divine service to humans is utterly unique in antiquity. No wonder the late German New Testament scholar Martin Hengel wrote, "The discrepancy between the shameful death of a Jewish state criminal and the confession that depicts this executed man as the pre-existent divine figure who becomes man and humbles himself to a slave's death is, as far as I can see, without analogy in the ancient world."[9]

Once a Muslim expressed to me his disbelief and even scorn at the idea of Christians wearing crosses: "How can Christians wear with pride the instrument of torture and humiliation? If your brother were killed in an electric chair, would you wear an electric chair around your neck?" I replied that it depends: "If my brother happened to be Jesus of Nazareth and his death in an electric chair brought about my salvation and was the means by which evil was defeated and creation renewed, then he would have transformed a symbol of shame and punishment into something glorious."

One theologian puts it this way: it's "truly godlike to be humble as it is to be exalted."[10] The New Atheists wrongly assume that God must be an egalitarian deity—that he is just like us (see Ps. 50:21).[11] We can set aside the false accusation that God is a divine, pompous windbag seeking to have his ego stroked by human flattery. That's the argument of village atheists, not those who have seriously examined the Scriptures.

Further Reading

Bauckham, Richard. *Jesus and the God of Israel: God Crucified and Other Studies on the New Testament's Christology.* Grand Rapids: Eerdmans, 2008.

Lewis, C. S. "The Weight of Glory." In *The Weight of Glory and Other Addresses.* New York: Macmillan, 1965.

4

Monumental Rage and Kinglike Jealousy?

Understanding the Covenant-Making God

Recall Richard Dawkins's put-down of God, claiming that he breaks into a "monumental rage whenever his chosen people flirted with a rival god."[1] Popular TV icon Oprah Winfrey said that she was turned off to the Christian faith when she heard a preacher affirm that God is jealous. Bill Maher of *Religulous* fame (or infamy) has said much the same thing—that being jealous about having other gods before you just isn't "moral." The New Atheists likewise consider Yahweh to be impatient, jealous, and easily provoked—a petty and insecure deity.

Good Jealousy and Bad Jealousy

As I said in the previous chapter, it's important to define our terms. Jealousy can be a bad thing *or* a good thing. It's bad to protect the petty; it's good to fiercely guard the precious. If jealousy is rooted in self-centeredness, it is clearly the wrong kind of jealousy. A jealousy that springs from concern for another's well-being, however, is appropriate. Yes, jealousy can be a vice (Gal. 5:20—"enmities, strife, jealousy, outbursts of anger"). Yet it can also be a virtue, a "godly jealousy," as Paul put it: "For I am jealous for you with a godly jealousy; for I betrothed you to one husband, so that to Christ I might present you as a pure virgin" (2 Cor. 11:2). Paul was concerned for the well-being of the Corinthians. His jealousy didn't spring from hurt pride or self-concern.

Throughout the Bible, we see a God who is a concerned lover. He's full of anguish and dismay when his covenant people pursue non-gods. In the prophetic book of Hosea, God—the loving husband—gets choked up when his wife, Israel, continually cheats on him: "My heart is turned over within Me, all My compassions are kindled" (Hosea 11:8).

When can jealousy be a good thing? In God's case, it's when we're rummaging around in the garbage piles of life and avoiding the ultimate source of satisfaction. It reminds me of a comic strip I once saw of a dog who had been drinking out of a toilet bowl. With water dripping from his snout, Fido looks up to tell us, "It doesn't get any better than this!"

Instead of enjoying fresh spring water, we look for stagnant, crummy-tasting substitutes that inevitably fail us. God laments over Israel: "For My people have committed two evils: They have forsaken Me, the fountain of living waters, to hew for themselves cisterns, broken cisterns that can hold no water" (Jer. 2:13).

The Marriage Analogy

A friend of mine who worked in Christian ministry in Europe for many years told me about a Christian couple he had gotten to know. Somehow the subject of adultery came up in conversation. The seemingly unassuming Dutch wife said that if her husband ever cheated on her, "I vill shoot him!" He knew she wasn't kidding.

A wife who doesn't get jealous and angry when another woman is flirting with her husband isn't really all that committed to the marriage relationship. A marriage without the potential for jealousy when an intruder threatens isn't much of a marriage. Outrage, pain, anguish—these are the appropriate responses to such a deep violation. God isn't some abstract entity or impersonal principle, as Dawkins seems to think he should be. He is an engaging, relational God who attaches himself to humans. He desires to be their loving Father and the wise ruler of their lives. In Israel's case, God's love is that of a passionate husband. We should be amazed that the Creator of the universe would so deeply connect himself to human beings that he would open himself to sorrow and anguish in the face of human betrayal and rejection.

God opened himself to repeated rejection from his people. He was continuously exasperated with and injured by his people: "How I have been hurt by their adulterous hearts which turned away from Me, and by their eyes which played the harlot after their idols" (Ezek. 6:9). God endured much defiance, despite his loving concern for his people: "I have spread out My hands all day long to a rebellious people, who walk in the way which is not good, following their own thoughts, a people who continually provoke Me to My face" (Isa. 65:2–3).

Spiritual adultery is no petty matter, as Dawkins seems to think. Notice God's perspective of Israel's unfaithfulness in Ezekiel 16 and 23. The scenarios described there aren't exactly suitable for G-rated audiences! In chapter 16, intimate, marital language is used for God's "marriage" to his people at Mount Sinai—the "time for love." God entered into a covenant with Israel so that "you became Mine." God provided lavishly for Israel, but she despised this privilege. Rather than trusting in God, she allied herself with other nations, trusting in their military might and foreign idols rather than in God. "But you trusted in your beauty and played the harlot because of your fame"; "you spread your legs to every passer-by to multiply your harlotry" (vv. 15, 25). This graphic language expresses the deep betrayal in Israel's spiritual adultery and prostitution.

We shouldn't be surprised that God wanted to wipe out Israel after the golden calf betrayal: "Let Me alone, that My anger may burn against them and that I may destroy them; and I will make of you [Moses] a great nation" (Exod. 32:10). This took place just after Israel had made "vows" to attach herself to Yahweh at Sinai: "All that the LORD has spoken we will do, and we will be obedient" (Exod. 24:7; cf. v. 3). Israel's idolatry was like a husband finding his wife in bed with another man—*on their honeymoon*! The reason God is jealous is because he binds himself to his people in a kind of spousal intimacy. So worshiping idols and other gods is a rejection of who he is, just as adultery is a rejection of one's spouse in marriage.[2]

When the word *jealous* describes God in Scripture, it's in the context of idolatry and false worship.[3] When we choose this-worldly pursuits over our relationship with God, we engage in spiritual adultery (James 4:4; cf. 2 Cor. 11:2), which provokes God's righteous jealousy. Unfortunately, a lot of Yahweh-critics who dislike the notion of divine jealousy—especially the New Atheists—just don't understand why idolatry's such a problem. After all, what's the big deal about bringing a hunk of meat to a statue, right? As has been said, ignorance may be bliss, but it isn't a virtue!

Idolatry is—and always has been—a very seductive enterprise that can get the best of any of us. Idolatry in the ancient Near East involved manipulating reality ("the gods") through certain rituals and sacrifices to get more kids, crops, and cattle. Chanting to an idol would get people into immediate contact with a god's very essence. And who wants to travel to Yahweh's Jerusalem three times a year when you can conveniently go to the shrine of a personal or family god (like Dagon or Baal) at a nearby grove or high hill (Deut. 12:2; 1 Kings 14:22–24)? Idolatry in the ancient Near East also appealed to the sensual and the indulgent side. Rather than self-restraint in Yahweh worship, one could get drunk at idol feasts as well as engage in ritual sex, gluttony, and adultery, all in the name of "religion." Furthermore, idolatry in the ancient

Near East didn't commit one to improved ethical behavior. As long as you kept your idol "fed," you didn't have to change your lifestyle. Contrast this with the moral behavior required by Yahweh's people: "all the words which the LORD has spoken we will do!" (Exod. 24:3).[4]

So calling Israel a mere "flirt" in these idolatrous scenarios reflects Dawkins's utter lack of awareness. We could perhaps ask Dawkins, "How strong should a spouse's commitment to a marriage be? How seriously should one treat adultery in a marriage?" Whichever way he'd answer, it would no doubt be revealing.

Divine Vulnerability

Throughout the Old Testament, God is not only passionately concerned for Israel but also frequently in pain at her rebellion and longing for reconciliation. God is a wounded husband who continually attempts to woo his people back into harmony with him. Isaiah 5 portrays God as a vineyard owner who had busied himself with the task of "planting" his people Israel—"the choicest vine"—on a fertile hill, digging all around it, removing its stones. Despite the legitimate expectation of Israel's bearing "good" fruit after all he had done, God is exasperated at Israel's "worthless" yield: "What more was there to do for My vineyard that I have not done in it?" (5:4). Jeremiah similarly writes of God's planting Israel as a "choice vine" and "faithful seed," but Israel rejects God (Jer. 2:21). The same theme of God's legitimate expectation of repentance and righteousness from Israel is found in Zephaniah 3:7: "I said, 'Surely you will revere Me, accept instruction.' So her dwelling will not be cut off according to all that I have appointed concerning her. But they were eager to corrupt all their deeds."

The psalmist articulates something similar: "I, the LORD, am your God, who brought you up from the land of Egypt; open your mouth wide and I will fill it. But My people did not listen to My voice, and Israel did not obey Me" (81:10–11). Israel's continual faithlessness exasperates God. In Amos 4:6–11, God tries to get the attention of his people by sending plagues, famine, drought, and the like. But despite each divine attempt, the same line is uttered: "Yet you have not returned to Me."

Likewise in Isaiah 66:4, God says, "I called, but no one answered; I spoke, but they did not listen. And they did evil in My sight and chose that in which I did not delight." Again, in Ezekiel 18:23, 31–32, God asks, "Do I have any pleasure in the death of the wicked? . . . Why will you die, O house of Israel? For I have no pleasure in the death of anyone who dies. . . . Therefore, repent and live." This theme of divine vulnerability[5] runs throughout the Old Testament, where God is presented as a wounded lover who is reluctant to bring judgment.

Jealousy implies vulnerability and the capacity to experience pain—not the pettiness of a power-hungry deity obsessed with dominating people. Amazingly, the disappointed Husband of Israel only requires her repentance to restore the relationship.[6]

An Anger That Cares

Most Americans are familiar with Warner Sallman's *Head of Christ* painting. This picture is commonly found on nursing home walls or memorial cards given out at funeral homes. Sallman's portrayal is one of an easily caricatured "meek and mild" Jesus. Though perhaps depicting his approachability and kindness toward children, such pictures can often leave us with a lopsided, sentimental impression of Jesus. No, the real Jesus was not only a friend of sinners and a welcomer of children; he was also a radical, a controversialist, a convicting and even frightening character. He is the Lion of the tribe of Judah (Rev. 5:5). The *Head of Christ* is a far cry from the temple-clearing, storm-calming Jesus, who evokes sometimes troubled, sometimes terrified responses: "Who then is this, that even the wind and the sea obey Him?" (Mark 4:41).[7]

Speaking of the temple cleansing, we see genuine, justified anger when Jesus drives out moneychangers from the temple (Mark 11; John 2). They had turned a house of worship for God-fearing Gentiles into a place of noise, commercial gain, and nationalistic pride. In our age of pseudotolerant true-for-you-but-not-for-meism, we could use considerably more righteous anger—at the world's injustices, the greed, the tyrannies, the lies, the spin . . . and our own proud, rationalizing hearts. And the various religious hucksters and exploiters of our day could stand to be driven out of the sphere of public influence.

If we're not directly touched by any of the world's many sufferings, sadnesses, and oppressions, our response may be indifferent and apathetic, and a person's flare-up of anger will make us very uncomfortable. Yet anger is often the first indication that we care. The tragedy is that we're not angered, not shocked enough.

Anger isn't necessarily wrong (Eph. 4:26)—indeed, at times it is virtuous. The never-angered person is morally deficient. The slow-to-anger person is the virtuous one. He's better able to calm disputes or listen well (Prov. 15:18; 16:32; 19:11; cf. James 1:19), but he also opposes injustice and tyranny. Likewise, God is frequently described as being "slow to anger" (e.g., Exod. 34:6). As with jealousy, so with anger: is the anger self-centered or other-centered? Does it reflect profound selfishness or concern for others? On closer inspection, God's anger doesn't reflect a self-centeredness.

God's jealousy and anger spring from love and concern, not from hurt pride or immaturity. The New Atheists resist the notion of God's rightful prerogatives over humans. The idea of divine judgment or anger or jealousy somehow makes them uncomfortable. But like Narnia's Aslan, Yahweh, though gracious and compassionate, isn't to be trifled with. God gets jealous or angry precisely because he cares.

Divine Jealousy to Protect and Benefit Humans

Those claiming that God's jealousy is petty and constricting might liken God to a husband who won't let his wife even *talk* to another man. A more appropriate analogy, however, is a husband who is concerned that his wife is being emotionally drawn toward another man. He wants to protect the preciousness of marital intimacy, which is in the best interests of his wife and their marriage.

Critics like the New Atheists tend to create a false dichotomy between God's gracious rule and human well-being, as though these are opposed to each other.[8] The Westminster Shorter Catechism (1647) begins with this question: "What is the chief end of man?" The famous response is: "to glorify God and enjoy Him forever." For many in the West (including professing Christians), the chief goal of many individuals is "to further my interests and to enjoy myself forever." Or if God exists, then the Catechism's answer is subconsciously revised to this: "The chief end of *God* is to make me as comfortable and pain-free as possible."

Philosopher Thomas Nagel has admitted that he doesn't want there to be a God. He acknowledges that in academic circles today there exists a "cosmic authority problem."[9] If people like Nagel don't want there to be a God (or they want a god who will let them do exactly what they want), then we're back to the problem of denying reality in order to pursue our own agendas. But obviously, God's ultimate role isn't to advance my own (or human) interests and freedom. The existence of God is no mere abstraction or armchair topic. The living God's existence and claim on our lives mean that something has to change!

On the other hand, God's relationship with us isn't a commander-commandee arrangement (similar to the "divine cop in the sky" notion). In that kind of relationship, God's will merely coerces, overriding the choices of human agents. Rather, God seeks the interpersonal intimacy with us in the context of covenant-making. Critics typically paint the picture of two false alternatives: sovereign coercion or total human autonomy. However, if we see God's activity and human nature as harmonious rather than in conflict, a new perspective dawns on us. When God's intentions for us are realized and when we're alert to the divinely given boundaries built into our nature and the world around us, we human beings flourish—that is, we enjoy loving, trusting relationships with God and one another because we're living out the design-plan.

God's jealousy isn't capricious or petty. God is jealous for our best interests. His commands are given "for your good" (Deut. 10:13; cf. 8:16; 30:9). In fact, we only harm ourselves when we live for ourselves and create our own idolatrous God-substitutes. So for God to block the possibility of our knowing him would actually be to *deprive us* of the *greatest possible good*. Author and pastor Tim Keller illustrates how this works for postmoderns:

> Instead of telling them they are sinning because they are sleeping with their girl-friends or boyfriends, I tell them that they are sinning because they are looking to their romances to give their lives meaning, to justify and save them, to give them what they should be looking for from God. This idolatry leads to anxiety, obsessiveness, envy, and resentment. I have found that when you describe their lives in terms of idolatry, postmodern people do not give much resistance. Then Christ and his salvation can be presented not (at this point) so much as their only hope for forgiveness, but as their only hope for freedom.[10]

When we apply this to God's jealousy, we can say that it's aroused not just to protect a *relationship*. God seeks to protect his *creatures* from profound self-harm. We can deeply damage ourselves by running after gods made in our own image. God's jealousy is other-centered. As we saw with God's humility, divine jealousy reacts to the human denial that God is God, to the false idea that a relationship with him isn't really needed for ultimate human well-being (John 10:10).

God is the all-good Creator and Life-giver. He desires that his creatures live life as it should be. When a person acts in life-denying ways (e.g., engaging in adultery, pornography, or promise breaking—or simply suppressing the truth about God), God's jealousy surfaces so that the person might abandon his or her death-seeking goals and return to an abundant life found in a life abandoned to God.

Divine jealousy should be seen in light of God's willing the best for his creatures. C. S. Lewis's insightful perspective puts divine jealousy and human idolatry into proper perspective:

> If we consider the unblushing promises of reward and the staggering nature of the rewards promised in the Gospels, it would seem that Our Lord finds our desires, not too strong, but too weak. We are half-hearted creatures, fooling about with drink and sex and ambition when infinite joy is offered us, like an ignorant child who wants to go on making mud pies in a slum because he can-not imagine what is meant by the offer of a holiday at the sea. We are far too easily pleased.[11]

Further Reading

Copan, Paul. *Loving Wisdom: Christian Philosophy of Religion*. St. Louis: Chalice Press, 2007. See esp. part 1, "God."

Kirkpatrick, Frank G. *A Moral Ontology for a Theistic Ethic: Gathering the Nations in Love and Justice*. Burlington, VT: Ashgate, 2004.

Lane, Nathan C. *The Compassionate but Punishing God*. Eugene, OR: Wipf & Stock, 2010.

Lewis, C. S. "The Weight of Glory." In *The Weight of Glory and Other Addresses*. New York: HarperOne, 2001.

Phillips, J. B. *Your God Is Too Small*. New York: Touchstone, 1997.

Stuart, Douglas K. *Exodus*. New American Commentary 2. Nashville: B & H Publishing, 2008.

5

Child Abuse and Bullying?

God's Ways and the Binding of Isaac

Now it came about . . . that God tested Abraham, and said to him, "Abraham!"
And he said, "Here I am." He said, "Take now your son, your only son, whom
you love, Isaac, and go to the land of Moriah, and offer him there as a burnt
offering on one of the mountains of which I will tell you." So Abraham rose
early in the morning and saddled his donkey, and took two of his young men
with him and Isaac his son; and he split wood for the burnt offering, and arose
and went to the place of which God had told him.

On the third day Abraham raised his eyes and saw the place from a distance.
Abraham said to his young men, "Stay here with the donkey, and I and the lad
will go over there; and we will worship and return to you." Abraham took the
wood of the burnt offering and laid it on Isaac his son, and he took in his hand
the fire and the knife. So the two of them walked on together. Isaac spoke to
Abraham his father and said, "My father!" And he said, "Here I am, my son."
And he said, "Behold, the fire and the wood, but where is the lamb for the burnt
offering?" Abraham said, "God will provide for Himself the lamb for the burnt
offering, my son." So the two of them walked on together.

Then they came to the place of which God had told him; and Abraham built
the altar there and arranged the wood, and bound his son Isaac and laid him
on the altar, on top of the wood. Abraham stretched out his hand and took
the knife to slay his son. But the angel of the LORD called to him from heaven
and said, "Abraham, Abraham!" And he said, "Here I am." He said, "Do not
stretch out your hand against the lad, and do nothing to him; for now I know
that you fear God, since you have not withheld your son, your only son, from

Me." Then Abraham raised his eyes and looked, and behold, behind him a ram caught in the thicket by his horns; and Abraham went and took the ram and offered him up for a burnt offering in the place of his son. Abraham called the name of that place The LORD Will Provide. (Gen. 22:1–14)

Occasionally, we'll read in the newspaper or hear on the evening news about certain deluded persons who've murdered someone. Their justification? "God told me to do it!" I've heard some use this line to justify divorcing a spouse in order to marry their personal assistant at work. God's name gets dragged into circumstances or actions that are wholly contrary to his good character. He certainly doesn't want the credit in such cases.

So what do we do with God's startling command to Abraham in Genesis 22:2: "Take now your son, your only son, whom you love . . . and offer him . . . as a burnt offering"? As we'll discuss later in this book, the law of Moses condemned child sacrifice. In fact, this was one of the horrible practices for which God judged the Canaanites. So then doesn't it seem that God's commands are whimsical and capricious in Genesis 22? Why can't God just as well command murder as prohibit it? After all, it looks like he's doing just that to Abraham. This is what one biblical scholar calls "a monstrous test."[1]

The bestselling author Bart Ehrman (an agnostic) comments on the *Aqedah,* or "binding," of Isaac: "The idea that suffering comes as a test from God simply to see if his followers will obey" is illustrated perhaps "more clearly and more horribly" in the offering of Isaac.[2] Some scholars claim that Abraham *failed* the test by being willing to sacrifice his son; others wonder how this act could serve as a test for godliness. Should Abraham be loved or hated for what he did?

The Danish Christian philosopher Søren Kierkegaard had a lot to say about this portion of Scripture. Abraham had a "right" to be a great man and thus to do what he did, but "when another does the same, it is sin, a heinous sin."[3] Kierkegaard said that God's command to Abraham *suspended* typical ethical obligations. God appears to use his authority to violate basic moral standards. God seems to be a relativist of sorts.

If we look at the bigger picture, perhaps we can place some of these troubling matters in proper context. Only then should we look at the specifics in Genesis 22.

The Broader Context

The Theme of the Pentateuch: Abraham's Faith and Moses's Unbelief

Biblical scholars have pointed out that the theme of faith holds the Pentateuch (Genesis–Deuteronomy) together at its seams.[4] The two major players are Abraham and Moses. Abraham is the positive example of faith, while Moses is the negative example. Abraham had faith without the law of Moses, which was given at Mount Sinai. Despite his wavering, he trusted God's promise, and so he was declared righteous by God (Gen. 15:6). By contrast, Moses actually failed in his faith—even though he lived under the law given at Sinai. Yes, he played a crucial role in Israel's history, but we see a critical failure of faith in Moses.

It's no coincidence that when "have faith/believe" is mentioned in the Pentateuch, it is used positively *before* the giving of the law at Sinai in Exodus 20 (Gen. 15:6; Exod. 4:5; 14:31; 19:9). However, these words are used negatively ("did not believe") *after* Sinai (Num. 14:11; 20:12; cf. Deut. 1:32; 9:23). The Pentateuch is in large part a contrast between Abraham and Moses. Though Abraham's faith wavered at times, it continued to grow.

It's significant that Abraham trusted God—and was declared righteous— *before* the law of Moses came. Even without the law, Abraham kept the intention or purport of the law because he lived *by faith*: "Abraham obeyed Me and kept My charge, My commandments, My statutes and My laws" (Gen. 26:5). Notice the words used: these are post-Sinai law terms used in Deuteronomy ("obeyed," "charge," "commandments," "statutes," "laws"), yet they apply to Abraham before the law was given. The point is to show how Abraham essentially kept the law and pleased God because he lived by faith (Gen. 15:6).

This connection wasn't lost on Paul in the New Testament (Rom. 4; Gal. 3–4). As he reread the Scriptures in light of his encounter with Christ, he discovered that Abraham lived by faith and was declared righteous by God. That's Genesis 15. In Genesis 17 came the covenant of circumcision, and over four hundred years later the law was given at Sinai. In other words, Abraham didn't need circumcision or the law to be right with God.

On the other hand, Moses had the law, but he failed in his faith; this prevented him from entering the land across the Jordan. He is the negative contrast to Abraham. Though Moses had the law, he died in the wilderness because of his and Aaron's lack of faith at Kadesh (Num. 20). Moses wasn't barred from the Promised Land just because he struck a rock. He had struck rocks before! The Hebrew text makes clear that both Moses and Aaron displayed unbelief in their exasperation. They weren't trusting in God. Moses (along with Aaron, apparently) cried out in frustration, "Listen now, you rebels; shall we bring forth water for you out of this rock?" (Num. 20:10). Psalm 106:32–33 reinforces the theme of Moses's *unbelief*. The rebellion of the people prompted Moses to speak rashly (not *act* rashly): "rash words came from Moses' lips" (NIV). So because of the unbelief of both Moses and Aaron, God rebuked both of them: "Because you [Moses and Aaron; the pronoun is plural] have not believed Me, to treat Me as holy" before Israel, "you shall not bring this assembly into the land which I have given them" (Num. 20:12; cf. v. 24). Later in Deuteronomy 32:51, we read again that at Meribah in Kadesh Moses "broke faith" with God. As a result of this failure of faith, Moses couldn't enter the Promised Land.

God used Abraham as a picture of trust—without the benefit of the law. Abraham serves as an illustration across the ages of how God's people should live. Moses turns out to be a negative example—and a sobering reminder to legalistically minded Jews—that having the law and keeping it scrupulously are inadequate for being right with God. Rather, we're to approach him trustingly, depending on his grace and sufficiency rather than putting confidence in our own sufficiency.

This important theme of Abraham's deep trust in God's promise and faithfulness helped shape Israel's own self-understanding and identity. So it's not surprising to hear Moses's words to Israel at Sinai: "Do not be afraid; for God has come in order to test [the Hebrew verb is *nasah*] you, and in order that the fear [*yir'ah*] of Him may remain with you, so that you may not sin" (Exod. 20:20). These two key verbs link back to Genesis 22. Abraham was *tested* by God (Gen. 22:1) and through this ordeal demonstrated his *fear* of God (v. 12). Abraham's obedience is intended to serve as a model for Israel and to inspire Israel's obedience and solidify their relationship with ("fear of") God.[5]

In fact, one can make the case that the entire Pentateuch speaks to the success of faith in Abraham and the failure of faith in Moses (despite having God's law). So to focus only on God's single command to offer up Isaac misses the big picture.

The Context of Abraham's Call

Let's now take a look at how God begins dealing with Abraham in light of his overarching plan for Israel. If we do so, we'll have a firmer grasp of what is going on with Abraham and Isaac. Otherwise, we'll likely distort the story in Genesis 22.

The first time God told Abr(ah)am to "go" (literally, "going go" [*lek-leka*]) was when he left his home in Ur of the Chaldeans (Babylonians) to go "to the land [*'el-'erets*] which I will show you" (Gen. 12:1). This remarkable act of trust was based on this promise—that God would make through him and his descendants a great nation (12:2–3). But in Genesis 22:2, God commanded Abraham once again to "go," using the *same* construction (literally, *going go* [*lek-leka*]) followed by the familiar-sounding to "one of the mountains of which I will tell you." Indeed, he is to go to the *land* (*'el-ha'arets*: "region") of Moriah. This time Isaac, the covenant son of the promise, is involved. Abraham couldn't have missed the connection being made. Bells are going off in Abraham's mind. God is clearly reminding him of his promise of blessing in Genesis 12 even while he's being commanded to do what seems to be utterly opposed to that promise.

In chapter 12, God had *promised* he would make Abraham's descendants as numerous as the stars. After Abraham's obedience here, God *confirms* his promise that he will make his offspring as numerous as the stars and the sand on the seashore (22:17). Genesis makes a connection between Abraham's *call* (Gen. 12) and his subsequent *obedience* (Gen. 22). The firmness of faith of Abraham, the father of Israel, was being tested, and this moment would shape the thinking and identity of subsequent generations of Israelites.[6] As one biblical scholar wrote, "Any Israelite who heard this story would take it to mean that his race owed its existence to the mercy of God and its prosperity to the obedience of their ancestor."[7]

Abraham had left his home in Ur and given up his *past* for the sake of God's promise. Now he was being asked if he would trust God by apparently surrendering his *future* as well. Everything Abraham ever hoped for was tied up in this son of promise.[8]

The Nearer Context: Hagar and Ishmael

Here we come to the more immediate narrative context—namely, what took place with Abraham's first son, Ishmael, and his mother, Hagar. The Ishmael story turns out to be the preliminary testing ground that informs Abraham's later experience.[9] Let's not forget that Ishmael was born to Hagar, Sarah's maidservant. Sarah, with Abraham, assumed that her having a *biological* son of promise in her old age wasn't going to work out (16:1–4). So Sarah, figuring that surrogate motherhood must be the way God wanted to fulfill his promise, told Abraham to take Hagar as her substitute—as a second-tier "wife" (v. 3). This, however, turned out to be an ill-conceived plan—a mis-conception! (We'll talk about this verse later in a future chapter.)

When Hagar conceived and began to despise her mistress, Sarah, this caused much tension, and Sarah drove her away. Yet God met Hagar in her desperation in the wilderness and told her to go back to live with Sarah and Abraham. There Hagar gave birth to Abraham's first son. As Ishmael grew up, Abraham unquestionably became quite attached to his son.

God, however, had different plans. He assured Abraham and Sarah that he wanted the son of promise to come from *both* their bodies, not just Abraham's. Through God's miraculous fulfillment of his promise, Isaac was born. But at the feast held when Isaac was weaned, Ishmael, now a teenager, mocked Isaac (21:9). It had been painful enough for Sarah to have her handmaiden Hagar—rather than herself—give birth to Abraham's first son. But for Ishmael to then scorn Sarah's own biological child was just too much to take. Sarah wanted to send away not only Ishmael but also his mother, Hagar. This created a dilemma for Abraham (21:11). Sending them off would calm Sarah down, but sending Hagar and Ishmael into the wilderness meant encountering harsh circumstances and risks—possibly even death.

But God allayed Abraham's fears, reassuring him that Ishmael wouldn't die (21:12–13). In fact, Yahweh had already told him, "I will make him a great nation" (17:20). Hagar herself had been told that God would "greatly multiply" her descendants (16:10). So Abraham could confidently send Ishmael away with Hagar and entrust them to God's care.

Then we come to God's command to Abraham to sacrifice Isaac. Abraham had endured a difficult challenge regarding Ishmael, and he was aware of the promise God had made concerning Ishmael. Though Abraham had sent Ishmael away into the wilderness, God had promised that he would live and become a great nation. Without God's promise, Abraham would have been wrong to send Hagar and Ishmael away to almost-certain death. So despite Sarah's anger at Hagar and Ishmael, God assured Abraham that he would provide for Ishmael and that Abraham need not worry that he was doing wrong. God would care for Ishmael (and Hagar) and would fulfill his promises to them. So Abraham "rose early in the morning" (21:14)—just as he would do with Isaac (22:3)—and sent them both away.

In the background was not only God's assurance regarding Ishmael. God had also provided a miracle son to Abraham—a son who had come from Sarah's own body—"your *only* son" (Gen. 22:2). This long-awaited son of promise would also become a great nation. Ishmael had been a preliminary test; Isaac would bring an even greater test. Abraham knew that God would fulfill his promise regarding Isaac, but he didn't know what God would do in the end. All he could do was trust God's promises and obey. Somehow God *had* to come through! Abraham's obedience, we now see, was carried out in the context of his awareness of God's earlier deliverance of Ishmael and of God's act of providing the miracle child of promise through Sarah.

The Text of Genesis 22

Having looked at the surrounding biblical text, we can hone in on Genesis 22. This text contains additional clues—some of them subtle—to help us better understand what takes place in this powerful, perplexing narrative. Because Abraham already knew God's faithful—and even tender—character and promises, he was confident that God would somehow fulfill his promise to him, however this would be worked out.

Four things about God's character emerge as we work through Genesis 22. First, we're immediately tipped off to the fact that God is *testing* Abraham (v. 1). God doesn't intend for Isaac to be sacrificed. No, Abraham isn't yet aware of what the reader knows—namely, that this is only a test.

Second, even the hard command to Abraham is cushioned by God's tenderness. God's directive is unusual: "*Please* take your son"—or as another scholar translates it, "Take, *I beg of you*, your only son."[10] God is remarkably gentle as he gives a difficult order. This type of divine command (as a plea) is rare. Old Testament commentator Gordon Wenham sees here a "hint that the LORD appreciates the costliness of what he is asking."[11] God understands the magnitude of this difficult task. In fact, one commentator states that God is not demanding here; thus, if Abraham couldn't see God's broader purposes and so couldn't bring himself to do this, he wouldn't "incur any guilt" in declining God's pleas.[12]

A third indication of God's good character highlights his faithfulness. God reminded Abraham of "your son, your only son, whom you love, Isaac" (v. 2). God's covenant acknowledgment is apparent: the divine promise to Abraham can't be fulfilled without Isaac. Abraham is struggling to keep two things in mind: his deep love for Isaac is good and right, and the circumstances surrounding Isaac's birth clearly showed that God was fulfilling his covenant promise to Abraham. While this is the most fearful and dreadful thing Abraham would ever have to do, he is trying to come to terms with just how God would fulfill his promise through Isaac.

A fourth reminder of God's faithful character is that God is sending Abraham to a mountain in the region of *Moriah*—derived from the Hebrew word *ra'ah*, "provide, see, show." As we noted earlier, the place "which I will tell you" is linked back to God's initial call to Abram to "go" to "the land which I will *show* you" (12:1, emphasis added). Abraham was also aware of God's provision for Hagar and Ishmael when they first fled. Hagar said (using the same Hebrew word *ra'ah*), "You are a God who *sees*" (16:13). So in the very word *Moriah* ("provision") we have a hint of salvation and deliverance. Wenham helpfully observes, "Salvation is thus promised in the very decree that sounds like annihilation."[13]

In all of these ways, we see God's faithful tenderness cushioning the startling harshness of God's command. It's as though God is saying to Abraham, "I'm testing your obedience and allegiance. You don't understand, but in light of all I've done and said to you, trust me. Not even death can nullify the promise I've made."

God himself told Abraham that it wasn't Hagar who would bear the child of promise—even though Abraham (with Sarah) thought it would be a good idea: "Oh that Ishmael might live before You!" (Gen. 17:18). God replied, "No, but Sarah your wife will bear you a son . . . and I will establish My covenant with him for an everlasting covenant for his descendants after him" (17:19). God assured Abraham that Isaac, not Ishmael, was the promised son.

So we can't separate God's *promise* in Genesis 12 and 17 from God's gentle *command* in Genesis 22. Abraham had confidence that even if the child of promise died, God would somehow accomplish his purposes through that very child. Abraham believed God could even raise Isaac from the dead. That's why Abraham told his servants before he headed to Mount Moriah with Isaac, "*We* will worship and then *we* will come back to you" (Gen. 22:5 NIV, emphasis added). No wonder the author of Hebrews observed that since Abraham "had received the promises," he "considered that God is able to raise people even from the dead" (11:17, 19). In *some* way, God would fulfill his promises. Abraham was confident of this—and commended for it. After all, Abraham confidently affirmed a few chapters earlier, "Shall not the Judge of all the earth deal justly?" (Gen. 18:25).

Abraham knew that God's faithful character meant that God wouldn't break his promises. Not only is it "impossible for God to lie" (Heb. 6:18; cf. Titus 1:2), but after promising to make Abraham into a great nation and to bring his descendants into the Promised Land, God himself "passed between the pieces" of animals in a dramatic display of pyrotechnics (Gen. 15:17 NIV). According to some scholars, this puzzling gesture of "cutting" a covenant indicates a self-curse: May I be like this cut-up animal if I don't fulfill my promise (see Jer. 34:18). Whatever a *divine* self-curse might mean, it shows how supremely dedicated God was to keeping his covenant (e.g., Jer. 33:19–26).

Philosophical Reflections on God's Command to Abraham

If Abraham was commanded to take an innocent life, should we revise the sixth commandment, "You shall not murder"? We're left with the question: "Could taking an innocent life ever be morally permitted?"[14]

Consider the following statements:

1. God's command to do X obligates person Y to do X.
2. It is wrong to kill innocent human beings.
3. God commanded Abraham to take an innocent life.

Can we hold all three of these statements with consistency? We can accept statement 1—that we should do what a good God commands. (After all, God's commands are rooted in his good nature and purposes.) On the other hand, statement 2 *normally* holds, but we must consider the specific context to see whether it always holds—apart from God's command. Could it be that under certain conditions taking an innocent life might be morally justified?

Take the specific case of an ectopic pregnancy: the fertilized human egg remains and grows in the woman's fallopian tube. If the embryo continues to grow without intervention, the mother will surely die. Ethicists generally agree that in this tragic case, it is morally permissible to take an innocent human life. The reason given is a self-defense argument—in order to protect the mother's life. Without intervention, both will die.

Now take the September 11 terrorist attacks. When four planes were hijacked, putting many more lives at risk than those of the innocent passengers, the president gave orders to shoot down the planes, which had suddenly become weapons. Again, while tragic, such a command was justified in an attempt to stop the killing of many more innocent persons.

These exceptional cases permit the taking of innocent human life. All things being equal, such actions would be morally permissible. But let's explore further.

What if the world of humans turned out to be different from the way we happen to find it? The philosopher John Hare provides this thought experiment. What if God rearranged the world so that it had different features and thus different ways to apply moral principles? Say that God willed that at the age of eighteen, humans should kill each other but that God would immediately bring them back to life and in robust health. In that case, killing people at this age wouldn't be a big deal—or *that* big a deal.[15] Yes, in this world, dead people stay dead (we're setting aside supernatural intervention, of course!). That is one of the reasons that killing innocent people in the actual world is wrong.

Let's shift to the unique historical setting of Genesis 22. We've seen that the narrative context of Genesis reveals repeated divine assurances and confirmations that Isaac was the child of promise and instrument of blessings to the nations. Abraham truly knew that Isaac would live to adulthood and have offspring in fulfillment of God's promise; so, if necessary, God would bring Isaac back from the dead: "*we* will return," Abraham promised his servants. So if Abraham *knew* God would fulfill his covenant promise, then Abraham's taking innocent human life in this case—according to God's command—was morally permissible.

Keep in mind that our ethical understanding is partly shaped by certain facts about the world. If we lived in a world in which hitting people in the head helped improve their health rather than causing harm and pain, then such actions would be encouraged. Yes, in the actual world, hitting people in the head usually causes harm. However, this illustration shows that the command "Don't hit people in the head" depends on certain givens in the world. If certain facts about the world were different, then the command wouldn't be binding on us.

So what if the facts about the world include a good God who specifically reveals himself and may issue extraordinary commands in specific, unique contexts and with morally sufficient reasons? Even if the critic believes the story of Abraham to be historically unreliable, that is irrelevant for our purposes. The critic's argument is based on the assumption that this event took place in accordance with the text. The critic's task, then, is to show why Abraham, given what he knew, shouldn't obey God's command. After all, Abraham knew the outcome: taking Isaac's life would only mean that God would resuscitate him so that God's covenant promise would be fulfilled. Yes, without God's command, which assumes covenant promises, Abraham would have been murdering his son, but that's not what we have here.

We've seen that statement 2—taking innocent human life is morally wrong—has its own set of exceptions (e.g., an ectopic pregnancy). Such exceptions aside, the critic wrongly assumes that this statement is absolutely correct while ignoring or rejecting certain truths about reality. He is ignorant of a supernatural being who is able to bring people back from the dead. He rejects the fact that God acts in history, makes promises, makes good on them, and has morally sufficient reasons for doing what he does. Statement 2 applies in a world in which dead people don't come back to life after being killed. So God's command wasn't immoral or contradictory.

The New Testament Perspective on Abraham and Isaac

Jesus as the Second Isaac

Commenting on Genesis 22, Bart Ehrman observes, "The God who had promised [Abraham] a son now wants him to destroy that son; the God who commands his people not to murder has now ordered the father of the Jews to sacrifice his own child."[16] Yet just as Caiaphas the high priest spoke better than he knew about Jesus (John 11:47–52), so Ehrman is speaking better than he knows without embracing the theological implications. Let's back up a bit, though, to put things into perspective.

In his book *The Crucified God*, German theologian Jürgen Moltmann quotes the Jewish writer Elie Wiesel, who powerfully wrote in his book *Night* on his own horrifying experiences at Auschwitz, the infamous Nazi concentration camp. Wiesel recounts one event that is particularly moving:

> The SS hanged two Jewish men and a youth in front of the whole camp. The men died quickly, but the death throes of the youth lasted for half an hour. "Where is God? Where is he?" someone asked behind me. As the youth still hung in torment in the noose after a long time, I heard the man call again, "Where is God now?" And I heard a voice inside myself answer: "Where is he? He is here. He is hanging there on the gallows."

What is Moltmann's profound response to Wiesel's assessment? "Any other answer would be blasphemy." The Christian takes strength and comfort in the fact that God suffers with us and even enters into our suffering—particularly in the person of Jesus of Nazareth on the shameful, humiliating cross. Indeed, a God who doesn't suffer "would make God a demon." An indifferent God would condemn human beings to indifference as well.[17]

The story of Abraham and his "one and only son" Isaac actually foreshadows God the Father's offering the redemptive sacrifice of the "second Isaac"—his "one and only Son" (John 3:16 NET). Rather than this being forced upon the Son—divine "child abuse," as Richard Dawkins calls it—the Father is not pitted against the Son. Christ willingly laid down his life and then took it up again (John 10:15, 17–18). God *sent* his Son into the world (John 3:17) to bear Israel's and humanity's curse and alienation on the cross. Yet, God the Son himself *came* into the world (John 9:39) to save it. With three wills of Father, Son, and Spirit united as one, the Triune God gave his very self to rescue and redeem humankind: "God was in Christ reconciling the world to Himself" (2 Cor. 5:19).

Abraham's unquestioning yet difficult obedience to the covenant God not only helped shape and confirm Israel's identity in Abraham but also provided a context for understanding God's immense self-giving love in the gift of his Son. When Abraham's dedication to God's command was confirmed, God said, "Now I know that you fear God, since you have not withheld your son, your only son, from Me" (Gen. 22:12).[18] Harking back to Abraham's sacrifice of Isaac, Paul uses this story to remind believers of God's supreme dedication to them: "He who did not spare His own Son, but delivered Him over for us all, how will He not also with Him freely give us all things?" (Rom. 8:32). Abraham's sacrifice of Isaac anticipated God's self-sacrifice in Christ. Abraham demonstrated his faithfulness to God, and God's sacrifice demonstrated his faithfulness to us.[19] The kind of demand God made of Abraham was one the Triune God was willing to carry out himself. So deep is God's love for us (Rom. 8:31–32) that the late Scottish theologian Thomas Torrance was willing to go so far as to say that "God loves us more than he loves himself."[20]

Was the Crucifixion Divine Child Abuse?

Dawkins, we've seen, considers the command for Abraham to sacrifice his son Isaac as tantamount to "child abuse and bullying." We've responded to this charge, but we should go further: was the crucifixion an instance of divine child abuse? Does the crucifixion justify violence or perhaps passivity in the face of injustice?

We've seen that the charge of "abuse" doesn't take into account the full scope of the biblical evidence—as though crucifixion was forced on the Son. Consider 1 Peter 2:21–25:

> To this you were called, because Christ suffered for you, leaving you an example, that you should follow in his steps. "He committed no sin, and no deceit was found in his mouth." When they hurled their insults at him, he did not retaliate; when he suffered, he made no threats. Instead, he entrusted himself to him who judges justly. He himself bore our sins in his body on the tree, so that we might die to sins and live for righteousness; by his wounds you have been healed. For you were like sheep going astray, but now you have returned to the Shepherd and Overseer of your souls. (NIV)

We have no passive victim here. Jesus's death on the cross was part of the predetermined plan of the Triune God—Father, Son, and Spirit. Each one suffered in this reconciling work. In *weakness*, Jesus actually *conquered* sin and the powers of darkness (John 12:31; Col. 2:15).

According to John's Gospel, as we've seen, Jesus's moment of being "lifted up" or "glorified" comes in the hour of God's great humiliation. Rather than thinking of the crucifixion as the *absence* of God—with the darkening skies

and the cry of dereliction ("My God, My God, why have you forsaken Me?")—
this is actually the moment when God's presence is most evident.

God shows himself in the crucifixion through a palpable darkness, an earth-quake, and the tearing of the temple curtain in two. (Compare this event with the darkening skies, thundering, and God's voice at Mount Sinai.) God's great moment in history comes when all seems lost, when God seems defeated. God's glory is revealed in God's self-humiliation. No, the crucifixion was no act of divine child abuse. It was the history-defining event in which God gave his very self for humanity's sake.

Further Reading

Crenshaw, James L. *A Whirlpool of Torment*. Minneapolis: Fortress, 1984. See esp. chap. 1.

Kierkegaard, Søren. *Fear and Trembling*. Various editions.

Moberly, R. W. L. *The Bible, Theology, and Faith: A Study of Abraham and Jesus*. Cambridge: Cambridge University Press, 2000.

Sailhamer, John H. *The Pentateuch as Narrative*. Grand Rapids: Zondervan, 1992. See esp. pp. 33–79.

———. *The Meaning of the Pentateuch*. Downers Grove, IL: InterVarsity Press, 2009.

Wenham. Gordon J. *Genesis 16–50*. Word Biblical Commentary 2. Dallas: Word, 1994.

Life in the Ancient Near East and in Israel

6

God's Timeless Wisdom?

Incremental Steps for Hardened Hearts

Someone posted an "Open Letter to Dr. Laura" on the internet.[1] Dr. Laura Schlessinger, of course, is the Jewish author and (until recently) radio talk show host who offers practical advice about relationships, parenting, and ethical dilemmas based on Old Testament principles. Here's part of that letter, which is saturated with sarcasm:

> Dear Dr. Laura:
>
> Thank you for doing so much to educate people regarding God's Law. I have learned a great deal from your show, and I try to share that knowledge with as many people as I can. When someone tries to defend the homosexual lifestyle, for example, I simply remind them that Leviticus 18:22 clearly states it to be an abomination. End of debate.
>
> I do need some advice from you, however, regarding some of the specific laws and how to follow them:
>
> - I would like to sell my daughter into slavery, as sanctioned in Exodus 21:7. In this day and age, what do you think would be a fair price for her?
> - I have a neighbor who insists on working on the Sabbath. Exodus 35:2 clearly states he should be put to death. Am I morally obligated to kill him myself?
> - A friend of mine feels that even though eating shellfish is an abomination (Lev. 11:10), it is a lesser abomination than homosexuality. I don't agree. Can you settle this?
> - Leviticus 21:20 states that I may not approach the altar of God if I have a defect in my sight. I have to admit that I wear reading glasses. Does my vision have to be 20/20, or is there some wiggle room here?

- Most of my male friends get their hair trimmed, including the hair around their temples, even though this is expressly forbidden by Leviticus 19:27. How should they die?
- I know from Leviticus 11:6–8 that touching the skin of a dead pig makes me unclean, but may I still play football if I wear gloves?
- My uncle has a farm. He violates Leviticus 19:19 by planting two different crops in the same field, as does his wife by wearing garments made of two different kinds of thread (cotton/polyester blend). . . .

I know you have studied these things extensively; so I am confident you can help. Thank you again for reminding us that God's word is eternal and unchanging. Your devoted disciple and adoring fan.

Twelfth-century rabbi Moses ben Maimon (Maimonides) counted out 613 distinct laws (365 prohibitions, 248 positive commands) in the Pentateuch. Talk about dos and don'ts! It's no secret that Westerners find many of these commands—and the ancient Near Eastern world in general—baffling. They seem millions of miles removed from us—all the regulations about food laws and skin diseases, not to mention prohibitions against cutting the edges of one's beard, wearing tattoos, or cooking a kid goat in its mother's milk. Israel's perplexing precepts, principles, and punishments seem odd, arbitrary, and severe.

When the New Atheists refer to the "ubiquitous weirdness" of the Bible, this may simply be the knee-jerk reaction of cultural snobbery or emotional dislike. It may also reflect a lack of patience to truly understand a world different from ours. C. S. Lewis warns against *chronological snobbery*—the "uncritical acceptance of the intellectual climate common to our age and the assumption that whatever has gone out of date is on that count discredited."[2]

How would *you* respond to the challenges of the open letter? Our discussion in part 3 will look at laws that may strike us as random, bizarre, and harsh. While the Old Testament world *is* in many ways a strange world to us moderns, to be fair-minded, we should at least try to understand it better.

After some introductory thoughts to frame the discussion, we'll look at issues related to cleanliness and the treatment of women and slaves, concluding our discussion with Israelite warfare. Hopefully, this lengthy but popular-level discussion will help put Israel's laws and ancient Near Eastern assumptions into proper perspective.

The Law of Moses: Inferior and Provisional

On Palm Sunday in 1865, the brilliant Confederate general Robert E. Lee surrendered to the tenacious, gritty Northern general Ulysses S. Grant—sometimes called "Unconditional Surrender" Grant. This day at the Appomattox Court House was the decisive end to a costly war. Well over six hundred thousand men were killed in the Civil War—2 percent of the United States' population—and three million fought in it.

Despite the North's victory, the Emancipation Proclamation that preceded it (January 1, 1863), and the attempt at Reconstruction in the South, many whites did not change their mind-set in regard to blacks. As a nation, we've found that proclamations and civil rights legislations may be law, but such legalities don't eradicate racial prejudice from human minds. A good deal of time was required to make significant headway in the pursuit of racial justice.

Let's switch gears. Imagine a Western nation or representatives from the West who think it best to export democracy to, say, Saudi Arabia. Think of the obstacles to overcome! A radical change of mind-set would be required, and simply changing laws wouldn't alter the thinking in Saudi Arabia. In fact, you could probably imagine large-scale cultural opposition to such changes.

When we journey back over the millennia into the ancient Near East, we enter a world that is foreign to us in many ways. Life in the ancient Near East wouldn't just be alien to us—with all of its strange ways and assumptions. We would also see a culture whose social structures were badly damaged by the fall. Within this context, God raised up a covenant nation and gave the people laws to live by; he helped to create a culture for them. In doing so, he adapted his ideals to a people whose attitudes and actions were influenced by deeply flawed structures. As we'll see with regard to servitude, punishments, and other structures, a range of regulations and statutes in Israel reveals a God who accommodates. Yet contrary to the common Neo-atheists' caricatures, these laws weren't the permanent, divine ideal for all persons everywhere. God informed his people that a new, enduring covenant would be necessary (Jer. 31; Ezek. 36). By the Old Testament's own admission, the Mosaic law was inferior and future looking.

Does that mean that God's ideals turn up only in the New Testament? No, the ideals are established at the very beginning (Gen. 1–2). The Old Testament makes clear that *all* humans are God's image-bearers; they have dignity, worth, and moral responsibility. And God's ideal for marriage is a one-flesh monogamous union between husband and wife. Also, certain prohibitions in the law of Moses against theft, adultery, murder, and idolatry have enduring relevance. Yet when we look at God's dealings with fallen humans in the ancient Near East, these ideals were ignored and even deeply distorted. So God was at work in seeking to restore or move toward this ideal.

We know that many products on the market have a built-in, planned obsolescence. They're designed for the short-term; they're not intended to be long-lasting and permanent. The same goes for the law of Moses: it was never intended to be enduring. It looked forward to a new covenant (Jer. 31; Ezek. 36). It's not that the Mosaic law was bad and therefore needed to be replaced. The law was good (Rom. 7:12), but it was a temporary measure that was less than ideal; it was in need of replacement and fulfillment.

Though a necessary part of God's unfolding plan, the Sinai legislation wasn't God's final word. As the biblical scholar N. T. Wright affirms, "The Torah [law of Moses at Sinai] is given for a specific period of time, and is then set aside—not because it was a bad thing now happily abolished, but because it was a good thing whose purpose had now been accomplished."[3] This is the message of the New Testament book of Hebrews: the old Mosaic law and other Old Testament institutions and figures like Moses and Joshua were prefiguring "shadows" that would give way to "substance" and completion. Or as Paul put it in Galatians 3:24, the law was a "tutor" for Israel to prepare the way for Christ.

Incremental Steps toward the Ideal

How then did God address the patriarchal structures, primogeniture (rights of the firstborn), polygamy, warfare, servitude/slavery, and a number of other fallen social arrangements that were permitted because of the hardness of human hearts? He met Israel partway. As Jesus stated it in Matthew 19:8, "Because of your hardness of heart Moses permitted you to divorce your wives; but from the beginning it has not been this way." We could apply this passage to many problematic structures within the ancient Near Eastern context: "Because of your hardness of heart Moses permitted *servitude* and *patriarchy* and *warfare* and the like, but from the beginning it has not been this way." They were not ideal and universal.

After God invited all Israelites—male and female, young and old—to be a nation of priests to God, he gave them a simple covenant code (Exod. 20:22–23:19). Following on the heels of this legislation, Israel rebelled against God in the golden calf incident (Exod. 32). High priests would also have their own rebellion by participating in deviant, idolatrous worship (Lev. 10). As a result of Israel's turning from God, he gave them more stringent laws (Jer. 7; cf. Gal. 3:19). In the New Testament, Paul assumes that God had been putting up with inferior, less-than-ideal societal structures and human disobedience:

- Acts 17:30: Previously, God "overlooked the times of ignorance" and is "now declaring to men that all people everywhere should repent."
- Romans 3:25: God has now "demonstrate[d] His righteousness" in Christ, though "in the forbearance of God He passed over the sins previously committed."

Like two sides of the same coin, we have *human* hard-heartedness and *divine* forbearance. God *put up with* many aspects of human fallenness and adjusted accordingly. (More on this below.)

So Christopher Hitchens's reaction to Mosaic laws ("we are not bound by any of it because it was put together by crude, uncultured human animals") actually points us in the *right* direction in two ways. First, the Mosaic law was temporary and, as a whole, isn't universal and binding upon all humans or all cultures. Second, Mosaic times were indeed "crude" and "uncultured" in many ways. So Sinai legislation makes a number of moral improvements without completely overhauling ancient Near Eastern social structures and assumptions. God "works with" Israel as he finds her. He meets his people where they are while seeking to show them a higher ideal in the context of ancient Near Eastern life. As one writer puts it, "If human beings are to be treated as real human beings who possess the power of choice, then the 'better way' must come gradually. Otherwise, they will exercise their freedom of choice and turn away from what they do not understand."[4]

Given certain fixed assumptions in the ancient Near East, God didn't impose legislation that Israel wasn't ready for. He moved *incrementally*. As stated repeatedly in the Old Testament and reinforced in the New Testament, the law of Moses was far from ideal. Being the practical God he is, Yahweh (the Old Testament title for the covenant-making God) met his people where they were, but he didn't want to leave them there. God didn't banish all fallen, flawed, ingrained social structures when Israel wasn't ready to handle the ideals. Taking into account the *actual*, God encoded more *feasible* laws, though he directed his people toward moral improvement. He condescended by giving Israel a jumping-off place, pointing them to a better path.

As we move through the Scriptures, we witness a moral advance—or, in many ways, a movement toward restoring the Genesis ideals. In fact, Israel's laws reveal dramatic moral improvements over the practices of the other ancient Near Eastern peoples. God's act of incrementally "humanizing" ancient Near Eastern structures for Israel meant diminished harshness and an elevated status of debt-servants, even if certain negative customs weren't fully eliminated.[5]

So when we read in Joshua 10:22–27 that Joshua killed five Canaanite kings and hung their corpses on trees all day, we don't have to explain away or justify such a practice. Such actions reflect a less morally refined condition. Yet these sorts of texts remind us that, in the unfolding of his purposes, God can use heroes such as Joshua within their context and work out his redemptive purposes despite them. And, as we'll see later on, warfare accounts in Joshua are actually quite tame in comparison to the barbarity of other ancient Near Eastern accounts.

So rather than looking at Scripture from a post-Enlightenment critique (which, as we'll see later, is itself rooted in the Christian influence on Western culture), we can observe that *Scripture itself* acknowledges the inferiority of certain Old Testament standards. The Old Testament offers national Israel various resources to guide them regarding what is morally ideal. God's legislation is given to a less morally mature culture that has imbibed the morally inferior attitudes and sinful practices of the ancient Near East.

Note too that common ancient Near Eastern worship patterns and rituals—sacrifices, priesthood, holy mountains/places, festivals, purification rites, circumcision—are found in the law of Moses. For example, we find in Hittite law a sheep being substituted for a man.[6] In his providence, God appropriated certain symbols and rituals familiar to Israel and infused them with new meaning and significance in light of his saving, historical acts and his covenant relationship with Israel.[7] This "redemption" of ancient rituals and patterns and their incorporation into Israel's own story reflect common human longings to connect with "the sacred" or "the transcendent" or to find grace and forgiveness. In God's historical redemption of Israel and later with the coming of Christ, the Lamb of God, these kinds of rituals and symbols were fulfilled in history and were put in proper perspective.

Instead of glossing over some of the inferior moral attitudes and practices we encounter in the Old Testament, we should freely acknowledge them. We can point out that they fall short of the ideals of Genesis 1–2 and affirm with our critics that we don't have to advocate such practices for all societies. We can also show that any of the objectionable practices we find in the Old Testament have a contrary witness in the Old Testament as well.[8]

The Redemptive Movement of Scripture

The Old Testament's laws exhibit a redemptive movement within Scripture. It's easy to get stuck on this or that isolated verse—all the while failing to see the underlying redemptive spirit and movement of Scripture that unfold and progress. For example, William Webb's book *Slaves, Women, and Homosexuals*[9] unpacks this "redemptive-movement" perspective found in Scripture. The contrast is the static interpretation that rigidly "parks" at certain texts without considering the larger movement of Scripture.

Some people might ask, "Is this some sort of relativistic idea—that certain laws were right for Old Testament Israel but now there's another standard that's right for us?" Not at all! Keep in mind the following thoughts we've already touched on:

- God's ultimate ideals regarding human equality and dignity as well as the creational standard of marriage made their appearance at the very beginning (Gen. 1–2).
- The ancient Near East displays a deviation from these ideals in fallen social structures and human hard-heartedness.
- Incremental steps are given to Old Testament Israel that tolerate certain moral deficiencies but encourage Israel to strive higher.

So the Old Testament isn't affirming relativism—that was true in the Old Testament but not in the New Testament. God's ideals were already in place at creation, but God accommodated himself to human hard-heartedness and

fallen social structures. Half a loaf is better than none—something we take
for granted in the give-and-take of the political process in the West. In other
words, the idea that you can make progress toward the ideal, even if you can't
get there all at once, is a far cry from relativism. Rather, your eye is still set
on the ideal, and you're incrementally moving toward it, but the practicalities
of life "on the ground" make it difficult to implement the ideal all at once.
Likewise, the Sinai laws were moving in the right direction even if certain
setbacks remained.

As we progress through Scripture, we see with increasing clarity how women
and servants (slaves) are affirmed as human beings with dignity and worth.
Let's take slaves, for instance:[10]

- Original ancient Near Eastern culture: The general treatment of slaves
  could be very brutal and demeaning, and slaves were typically at the
  mercy of their masters; runaway slaves had to be returned to masters
  on pain of death.
- Old Testament improvement on ancient Near Eastern culture: Though
  various servant/slave laws are still problematic, the Old Testament presents a redemptive move toward an ultimate ethic: there were limited
  punishments in contrast to other ancient Near Eastern cultures; there
  was a more humanized attitude toward servants/slaves; and runaway
  foreign slaves were given refuge in Israel.
- New Testament improvement on Old Testament: Slaves (in the Roman
  Empire) were incorporated into the body of Christ without distinction
  from masters (Gal. 3:28); masters were to show concern for their slaves;
  slaves were encouraged to gain freedom (1 Cor. 7:20–22). Note, though,
  that the Roman Empire had institutionalized slavery—in contrast to the
  Old Testament's humanized indentured servitude. So the New Testament writers had to deal with a new setting, one that was a big moral
  step backward.
- Ultimate ideal: This includes the genuine realization of creation ideals in
  Genesis 1:26–27, in which God's image-bearers live and work together
  harmoniously and are fairly, graciously treated; they are viewed as full
  persons and equals; and genuine humanness is restored in Christ, the
  second Adam/the new man.

While such a redemptive movement operates for women and servants/slaves
in Scripture, the same cannot be said for homosexual activity. This action is
consistently viewed negatively—a departure from God's creational design-plan.
Although I go into much detail elsewhere on the topic of homosexuality,[11] let
me briefly address it in this redemptive-movement discussion. Rather than revealing some progression in attitudes regarding homosexual activity, Scripture

from beginning to end is uniformly negative in its evaluation. Homosexual behavior, though quite common in the ancient Near East and the Greco-Roman world, was simply "alien to the Jewish and Christian ethos."[12]

Remember that homosexual *acts*—not simply *inclinations/tendencies*—were judged to be immoral by the biblical authors. No redemptive movement exists to advance homosexual acts toward increased moral acceptability.

Some claim that prohibitions against homosexual acts were "just cultural" or simply "on the same level" as the kosher or clothing laws given to Israel to set her apart from her pagan neighbors. This is too quick. Actually, the Mosaic law also prohibits adultery, bestiality, murder, and theft. Surely these go far beyond the temporary measures of eating shrimp or pork.

How then does this redemptive movement show itself in Scripture? As an illustration, consider the progression from Moses's permitting a certificate of divorce in Deuteronomy 24:1–4 to Jesus's discussion of this in Matthew 19. Jesus acknowledged the permitting—not commanding—of divorce in Deuteronomy 24 due to human hard-heartedness. Yet Jesus didn't simply "park" at this Old Testament passage and woodenly interpret it, as his religious opponents did. He considered the redemptive component of this legislation. The certificate of divorce was to protect the wife; a vulnerable divorced woman typically had to remarry to escape poverty and shame by coming under the shelter of a husband. This law took into consideration the well-being of the wife so that she wouldn't be divorced and taken back and then dumped once more at the whim of her former husband.

Many religious leaders of Jesus's day had a stilted interpretation of this passage, making it difficult for them to see that Moses wasn't commanding an absolute ethic. They couldn't see beyond the letter of the law to the spirit of the text. This conflict of interpretations is similar to the one in Mark 2:23–28: Jesus looked to the spirit of the Sabbath legislation, informing his critics that "the Sabbath was made for people, not people for the Sabbath" (v. 27 NET).

Jesus instructively pointed out that human hard-heartedness was behind such legislation on divorce (Matt. 19:8). After all, God hates divorce (Mal. 2:16); that's certainly *not* ideal. Instead, God desires that a husband and a wife cling to each other in lifelong love and commitment (Gen. 2:24). Yet the religious leaders of Jesus's day approached the Old Testament so legalistically that they missed the spirit behind the Mosaic legislation.

Throughout this book, we'll repeat the message: *Israel's Old Testament covenant wasn't a universal ideal and was never intended to be so.* The Mosaic covenant anticipated a better covenant. So when Sam Harris insists that consistent Bible believers should stone their children for believing heretical ideas, he's actually behind the times! As we move from Old Testament to New Testament, from national Israel to an interethnic Israel (the church), we see a shift from a covenant designed for a nation—with its own civil laws and judicial system—to a new arrangement for God's people scattered throughout the nations of the world and whose citizenship is a heavenly one. In the Old Testament, the death penalty could be carried out for adultery, for instance. Yet when we get to the New Testament, the people of God—no longer a national, civic entity—are to deal much differently with adultery. The professing Christian who refuses to stop his adulterous behavior after appropriate warning and loving concern is disciplined by (hopefully temporary) excommunication (1 Cor. 5:1–5). The Christian can agree that while adultery may be tolerated legally *by the state* (we don't jail people for it), it shouldn't be tolerated *in the church*. The goal of all such (hopefully temporary) discipline of removal is restoration to fellowship—that "his spirit may be saved" (v. 5).

So as we look at many of these Mosaic laws, we must appreciate them in their historical context, as God's gracious, temporary provision. Yet we should also look at the underlying spirit and movement across the sweep of salvation history.

Israel's History: Differing Stages, Different Demands

Israel's story involves a number of stages or contexts.[13]

Stage #1: Ancestral wandering clan (*mishpachah*): Genesis 10:31–32

Stage #2: Theocratic people/nation (*'am*, *goy*): Genesis 12:2; Exodus 1:9; 3:7; Judges 2:20

Stage #3: Monarchy, institutional state, or kingdom (*mamlakah*, *malkut*): 1 Samuel 24:20; 1 Chronicles 28:5

Stage #4: Afflicted remnant (*she'erit*): Jeremiah 42:4; Ezekiel 5:10

Stage #5: Postexilic community/assembly of promise (*qahal*): Ezra 2:64; Nehemiah 13:1

With these differing contexts come differing ethical demands. Each new situation calls for differing ethical responses or obligations corresponding to them. Don't get the wrong idea, however. It's not as though this view advocates "situation ethics"—that in some situations, say, adultery is wrong, but in other situations it might be "the loving thing to do."

Rather, the Old Testament supplies us with plenty of permanent moral insights from each of these stages. So during the wandering clan stage, we gain enduring insights about commitments of mutual love and concern as well as the importance of reconciliation in overcoming conflict. The patriarchs trusted in a covenant-making God; this God called for full trust as he guided them through difficult, unforeseeable circumstances. And during Israel's theocratic stage, an enduring insight is the need to acknowledge that all blessings and prosperity come from God's hand—that they aren't a right but a gift of grace. The proper response is gratitude and living holy lives in keeping with Israel's calling.

Again, what we're emphasizing is far from moral relativism; it's just that along with these historical changes came differing ethical challenges. During the wandering clan stage, for instance, Abraham and the other patriarchs had only accidental or exceptional political involvements. And even when Abraham had to rescue Lot after a raid (Gen. 14), he refused to profit from political benefactors. Through a covenant-bond, Yahweh was the vulnerable patriarchs' protector and supplier.

After this, Israel had to wait 430 years and undergo bondage in Egypt until the bag of Amorite sins was filled to the point of bursting (Gen. 15:16). God certainly didn't act hastily against the Canaanites! God delivered Israel out of slavery, providing a place for her to live and making her a political entity, a history-making nation. A theocracy was then formed with its own religious, social, and political environment.

To acquire land to live as a theocracy and eventually to pave the way for a coming Redeemer-Messiah, warfare (as a form of judgment on fully ripened sin) was involved. God used Israel to neutralize Canaanite military strongholds and drive out a people who were morally and spiritually corrupt—beyond redemption. The Canaanites had sunk below the hope of moral return, although God wouldn't turn away those who recognized God's justice and his power in delivering Israel from Egypt (such as Rahab and her family). This settling of the land was a situation quite different from the wandering clan stage, and it required a different response.

Later, when many of God's people were exiled in Babylon, they were required to handle this situation differently than in the previous theocratic stage. They were to build gardens, settle down, have children, and pray for the welfare of Babylon—the very enemy that had displaced them by carrying them into exile (Jer. 29:4–7). Israel's obligations and relationship to Gentile nations hardly remained fixed or static.

The "Is-Ought" Fallacy

Christopher Hitchens mentions "the ungrateful and mutinous children of Israel."[14] In fact, the Old Testament is full of characters who are deeply flawed and all too human. The critic wonders, "What kind of role model is Abraham (who lies about Sarah), or Moses (who murders an Egyptian), or David (who power-rapes Bathsheba and then arranges to have her husband, Uriah, killed)?" The critic has a point: this isn't the way things ought to be done. But the biblical authors often don't comment on such actions because (at least in part) they assume they don't need to. In other words, *is* doesn't mean *ought*;

the way biblical characters *happen to act* isn't necessarily an *endorsement* of their behavior.

Here's a question we should be careful to ask: What kind of example are they—morally excellent, evil/immoral, or somewhere in between? Indeed, 1 Corinthians 10 refers to the "ungrateful and mutinous" children of Israel who are full of stubbornness and treachery. They end up serving as vivid *negative* examples, and we should avoid imitating them. We can reject the notion that "if it's in the Bible, it must have God's seal of approval."

Take King David. He's more like a figure in Greek tragedies—a hero with deep flaws, a mixed moral bag. David is a lot like you and me. He illustrates the highs and lows of moral success and failure. Old Testament scholar John Barton puts it this way: "The story of David handles human anger, lust, ambition, and disloyalty without ever commenting explicitly on these things but by telling its tale in such a way that the reader is obliged to look them in the face and to recognize his or her affinity with the characters in whom they are exemplified."[15]

Biblical writers are often subtly deconstructing major characters like Gideon and Solomon, who are characterized by flawed leadership and spiritual compromise.[16] On closer inspection, the hero status accorded to Abraham, Moses, and David in the Old Testament (and echoed in the New Testament) is rooted not in their moral perfection but in their uncompromising dedication to the cause of Yahweh and their rugged trust in the promises of God rather than lapsing into the idolatry of many of their contemporaries.

Also, many of Israel's regulations are casuistic—instances of case law. That is, what rules are to be in place *if* such-and-such a scenario presents itself? These scenarios aren't necessarily being endorsed or applauded as good or ideal. For example, *if* someone steals another's possessions or *if* someone wants to get a divorce, *then* certain actions are to be taken in these inferior circumstances. Stealing *isn't* a good thing, and neither is divorce!

Unlike the abstracted ancient Near Eastern law codes, the Mosaic law is surrounded by lengthy narratives that often illustrate ethical life for Israel. Whether through failure, success, or something in between, biblical characters and events often put flesh and bones on ethical commands. Yes, the prologue and epilogue of Hammurabi's Code is full of self-exaltation and ethical promises, but it's fairly ahistorical. In fact, as we compare the Old Testament to other ancient Near Eastern worldviews—including beginnings, history, covenant, ethics, and theology—any surface differences fall away. As John Oswalt has recently argued, the Old Testament presents an utterly unique religious outlook that sets itself apart from its ancient Near Eastern counterparts.[17]

On another note, Hammurabi claims merely *to speak for* the deity Shamash; the Hittites claimed the sun god established the laws of the land. Moses, on the other hand, isn't the legislator on God's behalf. Rather, the law portrays a personally interactive God who throughout speaks in the first person:[18] "If you afflict him [the widow or the orphan] at all, and if he does cry out to Me, I will surely hear his cry; and My anger will be kindled" (Exod. 22:23–24); again, "You shall not defile the land in which you live, in the midst of which I dwell" (Num. 35:34). God's historical action of delivering enslaved Israel from Egypt becomes a model for how Israel is to live—for example, how to treat aliens and the disadvantaged in their midst.

Does this mean that humans can't use their judgment to create new laws? Not at all! Moses followed his father-in-law's advice to create a judicial hearing system so that he wouldn't be overworked (Exod. 18); David established a statute about giving a fair share to those who fought *and* to those who guarded their baggage (1 Sam. 30:22–25).

Of course, we should remember that just because the biblical text *claims* historicity and divine involvement, this doesn't yet *prove* anything. However, as Egyptologist Kenneth Kitchen and others have argued, as time goes on, the once-doubted historical claims of the Old Testament—whether the cost of slaves in the ancient Near East, camels on livestock lists during the time of Abraham, the kingship of David, the mines of Solomon, the metallurgy of the Philistines, or the existence of the Hittites—turn out to be anchored in ancient Near Eastern history.[19] The Old Testament portrays a God concerned enough to enter into and act in history, and these actual events and interactions are to shape and inspire the character and actions of the people of God.

These then are some important issues that will help us as we approach the law of Moses—a gracious gift temporarily given to national Israel that bridged God's ideals and the realities of ancient Near Eastern life and human hard-heartedness. Some of the troubling, harsh, and seemingly arbitrary Old Testament laws—though inferior and less than morally optimal—are often an improvement on what we see in the rest of the ancient Near East. God had to settle for less than the best with national Israel; however, he still desired moral improvement and spiritual obedience, despite fallen social structures and human rebellion.

Much in the Old Testament visibly reminds us of God's abundant grace despite human sin and fall-damaged social structures. We regularly see God work in and through sinful human beings—as inefficient as it seems!—to bring to pass his overarching purposes.

Further Reading

Copan, Paul. "Are Old Testament Laws Evil?" In *God Is Great, God Is Good: Why Believing in God Is Reasonable and Responsible*, edited by Chad Meister and William Lane Craig. Downers Grove, IL: InterVarsity, 2009.

Goldingay, John. *Theological Diversity and the Authority of the Old Testament*. Grand Rapids: Eerdmans, 1987.

Gundry, Stanley N., and Gary T. Meadors, eds. *Four Views of Moving beyond the Bible to Theology.* Grand Rapids: Zondervan, 2009.

Hoffmeier, James K. *The Archaeology of the Bible.* Grand Rapids: Kregel/Lion, 2008.

Webb, William J. *Slaves, Women, and Homosexuals: Exploring the Hermeneutics of Cultural Analysis.* Downers Grove, IL: InterVarsity, 2001.

Wenham, Gordon J. *Story as Torah: Reading Old Testament Narrative Ethically.* Grand Rapids: Baker Academic, 2004.

Wright, Christopher J. H. *Old Testament Ethics for the People of God.* Downers Grove, IL: InterVarsity, 2004.

7

The Bible's Ubiquitous Weirdness?

Kosher Foods, Kooky Laws? (I)

Imagine a triangle with the following categories: *God* at the top corner with *God's people* and *the land of Israel* at the bottom corners. The law given to Israel by Moses emphasized these three intimately connected angles—the *theological*, the *social*, and the *economic*. These intertwined themes undergirded God's covenant with Israel at Mount Sinai. The land (the economic) is a gift of God (the theological) to his covenant people (the social). So when a neighbor, say, moves boundary stones to enlarge his own territory, this has a social impact, affecting his neighbor's livelihood. This act of theft from a neighbor isn't just a societal violation; it's a violation against God as well. Or consider how adultery throws a family into upheaval, not to mention creating a tear in Israel's social fabric. It was an offense against God as well. So when the one God makes a covenant with his people (at Sinai) just before providing a land for them, he is attempting to reshape his people into a nation very much unlike their neighbors.

Regarding Israelite society, sociological research reveals that early on, Israel's identity was classified by tribes, clans, and households (extended families). In short, Israel had a tribal and kinship structure. Economic, judicial, religious, and even military aspects of life were oriented around this social formation. By contrast, Canaanites had a kind of feudal system with a powerful elite at the top and peasants at the bottom.

Regarding the land, many extended families were landowning households. These family units had considerable social freedom; Israelite society was "socially decentralized and non-hierarchical" until the time of Solomon onward. By contrast, Canaanite kings owned all the land. Peasants had to work the land as tenants and pay taxes.[1] Again we have dramatic improvements in Israelite law in contrast to the Canaanites.

At Sinai, the Creator bound himself to Israel in a loving covenant, the Mosaic law, which extends from Exodus 20 to Numbers 10 and is recapitulated in Deuteronomy (the "second law") for the next generation of Israelites about to enter Canaan. Included in this covenant are apparently odd and arbitrary Old Testament laws. The atheist Bertrand Russell wondered about the command not to boil a kid goat in the milk of its mother (Exod. 23:19; 34:26; Deut. 14:21); this demand seems arbitrary to our ears, he claimed, because it was rooted in some ancient ritual.[2] Like Russell, when we read commands regarding clothing laws, planting laws, food laws, laws prohibiting tattoos or ruining the corners of a beard, we may ask ourselves, "Why in the world . . . ? What's the point?" Apart from their purpose for national Israel in the Old Testament, what good are they for us today? Do they have any relevance for us? Even though Christians aren't under the Mosaic covenant "but under grace" (Rom. 6:14), what relationship does the Mosaic covenant have to those of us who live in the new covenant era initiated by Christ?

Keep in mind this statement that is worthy of full acceptance: the law of Moses is not eternal and unchanging. Despite what the New Atheists assume, Old Testament sages and seers themselves announced that the law of Moses was intentionally temporary. Yes, we see God saying things like "you shall not add to the word which I am commanding you, nor take away from it" (Deut. 4:2), but even here it is in the context of imageless worship (vv. 15–18).[3] We also see adaptation within the law itself, such as Zelophehad's daughters requesting an upgraded legislation to address their inheritance question (Num. 27:1–11). Furthermore, Old Testament saints awaited a new covenant (Jer. 31; Ezek. 36). Within the law itself, we're told that a time would come when God would circumcise the hearts of his people (Deut. 30:1–6). So let's not think that we're talking about the universal application of all Old Testament laws for post–Old Testament times.

Israel's History, God's Activity

The nineteenth-century British journalist William Ewer wrote, "How odd of God to choose the Jews." Well, grace is an amazing—and in some ways an odd—thing. Why did God select the nation of Israel and not another? Not because it possessed some right or had earned God's favor to be chosen. Israel owed its very existence to the saving activity of God in history. Israel's status as a theocracy (under "God's rule") was a privilege—and a responsibility—rooted in the grace of God.

The law of Moses didn't stand on its own as a mere ancient law code. It is unique in that it is interwoven into a dynamic historical narrative of a covenant-making God's activity through Israel from its beginnings: "I am the LORD your God, who brought you out of the land of Egypt, out of the house of slavery. You shall have no other gods before Me" (Exod. 20:2–3). God's act of gracious deliverance—along with his interaction with human beings in history—sets the context for God's giving the Mosaic law. In fact, the events in Israel's story often illustrate and clarify matters raised in the Mosaic law.

So we'll misunderstand these Mosaic matters if we think Israel's obligations consisted only in eating kosher foods, remaining ritually clean by staying away from corpses and carcasses, and going to the health inspector–priest to have skin diseases, scabs, and house mold examined. For one thing, God desired that Israel *love* him and *cling to* him (Deut. 6:5; 10:20), which isn't exactly reducible to keeping laws! Also, God's *actions* in history shaped his people's *identity* as God's covenant people; the deliverance from Egypt in turn was to shape the nation's inner motivation out of *gratitude*. For example, because God graciously rescued his people from Egypt, Israel was to remember to treat with compassion the strangers and less fortunate in their midst. His people were not to forget that they themselves were once slaves in a foreign land (Lev. 25:38, 42, 55; Deut. 15:15).

We've all met parents who think their kids can do no wrong. It's frustrating when you're the one trying to coach such kids in sports or teach them in a classroom. Some critics trump up this same charge against God—that he's treating Israel with a blind favoritism. Not so! In fact, God promised Israel that she would—and *did*—receive the same judgments God brought on morally corrupt nations surrounding her (Deut. 28:15–68; Josh. 23:14–16). God regularly reminded Israel that it wasn't her righteousness but rather God's grace that brought about her chosen status (Deut. 9:4–5); in response, they were to treat the poor and vulnerable with compassion and to be a blessing to the surrounding nations.

This picture expresses what one scholar calls the grace-gratitude ideal: "This is what God has done *for you*. Therefore, out of *gratitude* you should *do the same* for others."[4] The very context for the law was grace. Having "no other gods" (along with the other nine commandments) is preceded by the reminder that God had delivered Israel out of bondage (Exod. 20:2). Being God's graciously chosen people meant Israel's obligation to live wisely before the nations (Deut. 4:6–7).

Some atheist philosophers have objected to the idea of a "chosen people"—that this, by itself, is inherently immoral. Louise Antony asks, "What part of 'chosen people' do you not understand?"[5] Actually, she hasn't understood it all that well! Not only does God threaten Israel with the same judgments he brings on other nations, but he also reminds Israel that he is at work in the nations of the world: "Are you not as the sons of Ethiopia to Me, O sons of Israel? . . . Have I not brought up Israel from the land of Egypt, and the Philistines from Caphtor and the Arameans from Kir?" (Amos 9:7). When we encounter Melchizedek, Abimelech, Job, Rahab, Ruth, and other non-Israelites in the Old Testament, we are reminded of Paul's words—that a rescuing and redeeming God isn't far from each one of us (Acts 17:27), whether before or after Christ. And God's choosing Israel was not an end in itself but a means of blessing all the nations.

"One Nation under God"

The Manifest Destiny idea has shaped much of American life, though the term came into use in the 1840s to validate the United States' expansion into Texas, Mexico, and Oregon. Early in America's history, many Protestants who came to America believed that they were extending the Reformation; God's special hand of blessing was upon them as they hoped to realize the postmillennial dream: bringing God's kingdom to earth. The governor of the Massachusetts Bay Colony, John Winthrop (1588–1649), saw the New England colony as "a Citty upon a Hill" with "the eyes of all people . . . upon us."[6] The problem here was that the early colonists' vision was blurred; they didn't distinguish between church and state. They assumed that they were the new people of God embarking on a new exodus—an errand in the wilderness—to do theocracy the right way.

Today, many American Christians seem to mix up church and state. They believe the community of genuine believers in America is the people of God—both in heaven and on earth. But the nation of America isn't the people of God; we don't live in a theocracy. The sooner Christians realize this, the sooner the church can make a deeper impact as salt and light in society.

Things were different at Mount Sinai. A true theocracy was being created, the only one that would ever exist. Church and state were united.[7] Some readers may be thinking, "But Muslims have their theocracies too!" I'm not going to take the time here to argue for the Old Testament's unique authority as God's special revelation to Israel as opposed to, say, the Qur'an.[8] I'm just trying to help make better sense of difficulties found within the Old Testament.

Under the Mosaic covenant, national Israel uniquely existed as a theocracy, and even this arrangement wasn't intended to be ideal and permanent. This environment would help prepare the cultural and theological context for God's revelation of Jesus of Nazareth "when the fullness of the time came" (Gal. 4:4). The ministry, death, and resurrection of Jesus and the gift of the Spirit would lead to the creation of a new, interethnic community—the true Israel as the new royal priesthood and holy nation (1 Peter 2:9). The Old Testament theocracy gave way to a new covenant community from every nation and language—the church (see Matt. 8:11–12; 21:43). The fall of Jerusalem in AD 70 marked the finality of this transition, signaling the demise of national/ethnic Israel as the people of God.[9]

Again, Old Testament Israel was the one and only genuine theocracy ever to exist, and it was temporary at that. Furthermore, national Israel was established by God to help set the religious, cultural, and historical context for the saving work of Jesus the Messiah later in history. The ultimate goal is nothing less than God's salvation being brought to all the nations (Gen. 12:3) and seeing his righteous rule finally established (2 Pet. 3:13).

Holiness in All of Life

The Israelites seemed to have laws covering everything—food laws, clothing laws, planting laws, civil laws, laws regarding marriage and sexual relations. These weren't intended to be exhaustive. Rather, they were to be viewed first as visible reminders to live as God's holy people in every area of life. There wasn't any division between the sacred and the secular, between the holy and the profane. God was concerned about holiness in all things—the major and the minor, the significant and the mundane. In such legislation, Israel was being reminded that she was different, a holy people set apart to serve God.[10]

Holiness wasn't just for official priests; it was for the entire people of Israel. In fact, they were called "a kingdom of priests" and "a holy nation" (Exod. 19:6). Since God is holy or set apart, his people were to be so as well (Lev. 11:44). The Israelites were to be "marked off," just as the Sabbath day was "marked off" or "set apart as holy" to the Lord (Gen. 2:3). We could rephrase the command "be holy, for I the LORD am holy" (Lev. 19:2) this way: "You shall be my people and mine alone, for I am your God and yours alone."[11] This relationship can be compared to the serious marriage vows we talked about earlier. Being God's people meant living lives dedicated to God in every aspect of life.

This holiness wasn't religious pretense—a phoniness that looked intact and decent on the outside but was cracked and rotting within. When God prescribed rituals, he wanted them to represent humility of heart and love for God and neighbor (Ps. 51:15–19). God *hated* rites like "festivals . . . solemn assemblies . . . burnt offerings and . . . grain offerings" when God's people ignored "justice" and "righteousness" (Amos 5:21–24). Eating kosher foods and paying careful attention to rituals didn't matter if the worship of God and the treatment of others weren't kosher.[12]

Food, clothing, and planting laws weren't nitpicky commands God gave to oppress Israel. The prophets reminded her that God was primarily concerned about justice, mercy, and walking humbly before God (Deut. 10:12;

Mic. 6:8). This underlying *moral* concern, however, didn't cancel out *ritual* prescriptions—with their rich theological meaning—even much later in Israel's history after the Babylonian exile.[13]

The Christian (and we could throw in the non-Christian too) should learn the lesson God wanted to teach ancient Israel: living under God's reign should affect all of life. God's presence permeates and saturates our world. Heaven and earth are full of his glory (Ps. 19:1–2; Isa. 6:3). God isn't cordoned off to some private, religious realm. God is—either by direct control or divine permission so as not to violate human freedom—sovereignly at work in all the rhythms of creation and workings of human history. He's weaving together a tapestry to bring all things to their climax in Christ. As the hymn writer put it, God "speaks to me everywhere."[14]

Clean and Unclean

We've heard the line "cleanliness is next to godliness." In Old Testament times, this was closer to the truth than what we may think today. What does all this language of "cleanness" and "uncleanness" or "purity" and "impurity" mean? Why the ablutions for the pollutions? Why the need for purification? While we Westerners may think all of this strange, many other cultures—tribal, Islamic, Hindu—can more readily relate to such a picture. We'll be helped by thinking in terms of analogies and symbolism—not in terms of arguments—in our effort to better understand purity laws and the notions of clean and unclean.

Cleanness and uncleanness are symbols or pictures, and the Hebrew idea of life and death is behind these pictures. For the Hebrew, life wasn't mere biological existence. Humans could be biologically alive yet living in the realm of death—spiritual, moral, psychological/emotional ruin and alienation (e.g., Prov. 7:23–27). Uncleanness symbolizes loss of life.

Although many English translations use terms such as *(un)cleanness* or *(im)purity*, we shouldn't think these refer to health and hygiene. That isn't the case. Perhaps the term *taboo*—which suggests something nonmoral and perhaps mysterious that is off-limits regarding food, time, death, or sex—might capture this idea more effectively. A priest needed to be physically whole—without defect—so that the sanctuary of God might not become common. This doesn't mean that a physical defect is sinful or wrong; being polluted isn't identical to being immoral (although immorality brings pollution or is taboo). After all, animals that are taboo (unclean) are still part of God's good creation. And when unclean, Israelites weren't prohibited from worshiping God or even celebrating feasts—only from entering the sanctuary.[15]

Furthermore, sex is a good gift from God and not sinful (within marriage), yet purification was necessary after sex so as to show the distinction between God and human beings. (Keep in mind that the various ancient Near Eastern gods engaged in all kinds of sexual activity, unlike the biblical God.)[16]

Life, on the other hand, means being rightly connected to God and to the community—and properly functioning, whole, or well-ordered within (peace = *shalom*). As we'll see, carnivorous animals, whether predators or scavengers, are connected with death and are therefore unclean. Ritual uncleanness in Israel was inevitable and frequent but not in itself sinful.[17] Yet the ultimate concern behind cleanness, uncleanness, and holiness is the human heart—the very point Jesus made in Mark 7:14–23. And even though sin goes beyond ceremonial matters, it still defiles or pollutes us. Sin creates *moral* impurity or uncleanness before God. In the Old Testament, *ethical* concerns (sin) can't be separated from matters of *purity*.[18] Murder, for example, symbolically defiles or pollutes the land (Num. 35:33–34), and so it must be "cleansed." The same can be said about the language of abomination; it has the same kind of overlap as uncleanness. Sometimes it refers to *moral impurity*, other times *ceremonial impurity*—and these categories aren't always neatly distinguished in the Old Testament. To sum up, the law refers to two kinds of (im)purity: (1) *ritual* impurity (the result of contact with natural processes of birth, death, and sexual relations) and (2) *moral* impurity (through three serious sins in particular—idolatry, incest, and murder).[19]

Again, cleanness was ultimately a heart issue.[20] The nearer one came to God, the cleaner one had to be. Approaching God was serious business, and doing so called for self-scrutiny and preparation. The pursuit of cleanness was a kind of spiritual "dressing down"—an inner unveiling or internal examination of where one stood in relation to God.

Now, cleanness and uncleanness are opposite each other (Lev. 10:10), and Israelites could move in and out of these (temporary) states. In the course of life, they would become vulnerable to uncleanness. For example, an Israelite could touch a carcass or have a child and become unclean but then purify herself or offer a sacrifice and become clean again.

Cleanness and uncleanness are symbolic of life and death, respectively. Humans move between these two relative or temporary states (because of childbirth, male and female "issues," contact with death, sinful acts); these states represent being with or without life. The stable status of holiness, on the other hand, reflects closeness to life found in God, and an Israelite had to be "clean" (and closer to life) in order to approach the tabernacle's outer court; the high priest had to be clean and was specially set apart ("holy") to enter the Holy of Holies just once a year. Holy articles such as the ark of the covenant and the Holy of Holies remained holy and did not become unclean—even if the sanctuary might be cleansed under unusual circumstances (for example, 2 Chron. 28:19). More clearly in the New Testament, Jesus—"the Holy and Righteous One" (Acts 3:14)—touched lepers and a hemorrhaging woman but remained unpolluted. The relationship between life and death, holiness, and cleanness/uncleanness is illustrated in the figure below:[21]

Holiness came in degrees of set-apartness (e.g., the people, Levites, high priest). The closer an Israelite drew to a holy God (moving from the tabernacle's/temple's outer court to the Holy Place to the Holy of Holies), the more requirements he had to follow and precautions he had to take. At their consecration, high priests had special garments, washings, anointings with oil, and ceremonies that marked them as set apart. Nazirites (Num. 6) took sacred vows in consecration to God; this was shown by avoiding alcohol, haircuts, and contact with dead things. If someone from a priestly line couldn't give evidence of his ancestry, he was considered unclean (Ezra 2:62)—unfit for closely approaching God. There was a hierarchy of holiness in Israel.

Not Getting Mixed Up with Others

Attentive parents will regularly tell their kids to avoid getting mixed up with the wrong crowd. Bad company corrupts good character (1 Cor. 15:33; cf. Ps. 1:1–2). Likewise, God gave the Israelites certain actions to carry out as a way of *symbolically* telling them not to get mixed in with the false ways of the nations. Israel "wore" certain badges of holy distinction that separated them from morally and theologically corrupted nations surrounding them; they were not to get "mixed in" with those nations' mind-set and behavior.[22] Leviticus 19:19 and Deuteronomy 22:9–11 prohibit mixed breeding and other attempts at mixing: no cross-breeding of cattle; no planting of different crops ("two kinds of seed") in the same field (though this may refer to a Canaanite magical practice of the "wedding" of different seeds to conjure up fertile crops); no clothing with mixed fibers such as wool and linen (no polyesters!); and no plowing with both ox *and* donkey.[23]

The law also refers to improper *sexual* mixing as with adultery, incest, bestiality, and homosexuality, since these were viewed as *crossing boundaries* (Lev. 18:6–23).[24] Likewise, because God created male and female (Gen. 1:26–27), wearing the clothes of a person from the opposite sex (by which divinely ordained sexual distinctions could be blurred or spheres crossed) was prohibited (Deut. 22:5). As we'll see, the same applied to clean and unclean animals. These antimixing commands attempted to portray a sense of wholeness, completeness, and integrity. This is why the priest and the animal sacrifice weren't allowed to have any physical deformity (Lev. 21:18–24; 22:18–26).

A number of scholars reasonably claim that God was reminding Israel of her own distinctive, holy calling even in the very foods Israel was to eat. Animals that "crossed" or in a sense "transgressed" the individual and distinctive spheres of air, water, or land were considered unclean. Gordon Wenham puts it this way: "In creation God separated between light and darkness, waters and waters. This ban on all mixtures, especially mixed breeding, shows man following in God's steps. He must separate what God created separate."[25]

Food laws—interwoven with many other Mosaic commands regarding purity—symbolized the boundaries God's people were to keep before them:

- The sanctuary (tabernacle/temple): God's visible presence was manifested there; this was his "habitation." God gave laws to remind his people of their own set-apartness from all creation and how God was to be approached (e.g., priests as well as sacrificed animals had to be without defect or blemish).
- The land of Israel: The land of Israel was set in the midst of pagan nations with false gods, and thus there were certain commands that marked off the Israelites from other nations.

So Israel's land, Israel's sacrifices, and Israel's food all had social and theological significance. Israel's various boundaries were to remind her of her relationship to God and to the nations around her. Just as God was set apart from human beings, Israel was to be set apart in its behavior and theology from the surrounding nations. Just as the tabernacle represented sacred space within Israel, so the land of Israel itself represented a set-apartness in contrast to the nations around it.[26]

I've tried to set the stage for discussing food and other purity laws in more detail. I'll do so in the next chapter.

Further Reading

Hess, Richard S. "Leviticus." In *The Expositor's Bible Commentary*, vol. 1, edited by Tremper Longman III and David E. Garland. Rev. ed. Grand Rapids: Zondervan, 2008.

Kiuchi, Nobuyoshi. *Leviticus*. Apollos Old Testament Commentary 3. Nottingham, UK: Apollos; Downers Grove, IL: InterVarsity, 2007.

Miller, Patrick. *The Religion of Ancient Israel*. Louisville: Westminster John Knox, 2000.

Wenham, Gordon J. *Leviticus*. New International Commentary on the Old Testament. Grand Rapids: Eerdmans, 1979.

8

The Bible's Ubiquitous Weirdness?

Kosher Foods, Kooky Laws? (II)

Kosher Laws

The Hebrew word *kashrut* means to be proper or correct. Observant Jews will be alert to Kosher food labels with the letters *kshr* (in the Hebrew root form) on them. Israelites were to avoid foods such as pork, shrimp, and squid. Why were such foods unclean (not kosher)?

The listing of clean and unclean animals is found in Leviticus 11 and Deuteronomy 14. An interesting feature to these lists is that certain animals were unclean but still could be handled (for example, camels used for transportation). The issue arose when there was death. Unclean animal carcasses rendered a person impure, not necessarily touching the animals when they were alive.

Scholars have suggested various reasons for the distinction between clean and unclean. We'll look at a couple of unsatisfactory suggestions before zeroing in on a more likely solution.

- Health/hygiene: *Argument*: Israelites were to avoid eating vultures because these creatures eat roadkill and carnivores' "leftovers." And who knows what kinds of diseases these birds carry? We know that pigs can transmit diseases such as trichinosis, while the hare and coney/rock badger commonly carry tularemia. Shrimp shouldn't be eaten because they raise your cholesterol level! *Problem*: The health idea just isn't the concern in Leviticus 11 or elsewhere in the Old Testament. And why aren't poisonous *plants* considered unclean? To top it off, why did Jesus declare all these foods clean if health was really the issue in the kosher foods section of the Old Testament?[1]

- Association with non-Israelite religions: *Argument*: Animals were unclean because they were associated with non-Israelite religion in the ancient Near East. *Problem*: If that's the case, the bull should have been an abomination; after all, this animal was central to Canaanite and Egyptian religion. Yet the bull was the most valuable of Israel's sacrificial animals. As it turns out, the Canaanites sacrificed the same sorts of animals in their religious rituals as did the Israelites! (Hittites did sacrifice pigs, however.) On top of all this, ancient Near Easterners generally considered pigs detestable and typically avoided both eating them and sacrificing them in their religious rites. While Israel was to differentiate itself from neighboring nations in many aspects, animal sacrifice wasn't one of them.[2]

These two suggestions, therefore—health and religion—aren't good solutions. A couple of related angles will help us get at an answer: creation (Gen. 1) and the fall, death, and abnormality (Gen. 3).

Angle 1: Creation

Genesis 1 divides animals into three spheres: animals that walk on the land, animals that swim in the water, animals that fly in the air. Leviticus 11 lists as unclean certain animals that are connected to land (vv. 2–8), water (vv. 9–12), and air (vv. 13–25). As we've seen, these animals symbolize a mixing or blurring of categories. In contrast, the clean animal has all the defining features of its class given at creation. So animals that "transgressed" boundaries or overlapped spheres were to be avoided as unclean.

- Water: To be clean, aquatic animals must have scales *and* fins (Lev. 11:10; Deut. 14:10); so eels or shellfish, which don't fit this category, are unclean and thus prohibited.
- Land: Clean animals are four-footed ones that hop, walk, or jump. A clear indication of a land animal's operating according to its sphere is that it *both* (1) has split hoofs and (2) is a cud-chewer. These two features make obvious that an animal belongs to the land sphere (e.g., sheep and goat). Camels, hares, coneys (which chew the cud but don't have divided hoofs), and pigs (which have divided hoofs but don't chew the cud) are borderline cases; so they're excluded as appropriate land animals to eat.
- Air: Birds have two wings for flying. Birds like pelicans and gulls inhabit both water and sky, which makes them unclean. Insects that fly but

have *many* legs are unclean; they operate in two spheres—land and air. However, insects with four feet—two of which are jointed for hopping on the ground—are considered clean (Deut. 11:21–23). These insects— the locust, katydid, cricket, and grasshopper—are like birds of the air, which hop on the ground with two legs. Therefore they're clean.

Unclean animals symbolized what Israel was to avoid—mixing in with the unclean beliefs and practices of the surrounding nations. Israel was to be like the clean animals—distinct, in their own category, and not having mixed features. After all, the Israelites were God's set-apart people who were to reject the religion and practices of surrounding nations.[3]

But wasn't everything that God created "very good" (Gen. 1:31)? If so, doesn't this mean that no animal is inherently unclean or inferior? Yes, Jesus affirms this in Mark 7:19 (all foods are clean), and it is implied in Acts 10:10–16 (Peter's vision). However, as the people of God, the Israelites were reminded that holiness requires persons to conform to their class as God's set-apart people. So what the Israelites did in their everyday lives—even down to their eating habits—was to signal that they were God's chosen people who were to live lives distinct from the surrounding nations. Every meal was to remind them of their redemption. Their diet, which was limited to certain meats, imitated the action of God, *who limited himself to Israel from among the nations*, choosing them as the means of blessing the world.[4]

So no religious overlap, blurring distinctions, or compromise could exist between Israel and its neighbors. Israel was called to integrity and purity of life, to avoid what would restrict or inhibit drawing near to God. Holiness involved conformity to God's order of things. Just as clean animals belonged to their distinct sphere without compromise, so God's holy people were to belong to their distinct sphere; they weren't to mix their religion with surrounding pagan nations or intermarry with those who rejected the God of Israel (cf. Ezra 9:1–4; Neh. 13:23–30). Holiness wasn't merely a matter of eating and drinking but a life devoted to God in every area. The New Testament says the same thing: while all foods are ultimately clean (Mark 7:19), our eating and drinking matter to God, who is Lord of all (1 Cor. 10:31). Yet food matters shouldn't disrupt the church's joy and peace in the Spirit (Rom. 14:17).

Angle 2: The Fall, Death, and Abnormality

Not only do swarming and slithering creatures cut across the three spheres of classification and are thus unclean, but swarming and slithering animals in any sphere (eels, snakes, flying insects) were reminiscent of the fall in Genesis 3 and of the cursed slithering serpent. We can look at clean and unclean foods from another angle—that of curse and death. This connection with the fall is reinforced by the repetition of God's command in Genesis 2–3, "you may eat" (2:16; 3:2) or "you shall not eat" (2:17; 3:1, 3), in Leviticus 11 (vv. 2, 3, 9, 11, 21, 22).

Furthermore, the kinds of animals that were permitted and forbidden in the Israelites' diet were linked to the kind of people God wanted them to be. They weren't to be predators in their human relationships. Just as discharged blood and semen symbolized death and therefore uncleanness, so did predatory animals: "do not eat the meat of an animal torn by wild beasts" (Exod. 22:31 NIV).

A further aspect to cleanness and uncleanness seems to be an animal's appearance. An animal with either an odd-looking or abnormal appearance/feature or one that is weak and defenseless falls into the unclean category as well.

While specific kinds of food, clothing, planting, and sexual relations in their respective spheres serve as a picture of Israel's set-apartness from the nations, the distinction between clean and unclean animals in particular symbolizes how the Israelites were to act in relationship to their neighbors as well as to God. In the language of Leviticus, animals symbolize what God required from his people. For example, note the parallels between the kinds of animals offered in sacrifices in Leviticus 1, 3, and 23 ("without blemish," which resulted in a "pleasing aroma to the LORD") and the priest who is to be "without defect/blemish" (see Lev. 21:18–23). The parallel language between the unblemished priest and the unblemished sacrificial animal is striking (note the italicized words, emphasis mine):

Unblemished Priest (Lev. 21:18–20, 23)	Unblemished Animal (Lev. 22:18–22, 24)
For no one [of Aaron's priestly line] who has a *defect* shall approach: a *blind* man, or a lame man, or he who has a disfigured face, or any deformed limb, or a man who has a *broken* foot or *broken* hand, or a hunchback or a dwarf, or one who has a *defect* in his eye or *eczema* or *scabs* or *crushed testicles*. . . . He shall not go in to the veil or come near the altar because he has a *defect*, so *that he will not profane My sanctuaries*. For I am the LORD who sanctifies them.	[When anyone] presents his offering . . . it must be a male *without defect*. . . . Whatever has a *defect*, you shall not offer. . . . It must be perfect to be accepted; there shall be *no defect* in it. Those that are *blind* or *fractured* or maimed or having a running sore or *eczema* or *scabs*, you shall not offer to the LORD. . . . Also anything with its *testicles bruised or crushed or torn or cut*, you shall not offer to the LORD, or sacrifice in your land.

Getting more specific, Mary Douglas shows the connection between the kinds of animals that are permitted/forbidden to be eaten and the kind of people God wants Israel to be in its relationships.[5] The theme of (un)cleanness in Leviticus and Deuteronomy symbolizes creation's orderliness with everything in its own sphere. (So unclean animals represent a lack of wholeness or integrity in not belonging to their own sphere.) Yet something more is going on: animals that are unclean appear to be either (1) predatory animals or (2) vulnerable animals (defective in appearance or characteristics). This has a parallel to human relationships.

In regard to the predatory aspect, animals of the air (owls, gulls, hawks, and carrion-eaters such as vultures) are forbidden in Israel's diet because they themselves have consumed blood; they're predatory. Remember the prohibition against eating blood in Genesis 9:4, suggesting respect for life, which is in the blood: "the life of all flesh is its blood" (Lev. 17:14).

As for land animals, quadruped plant-eaters—rather than carnivores—may be eaten (once their blood has been drained). The fact that they (1) chew the cud and (2) have split hoofs (whether domestic or wild) are clear indications that they never eat blood and thus are not predatory (Lev. 11:3). The borderline cases—the pig, the camel, the hare, and the coney—are forbidden because they fit one but not both criteria. So land animals that are *predators* must be avoided because of their contact with blood. In a symbolic way, they "break the law."[6]

Some scholars point out another symbolic feature. Besides unclean animals that represent predation, there are others that represent *victims* of predation. For instance, prohibited aquatic animals (without scales and fins) symbolically lack something they "need"; this is a picture of vulnerability. The distinction between clean and unclean animals also serves as a picture of justice and injustice in personal relationships. Let me quote Douglas at length:

> The forbidden animal species exemplify the predators, on the one hand, that is those who eat blood, and on the other, the sufferers from injustice. Consider the list, especially the swarming insects, the chameleon with its lumpy face, the high humped tortoise and beetle, and the ants labouring under their huge loads. Think of the blindness of worms and bats, the vulnerability of fish without scales. Think of their human parallels, the labourers, the beggars, the orphans, and the defenceless widows. Not themselves but the behavior that reduces them to this state is an abomination. No wonder the Lord made the crawling things and found them good (Gen. 1:31). It is not in the grand style of Leviticus to take time off from cosmic themes to teach that these pathetic creatures are to be shunned because their bodies are disgusting, vile, bad, any more than it is consistent with its theme of justice to teach that the poor are to be shunned. Shunning is not the issue. Predation is wrong, eating is a form of predation, and the poor are not to be a prey.[7]

What's most clear in all of this is that holiness and predatory behavior don't mix. Holiness represents respect for human life, and the eating of blood (symbolizing violent death) represents predatory activity. Clean animals don't represent virtues in their own bodies, just as unclean animals' bodies don't represent vices. They just follow the "rule" of avoiding blood.[8] If scholars who claim that certain unclean animals symbolize vulnerability and defenselessness are correct, then this representation of the oppressed—the alien, the widow, the orphan (Deut. 14:29; 16:11; cf. Isa. 1:17)—would serve as a reminder that they ought to be respected.

Israel's entire way of life—down to the very food they ate (or didn't eat)—mattered to God. Their diet served as a reminder of the holy and the unholy: Israelites were to avoid the unholy activity of preying upon the vulnerable in society.

Dishonorable Discharges

Why do many levitical laws emphasize semen and blood? Leviticus 15 speaks of the emission of semen or the discharging of menstrual blood, both of which lead to impurity and the need for washing/purification. The reason? The life-death symbolism behind cleanness-uncleanness informs us that these discharges represented what was "outside" the wholeness of the human body, just as unclean foods entering the body would symbolically pollute or defile.

Vaginal blood and semen are powerful symbols of life, but their loss symbolizes death. To lose one of these life fluids represented moving in the direction of death.[9] Some scholars suggest that Exodus 23:19 prohibited cooking a kid goat in its mother's milk because this was a Canaanite fertility ritual. Others suggest that this is a case of clashing symbols. That is, life (mother's milk) and death (cooking a baby goat) collide in this scenario. Another such clash is found in Leviticus 22:28: "Do not slaughter a cow or a sheep and its young on the same day" (NIV). Likewise, life and death are symbolically at odds when semen or menstrual blood is lost from the body. This admixture of life and death represents a loss of wholeness.[10]

The symbolism doesn't stop here. Israel was surrounded by nations that had fertility cults. To have sex with a prostitute in a temple meant spiritually connecting with a particular deity. By contrast, Leviticus 15 presents something of an "emission control system"! The message to Israel was that sex has its proper place. God isn't prudish about sex. God is the author of mutually satisfying sex between husband and wife (Gen. 2:24; Prov. 5:15–19; Song of Songs). Yet, in contrast to her neighbors, Israel needed to take seriously restraint and discipline in sexual activity. Although sex brought temporary impurity, Israel was reminded that it was prohibited in the sanctuary as part of a religious ritual—unlike the sexual rituals in Canaanite religion. Again, sex within monogamous marriage is good, but adultery shouldn't be glorified by putting a religious label on it. To differentiate Israel from her neighbors, God provided certain "barriers" to keep sex in its proper place rather than degrading it—no matter how pious Israel's neighbor's made adultery appear.[11]

In contrast to the surrounding nations, wives in Israel weren't possessions to be used for sexual pleasure. Men had certain restrictions regarding when they could have sex with their wives, which was to help give women a greater measure of independence. As Richard Hess points out, such protective laws have no parallels in the ancient Near East.[12]

The Holiness Gap: Purity Laws and the Need for Grace

Being God's chosen nation was a privilege. However, a heavy burden came with it. As the peasant Tevye in *Fiddler on the Roof* tells God, "I know, I know. We are Your chosen people. But, once in a while, can't You choose someone else?" Now rewind to the Jerusalem Council (Acts 15). Many of the earliest Christians (who were Jewish) thought that one must become a good Jew in order to become a good Christian. Yes, Jesus was sufficient for salvation—sort of. But more was needed, some argued—namely, Jewishness! Peter replied to this claim: "Now therefore why do you put God to the test by placing upon the neck of the disciples a yoke which neither our fathers nor we have been able to bear?" (v. 10).

Serious-minded Old Testament Jews were regularly reminded of the gap between God and themselves. To approach God was no light thing, and throughout an Israelite's daily life were many reminders of defilement, impurity, and barriers in worshiping God. Attentive Israelites routinely experienced a "holiness gap" that existed between them and God.[13] Being placed in such a position could prompt an Israelite to seek God's grace and purification on his behalf.

Animal sacrifices were a small picture of this. The worshipers/priests would place their hands on the animal. This act symbolized that an animal was being put to death in the place of humans (Lev. 4:15; 8:14, 18, 22). Sacrifice served as a reminder of human sin and unholiness and the great need for outside assistance—that is, divine grace.

Richard Hess offers an illuminating perspective on sacrificial laws and the sequence of sacrifices in Leviticus. First is the *purification* (from sin) offering, then the *burnt* offering (indicating total dedication to God), and then the *fellowship* (or ordination) offering (chaps. 8–9, 16). This helps us better understand the nature of Christian discipleship in the New Testament epistles: first comes confession of sin, then dedication to God, and then fellowship with God. Though Christ fulfills these sacrifices (as Hebrews makes clear), they illustrate nicely what is involved in Christian discipleship.[14]

Galatians 3:24–25 mentions the law as a tutor to lead us to Christ. In other words, the law pointed *forward* toward the ultimate fulfillment of Israel's sacrifices, priesthood, and holy days. And as we've seen, such things pointed *backward* to Abraham, who turns out to be a picture of the need for grace apart from law keeping. Genesis 15:6 affirms that Abraham trusted God and was counted righteous by God because of his faith. Notice: this happened even before he was circumcised and before the Mosaic law was given. Living by faith, even without the law, enabled one to keep the heart of it (cf. Gen. 26:5).[15] The law—with all its purity requirements and sacrifices—actually revealed human inadequacy and thus the need for humans to look beyond their own resources to God's gracious assistance.

However one navigates through some of these Old Testament purity laws, the undergirding rationale behind these laws is Israel's call to live holy lives in everything. That's why the theme of holiness is explicitly mentioned in all the passages in which the prohibited food lists are given (Exod. 22:30–31; Lev. 11:44–45; 20:25–26; Deut. 14:4–21).

Upon reflection, the New Atheists' caricatures of the Mosaic law shouldn't be taken so seriously. We need patience to understand what's going on with the Old Testament's levitical laws, and we shouldn't see the law as the ideal standard for all humanity. However, we'll continue to see how it shows a greater moral sensitivity and a marked improvement over other ancient Near Eastern law codes.

Further Reading

Douglas, Mary. "The Forbidden Animals in Leviticus." *Journal for the Study of the Old Testament* 59 (1993): 3–23.

Hartley, John L. *Leviticus*. Word Biblical Commentary 4. Dallas: Word, 1992.

Hess, Richard S. "Leviticus." In *The Expositor's Bible Commentary*, vol. 1, edited by Tremper Longman III and David E. Garland. Rev. ed. Grand Rapids: Zondervan, 2008.

Kiuchi, Nobuyoshi. *Leviticus*. Apollos Old Testament Commentary 3. Nottingham, UK: Apollos; Downers Grove, IL: InterVarsity, 2007.

Wenham, Gordon J. *Leviticus*. New International Commentary on the Old Testament. Grand Rapids: Eerdmans, 1979.

———. "The Theology of Unclean Food." *Evangelical Quarterly* 53 (1981): 6–15.

9

Barbarisms, Crude Laws, and Other Imaginary Crimes?

Punishments and Other Harsh Realities in Perspective

In many ways, life in the ancient Near East was much like the "state of nature" described by philosopher Thomas Hobbes (1588–1679) in his *Leviathan*: "nasty, brutish, and short." It was no picnic, to be sure, and many of the ancient Near Eastern laws reflected this harsh, morally underdeveloped existence.

We've taken pains to show that the Old Testament laws weren't given in a vacuum. Though they presented a dramatic moral improvement, they also reflected the ancient Near Eastern social context. The punishments in the Mosaic law reveal aspects of that context. So when the New Atheists refer to barbarisms, crude laws, and other imaginary crimes found in the Old Testament, they no doubt have these kinds of passages in mind:

> If there is anyone who curses his father or his mother, he shall surely be put to death; he has cursed his father or his mother, his bloodguiltiness is upon him. (Lev. 20:9)

> Now the son of an Israelite woman, whose father was an Egyptian, went out among the sons of Israel; and the Israelite woman's son and a man of Israel struggled with each other in the camp. The son of the Israelite woman blasphemed the Name and cursed. So they brought him to Moses. . . . They put him in custody so that the command of the LORD might be made clear to

them. Then the LORD spoke to Moses, saying, "Bring the one who has cursed outside the camp, and let all who heard him lay their hands on his head; then let all the congregation stone him." (Lev. 24:10–14)

Now while the sons of Israel were in the wilderness, they found a man gathering wood on the sabbath day. Those who found him gathering wood brought him to Moses and Aaron and to all the congregation; and they put him in custody because it had not been declared what should be done to him. Then the LORD said to Moses, "The man shall surely be put to death; all the congregation shall stone him with stones outside the camp." So all the congregation brought him outside the camp and stoned him to death with stones, just as the LORD had commanded Moses. (Num. 15:32–36)

If any man has a stubborn and rebellious son who will not obey his father or his mother, and when they chastise him, he will not even listen to them, then his father and mother shall seize him, and bring him out to the elders of his city at the gateway of his hometown. They shall say to the elders of his city, "This son of ours is stubborn and rebellious, he will not obey us, he is a glutton and a drunkard." Then all the men of his city shall stone him to death; so you shall remove the evil from your midst, and all Israel will hear of it and fear. (Deut. 21:18–21)

The law of Moses seems so severe with all this death-penalty and harsh-punishment talk! Some Westerners utterly disapprove of even modest corporal punishment. In fact, it's illegal in places like Sweden and other Nordic countries. So when we come to some Old Testament laws, the punishments seem outrageous. Critics claim that stoning people is primitive and barbaric and that the death penalty itself is cruel and unusual punishment. Now I'm not advocating stoning people as a punishment, nor am I advocating a death penalty for those who reject the Bible. But we'll try to put some of this harsh-sounding legislation into perspective.

Ancient Near Eastern Law Codes and the Mosaic Law

We've repeated the theme that the Mosaic law was given to Israel in a morally inferior ancient Near Eastern context. Other ancient Near Eastern law codes existed in the second millennium BC and were known as "cuneiform" law. Cuneiform (kyoo-*nee*-i-form) refers to the wedge-shaped characters or letters inscribed on ancient Near Eastern clay tablets, typically with a reed stylus. Included in this list are the laws of Ur-Nammu (c. 2100 BC, during the Third Dynasty of Ur); the laws of Lipit-Ishtar (c. 1925 BC), who ruled the Sumerian city of Isin; the (Akkadian) laws of Eshnunna (c. 1800 BC), a city one hundred miles north of Babylon; the Babylonian laws of Hammurabi (1750 BC); and the Hittite laws (1650–1200 BC) of Asia Minor (Turkey).[1]

We shouldn't be surprised that there are parallels and overlap between various ancient Near Eastern laws and the Mosaic law. In fact, various sayings and maxims in the book of Proverbs sound a lot like adaptations or borrowings from the Egyptian *Instruction of Amenemope*. Biblical writers might quote a work of poetry—like the Book of Jashar (Josh. 10:13; 2 Sam. 1:18)—or they might consult official documents, as the chronicler does. Along these lines, we could view Moses as something of an editor of the Pentateuch who appropriates oral traditions and writings related to creation and Israel's patriarchal history. Later in the New Testament, Luke 1:1–4 reveals an orderly research project investigating the Jesus traditions that had accumulated in order to compile a trustworthy biography of Jesus. These human endeavors, writing styles, literary genres, and personalities are part of the Spirit-inspired enscripturation process. Some have compared the "making" of the Scriptures to the doctrine of the incarnation. In the person of Jesus of Nazareth, the divine and the human are brought together. Likewise, simply because a writer's personality or style or various processes are involved or because "outside" material was borrowed doesn't mean that God's inspiring Spirit wasn't involved in Scripture formation.

Again, various parallels and similarities exist between ancient Near Eastern laws and the Mosaic law (and more specifically, the covenant code of Exodus 20:21–23:33)—whether this be capital punishment for murder or legislation regarding a goring ox. And, yes, there were certain humanizing improvements in various ancient Near Eastern codes over time—for example, a softening of legislation from the Old Hittite laws (1650–1500 BC) to the New Hittite laws (1500–1180 BC). But at key points, whopping differences exist between the Mosaic law and other ancient Near Eastern codes. The Sinai legislation presents genuinely remarkable, previously unheard-of legal and moral advances. Not surprisingly, critics like the New Atheists focus on the negative while overlooking dramatic improvements. Why bother with nuance when you can score rhetorical points about the backward ways of the ancient Near East! Throughout the rest of part 2, we'll highlight these significant differences.

As we delve more deeply, we'll continue to affirm two things: (1) certain Old Testament laws and punishments were inferior to creational ideals (Gen. 1–2); (2) the Mosaic law is not permanent, universal, and the standard for all nations. So we should evaluate the severity of harsh laws and punishments in their ancient Near Eastern context instead of in light of Western culture. Indeed, to the minds of the ancient Near Eastern peoples, we Westerners would be considered a bunch of softies!

Sabbath-Breakers and Slanderers

The Sabbath-breaker story (Num. 15:32–36) comes on the heels of legislation regarding unintentional sins and defiant or "high-handed" sins. The stick-gathering Sabbath-breaker illustrates a defiant act; it's a direct violation of God's clear commands in Exodus 31 and 35. The one working on the Sabbath was to be put to death (Exod. 31:14–15). Then we have the son who blasphemes or slanders God—or "the Name" (Lev. 24)—as well as the stubborn, rebellious son (Deut. 21). These too are flagrant violations of what God had commanded.

Often, when first-time violations were committed in the midst of this fledgling nation, a harsh punishment came with it. Consider the high priests Nadab and Abihu, who [like father, like sons] imitated Aaron's idolatry in the golden calf incident (Exod. 32); they offered "strange fire"—a pagan ritual of Western Semitic cults that was associated with one's appointment to the priesthood—and were struck dead (Lev. 10).[2] And Israelite men, deliberately lured into adultery and idolatry by Midianite women, were struck down because of their disregard for God's covenant (Num. 25). During the Davidic monarchy, Uzzah tried to steady the tottering ark of the covenant as it was being transported (2 Sam. 6:1–7). How was he "thanked" for his efforts? God struck him dead! Even David was angered at God's actions.

Just think of Ananias and Sapphira in the New Testament (Acts 5), who were struck dead for lying about just how generous they were. The message wasn't lost on the early church: "great fear came over the whole church, and over all who heard of these things" (Acts 5:11). Especially in exemplary or first-time cases, God seems especially heavy-handed. God isn't to be trifled with. He takes sin seriously, and he is often setting a precedent with first-time offenses. For the people of God, these punishments were to be sobering reminders of what God expected.

So when Uzzah tried to steady the ark of the covenant, which David had placed on a "new cart," God was making very clear that his instructions in the law of Moses had been ignored. The ark was to be carried on poles by the Levites (Exod. 25:12–15; 30:4), not transported by oxcart. And certain holy things weren't to be touched on pain of death (Num. 4:15). As God told Aaron and Moses after Nadab and Abihu were struck dead, "By those who come near Me I will be treated as holy, and before all the people I will be honored" (Lev. 10:3).

The Glutton and the Drunkard: Deuteronomy 21:18–21

What about this harsh text, quoted earlier? We don't have any biblical record of this actually happening. But as with first-time offenses in Israel, the goal was to instruct: that "all Israel will hear of it and fear" (Deut. 21:21). What was the offense? We're not talking about a little practical joker or even about a teenager who won't clean up his room. No, he's an utter delinquent whose hardened, insubordinate behavior simply can't be corrected, despite everyone's best efforts. He's a repeat offender: "when they [his father and his mother] chastise him, he will not even listen to them" (Deut. 21:18). He's a picture of insubordination—"a glutton and a drunkard" (v. 20; cf. Prov. 23:20–21). This serious problem would have had a profoundly destructive effect on the family and the wider community. (Jesus was called "a glutton and a drunkard," a very serious offense in Israel.)

This son, probably a firstborn, would inevitably squander his inheritance when his father died; he would likely bring ruin to his present and future family. He was like a compulsive gambler who bets away his home and life savings right out from under his family's feet. Notice, though, that the parents don't take matters into their own hands. They confer with the civil authorities, who are responsible for keeping an orderly, functioning society. The parents aren't in the picture any longer; they're not taking charge of punishment. Rather, the community carries out this exercise of social responsibility. And when it takes this drastic action, it's a tragic last resort to deal with this trouble.[3]

Mediums, Sorcerers, and False Prophets

Mediums (or diviners) and sorcerers (or soothsayers) were prohibited from living in Israel on pain of death (Lev. 19:26). Those predicting the future through omens or signs, telling fortunes, and attempting to contact spiritual (demonic) beings were outlawed. Likewise, false prophets, who sought to lead Israel into idolatry, were to be capitally punished (Deut. 13:1–11).

The cult of the dead was common in the ancient Near East, including Canaan. Ancient Near Eastern peoples attempted to consult or connect with the dead so that they could step in and help the living. These ancient Near Eastern religions advocated mourning rituals like cutting one's body for the dead and putting tattoo marks on the body (Lev. 19:28). The act of men trimming their hair on the sides of their head or the edges of their beard (Lev. 19:27) was a Canaanite practice of offering one's hair to departed spirits to appease them (cf. Deut. 14:1).

None of that was to take place in Israel! God's people were to be different from the nations around them; they were to focus on life and the God of life, not the dead or false deities. No one was to "consult the dead on behalf of the living" (Isa. 8:19; cf. 2:5–6). Israel's priests couldn't even attend funerals, unless they were relatives of the deceased (Lev. 21:1–5). They were to be "holy to their God" (v. 6). So mediums and fortune-tellers and the like—those in the dying business—were to be capitally punished.[4]

In a democratic society like ours, all of this sounds intolerant. We're to respect the freedom of religion of others, aren't we? Yet Israel had bound herself to Yahweh, who had made a covenant with Israel—like a husband to a wife. The people of Israel themselves had vowed that they were God's and that they would keep his covenant (Exod. 24:3). They had willingly submitted to God's (theocratic) rule. So any intrusion into this relationship—whether in the form of foreign deities, political alliances, or consulting with the dead—that replaced trust in God was in violation of these covenantal vows. Even so, it's misleading for Sam Harris to speak of stoning to death a son or daughter coming home from a yoga class.[5] The point of Deuteronomy 13:6–16 is that of a false teacher who tries to "entice" the community by commanding worship of other deities ("let us go and serve other gods").

Of course, those not wanting to embrace Israel's God or obey his requirements were free to leave Israel and live in another nation. This was the obvious, preferable alternative. It was spiritually healthier for Israel and safer for theocracy opposers. Any remaining in the land were to respect the covenant and the laws that went with it.

Different Strokes for Different Folks

> If there is a dispute between men and they go to court, and the judges decide their case, and they justify the righteous and condemn the wicked, then it shall be if the wicked man deserves to be beaten, the judge shall then make him lie down and be beaten in his presence with the number of stripes according to his guilt. He may beat him forty times but no more, so that he does not beat him with many more stripes than these and your brother is not degraded in your eyes. (Deut. 25:1–3)

Remember when the American eighteen-year-old Michael Fay was jailed in Singapore back in 1994? He had gone on a rampage of theft and destruction, spray-painting cars at an auto dealership. Fay found out that you don't mess around like that in Singapore! After he and his parents pleaded with the authorities, he received four instead of six stinging lashes with a long cane.

Now the Singaporean strokes were less numerous but more severe than Semitic strokes. In Israel, rods were likely used. But, still, doesn't a punishment of forty strokes seem extremely harsh and overdone? Again, let's look more closely at this text to gain a greater appreciation for what is happening here:

1. A proper trial had to take place first.
2. No one was to exact punishment personally, taking matters into his own hands.
3. The process was to be supervised by the judge, who would ensure that the punishment was properly carried out; the punishment wasn't left up to the cruel whims of the punisher.
4. This was a maximum penalty, and offenders were typically punished with fewer strokes than forty. Yet the maximum number of lashes was fixed and wasn't to be exceeded.

5. The judge rendering the verdict and the punisher were to remember that the guilty party was a "brother." The criminal was to be protected from the overreaction of a mob or individual; he wasn't to be humiliated (so that "your brother is not degraded in your eyes").[6]

A beating with rods does sound harsh to modern ears. Yet the metaphor or image of the rod can have a gentler connotation of guiding, say, sheep (Ps. 23:4) and disciplining a child (Prov. 13:24; 22:15; 29:15).[7] Again, the law prescribed a maximum punishment of strokes, and a judge could determine a lesser punishment. Furthermore, Israel's punishments were tame compared to the more brutal law codes and ruthlessness of other ancient Near Eastern cultures. For certain crimes, Hammurabi's code insisted that the tongue, breast, hand, or ear be cut off. One severe punishment involved the accused being dragged around a field by cattle.[8] In ancient Egyptian law, punishments included cutting off the nose and the ear. The Code of Hammurabi insisted on death for a thief,[9] whereas the Old Testament demanded only double compensation for the loss (Exod. 22:4). This contrast is one of many reminders that persons mattered more in Israel's legislation than in other cultures in the ancient Near East. When punishing criminals (for perjury or libel, for example), Egyptian law permitted between one hundred and two hundred strokes; the hundred-stroke beating was the mildest form of punishment.[10] Regarding penalties for theft in the Old Testament, David Baker observes, they "are much more humane than in most [ancient Near Eastern] laws, and never involve mutilation, beating, or death."[11]

How does Deuteronomy 25:1–3 look to you now? Israel's legislation allowed no more than forty strokes for a criminal's punishment. This was the maximum penalty, one left up to the judge's assessment. By contrast, punishments in other places in the ancient Near East were extremely severe. On top of all this, in Babylonian or Hittite law, for example, status or social rank determined the kind of sanctions for a particular crime. By contrast, biblical law held kings and priests and those of social rank to the same standards as the common person.[12]

Some may point to the following example as a moral upgrade. Initially, Hittite law stated that if a person plowed a sown field and sowed his own seed in its place, he was to be put to death.[13] But in later legislation, the criminal needed ritual purification and to bring a sacrifice.[14] While we can be grateful for this improvement, it still came nowhere near Israel's strong emphasis on compensation for property crimes, not the death penalty. People mattered more than property in Israel, a noted contrast with the rest of the ancient Near East.

"An Eye for an Eye"?

What of Scripture's emphasis on "an eye for an eye and a tooth for a tooth"? Some consider such exacting punishments ruthless and barbaric. We should take another look, though. A much different picture emerges upon closer inspection.

Such exacting punishments—called *lex talionis*—are mentioned in several places: Exodus 21:23–25; Leviticus 24:17–22; and Deuteronomy 19:16–21. What's interesting is that in none of the cases is "an eye for an eye" taken literally. Yes, "a life for a life" was taken in a straightforward way when it came to murder. Yet each example in these passages calls for (monetary) compensation, not bodily mutilation. For example, following on the heels of the *lex talionis* passage of Exodus 21:23–25 comes, well, Exodus 21:26–27! And it illustrates the point we're making quite nicely: "If a man hits a manservant or maidservant in the eye and destroys it, he must let the servant go free to compensate for the eye. And if he knocks out the tooth of a manservant or maidservant, he must let the servant go free to compensate for the tooth" (NIV). We don't have a literal *eye* or *tooth* in view here, just compensation for bodily harm. Scholars such as Raymond Westbrook note that the *lex talionis* as a principle of compensation wasn't taken literally. [15]

The point of *lex talionis* is this: the punishment should fit the crime. Furthermore, these were the maximum penalties; punishments were to be proportional and couldn't exceed that standard. And a punishment could be less severe if the judge deemed that the crime required a lesser penalty.

Later in the New Testament, Jesus himself didn't take such language literally either. This language had been misapplied by Jesus's contemporaries *outside* the law courts as a pretext for personal vengeance (Matt. 5:38–39). At any rate, Jesus took this language no more literally than he did the language of plucking out eyes and cutting off hands if they lead one to sin (Matt. 5:29–30).

What's more, carrying out punishments that fit the crime protected the more vulnerable—the poor, the weak, the alienated. The wealthy and powerful couldn't dictate the terms of punishment; in fact, the socially elite could receive these proportional punishments like everyone else. In addition, this *lex talionis* principle served as a useful guide to prevent blood feuds and disproportionate retaliation (think Mafia methods here). When we compare Israel's punishments with other ancient Near Eastern legislation, the law of Moses presents a noteworthy moral development. As biblical scholar Brevard Childs points out, the *lex talionis* principle "marked an important advance and was far from being a vestige from a primitive age."[16]

Some people might bring up the point that the Code of Hammurabi already had its own *lex talionis*, what we could call "a bone for a bone" as well as "a tooth for a tooth." However, this applied when an aristocrat (a patrician)—not a common person (a plebian)—was injured by a peer.[17] Furthermore, we know that the Code of Hammurabi called for the cutting off of actual hands, noses, breasts, and ears! Middle Assyrian laws (around 1100 BC)—over two hundred years after the law of Moses was given at Sinai—were outrageously disproportionate. They included beatings up to one hundred blows as well as mutilations. So the expression "an eye for an eye" was a measure of justice, not something Israel took literally.

Ox-goring legislation provides an interesting contrast between the Mosaic law and other ancient Near Eastern codes. Codes like those of Hammurabi or Eshunna, for example, didn't reflect as high a regard for human life as did the Mosaic code. In the other codes, if an ox was in the habit of goring but the owner took no precautions to prevent it so that it gored and killed a free-born person, then a half mina (or two-thirds of a mina) in silver was paid to the victim's family and the ox lived.[18] By contrast, Exodus 21:28–36 presents a more severe maximum punishment because of the value of human life, which was reflected in Israel's laws. The requirement was to put a goring ox to death (cf. Gen. 9:4–6), and its meat couldn't be eaten. Furthermore, if an ox was in the habit of goring and the owner did nothing to prevent this so that the ox killed a man or a woman, then the *owner*—not just the ox—could be put to death as a maximum penalty (and we'll look at another angle on this shortly).

Likewise, Hammurabi insisted that if a homebuilder was careless and his construction collapsed and killed a minor, then the builder's *own child* would be killed.[19] By contrast, killing a child for the parents' offenses (or a parent for his child's offenses) wasn't permitted in Israel (Deut. 24:16).

Beyond all this, the ancient world lived by an unwritten code to take revenge for the killing of a family member. And it didn't matter whether or not the death was accidental: "You killed my family member; I'll kill someone in your family!" By contrast, Israel's law distinguished between *accidental* killing and *intentional* killing. It provided cities of refuge for those who had accidentally killed another (Exod. 21:12–13), a way of preventing ongoing blood feuds.[20]

The noted historian Paul Johnson commented on the Code of Hammurabi, though much the same could be said for other ancient Near Eastern law codes: the "dreadful laws are notable for the ferocity of their physical punishments, in contrast to the restraint of the Mosaic Code and the enactments of Deuteronomy and Leviticus."[21]

One further matter: We've seen that the various ancient Near Eastern laws we've explored are far more harsh in comparison to Israel's laws. Even so, a range of scholars argue that punishments in the Mosaic law—and even in various ancient Near Eastern law codes—are less fierce in actual practice. For example, Numbers 35:31 states, "You shall not take ransom [i.e., substitute payment] for the life of a murderer who is guilty of death, but he shall surely be put to death." This idea is reinforced in Exodus 21:29–30 (an ox goring a human to death as the result of owner negligence); since this isn't premeditated murder, verse 30 allows for the possibility of monetary payment instead of taking the owner's life: "If a ransom is demanded of him, then he shall give for the redemption of his life whatever is demanded of him."

Walter Kaiser points out the general observation of Old Testament scholars: There were some sixteen crimes that called for the death penalty in the Old

Testament. Only in the case of premeditated murder did the text say that the officials in Israel were forbidden to take a "ransom" or a "substitute." This has widely been interpreted to imply that in all the other fifteen cases the judges could commute the crimes deserving of capital punishment by designating a "ransom" or "substitute." In that case the death penalty served to mark the seriousness of the crime.[22] One could cite other scholars such as Raymond Westbrook, Jacob Finkelstein, and Joseph Sprinkle, who readily concur with this assessment.[23]

So if we take the severe Old Testament punishments literally, we observe that the Mosaic law is far *less* strict than other ancient Near Eastern law codes. If, on the other hand, we follow these scholars who take the Old Testament's capital punishment laws as allowing for a "ransom" payment instead (with the exception of premeditated murder), then this opens up a dramatically new perspective on these apparently severe punishments.

Infant Sacrifice in Israel?

Not a few critics will point out that the Old Testament assumes that infant sacrifice was acceptable in Israelite society and demanded as an act of worship by the God of Israel. Some will showcase Abraham and Isaac (though hardly an infant) as one such example. Such criticisms are off the mark, however.

For one thing, the Mosaic law clearly condemns child sacrifice as morally abhorrent (Lev. 18:21; 20:2–5; Deut. 12:31; 18:10). As Susan Niditch points out in *War in the Hebrew Bible*, the "dominant voice" in the Old Testament "condemns child sacrifice" since it opposes God's purposes and undermines Israelite society.[24]

Let's look at a couple of passages that allegedly suggest that human sacrifice was acceptable.

Mesha, King of Moab: 2 Kings 3:27

Then he took his oldest son who was to reign in his place, and offered him as a burnt offering on the wall. And there came great wrath against Israel, and they departed from him and returned to their own land. (2 Kings 3:27)

Here, Mesha, king of Moab, sacrifices his firstborn son on the wall of Kir Hareseth (in Moab). After this, the Israelite army withdrew because of "wrath." Some think this is *God's* wrath and that God is showing his *approval* of Mesha's sacrifice of his son by responding in wrath against Israel. This view, however, has its problems:

- This notion is at odds with clear condemnation of child sacrifice earlier in the Pentateuch (Deut. 12:31; 18:10) as well as repudiation of it within Kings itself (2 Kings 16:3; 17:7; 21:6).

- The word fury or wrath (*qetseph*) isn't *divine* wrath.[25] Elsewhere in 2 Kings, a cognate word (coming from the same root as *qetseph*) clearly refers to *human* fury (5:11; 13:19).

- Typically, commentators suggest several plausible interpretations: (1) This was Moab's fury against Israel because their king, Mesha, forced by desperation, sacrificed his son; Mesha's goal was to prompt Moab's renewed determination to fight. (2) The Israelites were filled with horror or superstitious dread when they saw this human sacrifice, causing them to abandon the entire venture. (3) Even though Mesha had failed in his attempt to break through the siege (perhaps to head north for reinforcements), he was still able to capture the king of Edom's firstborn son, whom he sacrificed on the wall, which demoralized Edom's army. The wrath of Edom's army ended the war because they withdrew from the military coalition of Israel, Judah, and Edom.[26]

Jephthah's Daughter: Judges 11:30–40

Israel's judge Jephthah made a rash vow: "whatever comes out of the doors of my house to meet me when I return in peace from the sons of Ammon [who were oppressing Israel], it shall be the LORD's, and I will offer it up as a burnt offering" (Judg. 11:31). Perhaps he was thinking it might be one of his servants, who would most likely come out to attend to him. Yet he was horrified to see that "his daughter was coming out to meet him with tambourines and with dancing" (v. 34).

Some Old Testament scholars argue that Jephthah didn't literally sacrifice his daughter. Most, however, are convinced that the text asserts this. So let's take for granted the worst-case scenario. Then come the inevitable questions: Wouldn't Jephthah have clearly known that child sacrifice was immoral and that God judged the Canaanites for such practices? Why then did he go ahead with this sacrifice? Was it because God really did approve of child sacrifice after all?

We've already affirmed that *is* doesn't mean *ought* in the Old Testament; just because something is *described* doesn't mean it's *prescribed* as a standard to follow. Certain behaviors are just bad examples that we shouldn't follow (cf. 1 Cor. 10:1–12). So let's make the necessary changes and apply our questioner's reasoning to another judge—Samson. As a judge of Israel, wouldn't he have clearly known that touching unclean corpses was forbidden (Judg. 14:8–9), especially given his (permanent) Nazirite vow (Num. 6)? Wasn't he fully aware that consorting with prostitutes was prohibited (Judg. 16:1)? You get the idea. Keep in mind that we're talking about the era of Israel's judges. To borrow from Charles Dickens, this was in large part the worst of times, an age of foolishness, the season of darkness, and the winter of despair. So critics should be careful about assuming that Jephthah (or Samson) was in peak moral condition.

Some might wonder, "Didn't 'the Spirit of the LORD' come on Jephthah?" (Judg. 11:29). Yes, but we shouldn't take this as a wholesale divine endorsement of all Jephthah did—no more so than the Spirit's coming on Gideon (Judg. 6:34) was a seal of approval on his dabbling with idolatry (Judg. 8:24–27), or of Ehud's, for that matter (Judg. 3:26). Yes, these judges of Israel would surely have known idolatry was wrong. Likewise, "the Spirit of the LORD" came upon Samson to help Israel keep the Philistines at bay (Judg. 14:6, 19; 15:14). Yet his plans to marry a Philistine woman, cavorting with a prostitute, and getting mixed up with Delilah all reveal a judge with exceedingly poor judgment! We can surely find a lesson in here somewhere about how God works *despite* human sin and failure.

The theology of Judges emphasizes a remarkable low point of Israelite morality and religion, with two vivid narratives at the book's end to illustrate this (chaps. 17–21). Israel continually allowed itself to be "Canaanized." And in light of Judges' repeated theme, "every man did what was right in his own eyes" (17:6; 21:25; cf. 2:10–23), we shouldn't be surprised that Israel's leaders were also morally compromised. We don't have to look hard for negative role models in Judges, when Israel was in the moral basement. The Jephthah story needs no explicit statement of God's obvious disapproval.

Some might press the point: doesn't the Old Testament refer to offering the firstborn to God (Exod. 22:29–30)? Following Ezekiel 20:25–26, they claim that God literally gave harmful ("not good") statutes by which Israel could not "live"—commands involving sacrificing the firstborn child in the fire. They assert that Yahweh just didn't like it when Israel sacrificed children to *other* gods!

However, no such distinction is made; infant sacrifice—whether to Yahweh or to Baal or Molech—is still detestable. Yes, this was a common practice in Israel and Judah (e.g., 2 Kings 17:17; 23:10), and kings Ahaz, Manasseh, and others made their sons and daughters "pass through the fire" (2 Kings 16:3; 2 Chron. 33:6). But commonality here doesn't imply acceptability. Exodus does refer to the "redemption"—not sacrifice—of the womb-opening firstborn child; God himself redeemed his firstborn Israel by bringing him up from Egypt (Exod. 13:13; cf. 4:23).

What then is Ezekiel talking about? The text clearly indicates that God gave the Sinai generation "statutes" (*chuqqot*) (e.g., Sabbath commands) by which an Israelite might "live" (20:12–13). Israel rejected these laws given at Sinai; they refused to follow them (v. 21). So God "withdrew [His] hand." God responded to the second (or wilderness) generation as he does in Romans 1: he "gave them over to statutes that were not good and laws they could not live by" (Ezek. 20:25 NIV). Ezekiel not only distinguishes this word *statutes* (the masculine plural *chuqqim*) from *statutes* elsewhere in the context (the feminine noun *chuqqot*). The text also involves quite a bit of irony. God sarcastically tells Israel to "go, serve everyone his idols" (Ezek. 20:39); to put it another way, "go, sacrifice your children." This ironic "statute" to stubborn Israel to continue in idolatry and infant sacrifice is comparable to God's sarcasm in Amos 4:4: "Go to Bethel and sin; go to Gilgal and sin yet more" (NIV). The same is true of the prophet Micaiah, who tells the disobedient, Yahweh-ignoring king of Israel, "Go up and succeed, and the LORD will give it into the hand of the king" (1 Kings 22:15). These are the sorts of sarcastic "commands" that aren't "good" and by which Israel can't "live."[27]

The Value of Unborn Life

One of the big differences between Old Testament laws and their ancient Near Eastern counterparts is the value of human life. Despite this, it's not unusual to hear that in ancient Israel unborn life wasn't as valuable as life outside the womb. Indeed, certain proabortion advocates have sought theological justification for permitting abortion in the following passage:

> If men who are fighting hit a pregnant woman and she gives birth prematurely [some advocate an alternate reading: "she has a miscarriage"] but there is no serious injury, the offender must be fined whatever the woman's husband demands and the court allows. But if there is serious injury, you are to take life for life, eye for eye, tooth for tooth, hand for hand, foot for foot, burn for burn, wound for wound, bruise for bruise (Exod. 21:22–25 NIV).

The key issue is this: should the Hebrew word *yalad* be translated "give birth prematurely" or "have a miscarriage"? If the mother miscarries, then the offender only has to pay a fine; the implication in this case is that the unborn child isn't as valuable and therefore isn't deserving of care normally given to a person outside the womb. Apparently, this Old Testament passage shows a low(er) regard for unborn life.

Let's skip to another passage, Psalm 139, which strongly supports the value of the unborn:

> For you created my inmost being;
>   you knit me together in my mother's womb.
> I praise you because I am fearfully and wonderfully made;
>   your works are wonderful,
>   I know that full well.
> My frame was not hidden from you
>   when I was made in the secret place.
> When I was woven together in the depths of the earth,
>   your eyes saw my unformed body.
> All the days ordained for me
>   were written in your book
>   before one of them came to be. (vv. 13–16 NIV)

Keep this text in mind as we go back to the Exodus 21 passage.

Contrary to the above claims, Exodus 21 actually supports the value of unborn human life. The word *yalad* means "go forth" or "give birth," describing a normal birth (Gen. 25:26; 38:28–30; Job 3:11; 10:18; Jer. 1:5; 20:18). It's always used of giving birth, not of a miscarriage. If the biblical text intended to refer to a miscarriage, the typical word for "miscarry/miscarriage" (*shakal/shekol*) was available (e.g., Gen. 31:38; Exod. 23:26; Job 21:10; Hosea 9:14). *Miscarry* isn't used here.

Furthermore, *yalad* ("give birth") is always used of a child that has recognizable human form or is capable of surviving outside the womb. The Hebrew word *nepel* is the typical word used of an unborn child, and the word *golem*, which means "fetus," is used only once in the Old Testament in Psalm 139:16, which we just noted: God knew the psalmist's "unformed body" or "unformed substance."

This brings us to another question: Who is injured? The baby or the mother? The text is silent. It could be either, since the feminine pronoun is missing. The gist of the passage seems to be this:

> If two men fight and hit a pregnant woman and the baby is born prematurely, but there is no serious injury [to the child or the mother], then the offender must be fined whatever the husband demands and the court allows. But if there is serious injury [to the baby or the mother], you are to take life for life, eye for eye.

These verses then actually imply the intrinsic value of the unborn child—that the life of the offender may be taken if the mother's or the child's life is lost. The unborn child is given the same rights as an adult (Gen. 9:6).

New Atheists and other critics often resort to caricatures or misrepresentations of the Old Testament laws. While Mosaic laws do not always reflect the ultimate or the ideal (which the Old Testament itself acknowledges), these laws and the mind-set they exhibit reveal a dramatic moral improvement and greater moral sensitivity than their ancient Near Eastern counterparts.

Further Reading

Longman III, Tremper, and David E. Garland, eds. *The Expositor's Bible Commentary*. Vol. 1. Rev. ed. Grand Rapids: Zondervan, 2008.

Stuart, Douglas K. *Exodus*. New American Commentary 2. Nashville: B & H Publishing, 2008.

Wright, Christopher J. H. *Deuteronomy*. New International Biblical Commentary 4. Peabody, MA: Hendrickson, 1996.

Wright, Christopher J. H. *Old Testament Ethics for the People of God*. Downers Grove, IL: InterVarsity, 2004.

10

Misogynistic?

Women in Israel

When we start talking about the treatment of women in the Old Testament, the pandemonium begins! Feminists accuse Old Testament writers of endorsing all kinds of sexism, patriarchy (socially oppressive structures favoring men over women), and even misogyny (hatred of women). *Misogynistic* is one of the adjectives Richard Dawkins uses to describe the Old Testament God.

Why does Sarah refer to her husband as "my master" (Gen. 18:12 NIV)? Why do Hebrew girls belong to their "father's house" (e.g., Lev. 22:13)? Why does an Israelite woman remain ceremonially unclean for only forty days after giving birth to a boy but eighty days after having a girl (Lev. 12:2–5)? Why can't women participate in the priesthood of Israel? What about all those concubines? What about levirate marriage? Why does God permit polygamy? Doesn't the Old Testament endorse a bride-price, which only reinforces the idea of women as property?

In this chapter, we'll look at the underlying male-female equality in the Old Testament and some passages that allegedly suggest otherwise. Then in the next chapter we'll review some key passages related to polygamy (multiple wives) and concubines as well as related passages that critics commonly mention.[1]

Genesis 1–2: The Original Ideal

However we understand the levitical laws and Old Testament narratives regarding women, Genesis 1–2 points us to the ideal view of women, which is far from a fallen, skewed, or demeaning attitude. God creates male *and female* in his image (Gen. 1:26–27). Eve is taken from Adam's rib (Gen. 2:22), a picture of equality and partnership, not one of a superior to an inferior. Marriage is to be a partnership of equals, and sex (the one-flesh union) is to be enjoyed within the safety of lifelong, heterosexual marriage (Gen. 2:24).

Although Genesis 1–2 spells out the ideal of male-female equality, laws regarding women in Israel take a realistic approach to fallen human structures in the ancient Near East. In Israel's legislation, God does two things: (1) he works within a patriarchal society to point Israel to a better path; and (2) he provides many protections and controls against abuses directed at females in admittedly substandard conditions. Do we see examples of oppressed women in the Old Testament? Yes, and we see lots of oppressed *men* as well! In other words, we shouldn't consider these negative examples *endorsements* of oppression and abuse.

The Equality of Women—from Various Angles

Reading the Old Testament reveals two important parallel features: (1) patriarchal social structures in Israelite families alongside (2) the honoring of women as equals, including a bevy of prominent matriarchs and female leaders in Israel.

On the one hand, fathers had legal responsibility for their households (often reaching fifteen to twenty members); this included matters of family inheritance, property ownership, marital arrangements of sons and daughters, and being spokesman for family matters in general. For instance, when a daughter or a wife took a vow, such solemn promises were to be approved by the father/ husband as the legal point person in the home (Num. 30). This represents more than just legal protection for a wife or a daughter, though. Embedded social attitudes and ideas die hard, especially in places like the ancient Near East. Patriarchal attitudes were strongly held in the ancient Near East—attitudes that were a far cry from the equality language at creation. Genesis 2:24 affirms that a man was to leave his parents and "cling" to his wife as an equal partner (NRSV). But the fall deeply affected human relationships. As a result, Sarah followed the ancient Near Eastern custom of calling her husband "lord ['*adon*]" (Gen. 18:12). She gave her handmaid Hagar to Abraham to produce a child (Gen. 16:3), a common ancient Near Eastern practice. Later king Abimelech "took" Sarah as his wife (Gen. 20:2–3). And when Sarah gave birth to Isaac, she "bore a son to Abraham" (Gen. 21:2–3).

On the other hand, these embedded patriarchal attitudes distorted the many strong biblical affirmations of female dignity and equality. Mothers/wives deserved honor equal to that of husbands/fathers, and strong matriarchs both helped lead Israel and had sway within their households. Yes, the husband was the legal point person for the Israelite family, but we shouldn't automatically assume that women considered this an oppressive arrangement. In fact, wives in many Old Testament marriages were, for all practical purposes, equal and equally influential in their marriages and beyond (e.g., Prov. 31).

In fact, many passages speak more of protection and care for those who are often taken advantage of, especially widows or divorced women. God is concerned about justice for widows and the other vulnerables of society such as orphans and non-Israelite strangers or aliens. God sternly warned would-be oppressors that he's on the side of the weak and defenseless (Exod. 22:22; Deut. 10:18; 14:29; 24:17, 19; etc.).

Now, feminists would dispute the claim that Israelite women/wives were considered equal in personhood and dignity to men/husbands. Let's address this point. Yes, patriarchal structures strongly influenced the mind-set of Israelite society. Yet we see undeniable affirmations of equality in the Old Testament from theological, historical, and legal perspectives.

Theological: Female equality is presumed in the following passages (emphasis added):

Genesis 1:27: "God created man in His own image, in the image of God He created him; *male and female* He created them."

Genesis 2:24: "For this reason a man shall leave *his father and his mother*, and be joined to his wife; and they shall become one flesh."

Exodus 20:12: "Honor *your father and your mother*, that your days may be prolonged in the land which the LORD your God gives you" (cf. 21:15; Deut. 5:16; 21:18–21; 27:16).

Leviticus 19:3: "Every one of you shall reverence *his mother and his father*" (cf. 20:9).

Proverbs 6:20: "My son, observe the commandment of *your father* and do not forsake the teaching of *your mother*."

Proverbs 18:22: "He who finds a wife finds a good thing and obtains favor from the LORD."

Proverbs 19:26: "He who assaults *his father* and drives *his mother* away is a shameful and disgraceful son."

Proverbs 23:22: "Listen to *your father* who begot you, and do not despise *your mother* when she is old."

Proverbs 23:25: "Let *your father and your mother* be glad, and let her rejoice who gave birth to you."

Song of Songs 6:3: "I am my beloved's and my beloved is mine" (cf. 7:10).

When it comes to Genesis 2:18, where Adam's wife is called a suitable "helper ['*ezer*]," we should recall that, rather than suggesting inferiority, the same word is used of God elsewhere in Scripture (Pss. 10:14; 30:10; 54:4). We could list more passages on these theological aspects, but you get the idea.

Historical: The Old Testament is full of powerful matriarchs who were highly valued and exerted a great deal of influence. The testimony of the Old Testament authors reveals a perspective that can hardly be called misogynistic. Consider the following list for starters: Sarah, Hagar, Rebekah, Rachel, Leah, and Tamar (all in Genesis); the Hebrew midwives Shiphrah and Puah (Exod. 1); the Egyptian princess (Exod. 2); Miriam and Jethro's seven daughters, including Zipporah, Moses's wife (Exod. 2, 4, 15); the daughters of Zelophehad (Num. 27); Deborah, Ruth, Naomi, Abigail, and Bathsheba (Judg. 4–5; Ruth 1–4; 1 Sam. 25; 1 Kings 1–2); and let's not forget that excellent Proverbs 31 woman. These strong women stepped forward and wielded influence with the best of the men.

Legal: The moral and ceremonial laws of Israel presumed that women were not only equal but also shared equal moral responsibility with the men. One author writes that the system of Israel's ritual impurity laws is "rather evenhanded in its treatment of gender."[2] Some might quibble with the ceremonial uncleanness of menstruation, which obviously affects women and not men. But as we'll see, men have their own issues! And the purity laws also address these (e.g., Lev. 15:16–18, 32; 22:4; Deut. 23:10).

The moral—not just ceremonial—aspects of the levitical laws that address incest and adultery (e.g., Lev. 18, 20) apply to men and women without distinction. In fact, those claiming that committing adultery against one's neighbor's wife was a "property offense" in Israel are incorrect. Both the man and the woman can be put to death for adultery, but, unlike the Code of Hammurabi, Old Testament law never requires the death penalty for property offenses.[3]

Texts That (Allegedly) Promote Female Inferiority

Now it's time to look at some of those potentially embarrassing passages that put down women.

The Trial of Jealousy: Numbers 5

Let's summarize the theme of this text. If a man suspected his wife of adultery, he could bring her before the priest to accuse her. In this case, two or three witnesses weren't available (Deut. 17:6–7); the only "witness" was the husband's suspicion that his wife had been cheating on him. Critics charge that this would have been a terrifying ordeal: a cheating wife's abdomen would swell and her thigh would shrivel after drinking "the water of bitterness." Critics raise the question, "Why couldn't *a woman* bring her husband before the priest if she suspected that *he* was guilty of adultery?"

As it turns out, critics have chosen a poor text to illustrate oppression of women. For one thing, consider the context, which gives us every reason to think that this law applied to *men* as well. Before and after this passage, the legislation concerns both men and women: "Israelites" (Num. 5:2 NIV), "a man or woman" (Num. 5:6), "a man or a woman" (Num. 6:2). It wasn't just the husband's prerogative to call for this special trial; the wife could as well.

Second, this priestly court was actually arranged for the protection and defense of women, not to humiliate them before proud husbands or prejudiced mobs. This law protected women from a husband's violent rage or arbitrary threat of divorce to get rid of his wife cheaply.[4] And if the woman happened to be guilty, then she'd *rightly* be terrified by a supernatural sign affecting her body. In fact, as with the deaths of Ananias and Sapphira in the early church (Acts 5), the Israelites would have a sobering warning regarding God's attitude toward adultery.

Some critics have compared this event to "the River Ordeal" practiced in non-Israelite ancient Near Eastern cultures (Babylon, Assyria, Sumer). How did this work? When criminal evidence was inconclusive, the accused would be thrown into a bitumen well—that is, a natural petroleum tar commonly used as a sealant and adhesive and as mortar for bricks. In Sumer, this tar "river" was the abode of the god Id (which means "river"). Sometimes these "jumpers" and "plungers," who went "into the god," were overcome by the liquid and its toxic fumes; most survived (they were "spat out" by the river god), but it was still a nightmare to endure. If one was overcome by the "river," he was guilty since his death was the river god's "judgment." If he survived, he was innocent and the accuser was guilty of making false charges.[5]

There's a big difference between this "ordeal" and Numbers 5, though. The river ordeal was the general treatment for inconclusive criminal evidence *across the board*. In the Mosaic law, however, a charge couldn't be established unless two or three witnesses were available; otherwise, the prosecuting side didn't have a case—end of story. (In the unique trial of jealousy in Numbers 5, though witnesses weren't available, it's understandable that certain clues might tip off a husband or a wife to something fishy going on with a spouse—strange behavior, irrational reactions, breaking out into sudden sweats, or simply the husband's belief that he wasn't involved in his wife's conception of a child.)

Second, if the accused couldn't swim and get out of the tar, he looked guilty even if he were innocent! Not so if an Israelite wife (or husband) was falsely accused. A telltale supernatural sign was provided to prove guilt. Third, the river ordeal assumed guilt until innocence was proven; in the trial of jealousy, the court assumed innocence unless guilt was exposed by a divinely given miracle.

Impurity at Childbirth: Leviticus 12:1–8

This passage, some claim, implies female inferiority: the woman is ceremonially impure for forty days (7 + 33 days) after giving birth to a *boy* but eighty days (14 + 66 days) after giving birth to a *girl*. Surely this reveals a lower social status for females.

Again, not so fast! Various sensible explanations have been proposed. Some scholars argue that more days for the female actually indicate a kind of protection of females rather than a sign of inferiority. Others suggest the motive may be to preserve Israel's religious distinctiveness over against Canaanite religion, in which females engaged in religious sexual rites in their temples.

In general, a Jewish mother's lengthier separation from the tabernacle (or temple) after giving birth to a girl made a theological and ethical statement. In ancient Near Eastern polytheism, the strong emphasis was on fertility rites, cult prostitution, and the dramatization of the births of gods and goddesses. The distance between the birth event and temple worship—especially with baby girls—was carefully maintained.

Another plausible explanation focuses on a natural source of uncleanness— namely, the flow of blood. Verse 5 refers to the reason: it's because of "the blood of her purification." The mother experiences vaginal bleeding at birth. Yet such vaginal bleeding is common in newborn girls as well, due to the withdrawal of the mother's estrogen when the infant girl exits the mother's womb. So we have *two* sources of ritual uncleanness with a girl's birth but *only one* with a boy's.

Notice also that when the time of purification is over, whether "for a son or for a daughter," the mother is to bring the identical offering (whether a lamb, pigeon, or turtledove); this is to be a *purification* offering (12:6)—not technically a sin offering—and its purpose is to take away the ritual (not moral) impurity.[6]

Levirate Marriage: Deuteronomy 25:5–10

If a man died without a son to carry on the family name, then his unmarried brother could marry his widow in order to sustain the family name. Legally, the firstborn son from this union was officially the deceased husband's son. Since the first husband was deceased, this wasn't considered incest (sexual relations with an in-law). The term *levirate* comes from the Latin word for "husband's brother" or "brother-in-law," *levir*. This legislation sounds quite strange to modern ears, and it certainly does reflect a patriarchal background. A similar practice was carried out by the Hittites. Their law stated that if a man has a wife and then dies, his brother must take the widow as his wife.[7]

While levirate marriage was an admittedly patriarchal arrangement, we should keep certain things in mind. First, if the widow did marry her deceased husband's brother, this would help keep the widow's property (which she may have brought to the marriage) within the family. Marrying *outside* the family meant running the risk of losing it.[8] Second, although the man could refuse, this was discouraged. And if he refused to comply, the widow herself could exert her role and her rights in the shaming "sandal ceremony." So the widow had a certain natural advantage in this arrangement.

It's instructive to place this levirate scenario next to the story of Zelophehad's daughters (Num. 27:1–11). In the ancient Near East, there existed patriarchal laws of primogeniture—the firstborn's right to receive property and inherit family headship from the father. Deuteronomy 21:17 reveals that this meant a double portion for the firstborn over his brothers. Yet primogeniture is subtly overturned at various points in the Old Testament. Though Mosaic legislation operated within patriarchal structures of the ancient Near East, the Old Testament reveals a certain dynamism and openness to change. The daughters of the deceased, sonless Zelophehad appealed to Moses regarding the male-favoring inheritance laws. In light of the women's particular circumstances, Moses took this matter before God, and the daughters' appeal was granted.

When humans sought to change social structures in light of a deeper moral insight and a determination to move toward the ideal, we witness an adaptation of ancient Near Eastern structures. Even earlier in the Old Testament, various narratives subtly attack the primogeniture arrangement; the younger regularly supersedes the elder: Abel over Cain, Isaac over Ishmael, Jacob over Esau, Joseph/Judah over Reuben.[9] This biblical sampling reveals a subversive and more democratic ethic; though not ideal, it's a drastic improvement over other ancient Near Eastern laws.[10]

Your Neighbor's Wife: Exodus 20:17

"You shall not covet" is the tenth commandment. It prohibits longing for what rightfully belongs to another. What's included in this prohibition? A neighbor's house, wife, male or female servant, ox, donkey, and "anything that belongs to your neighbor." Critics complain that a wife is unflatteringly and inappropriately viewed as property—in the same category as a neighbor's house, ox, or donkey!

One big problem: just a few commands earlier (Exod. 20:12), children are commanded to give their mother honor *equal to* that of the father. A mother was to have equal authority over her children. (Check out the string of verses cited earlier in this chapter.) Another big problem: women in Israel weren't saleable items like houses, oxen, or donkeys. A further revealing fact is that in other cultures in the ancient Near East, the mother was often under the control of the son.[11] Yet the Mosaic law presents a striking contrast in this regard. Leviticus 19:3 commands a son to revere mother and father alike—and the mother is even listed first.

No Female Priests?

Why couldn't women participate in the priesthood? Why was this restricted to males alone? Many critics have a beef with this males-only religious club.

But if you think about it, most Israelite males were excluded too! Priests had to be from the tribe of Levi and from the line of Aaron; also, non-Israelite males weren't allowed to be priests.

But it's not as though the Old Testament automatically places *female* and *priesthood* in opposite categories. The Bible says plenty about female priests. Back in Genesis, Eve herself had a priestly role in Eden's garden; biblical scholars see this location as a sanctuary that foreshadows the tabernacle (cf. Gen. 2:12). Both Adam and Eve carried out priestly duties of worship and service to God, who would walk and talk with them (Gen. 2:15; 3:8).

Later, the priesthood was extended to the entire nation of Israel—male *and female*. God desired that *all Israelites* approach him as a "kingdom of priests" (Exod. 19:6). However, they refused to go up to the mountain; so Moses went in their place (20:19, 21). As a result, an official male priesthood was formed to function within the tabernacle/temple structure.[12]

So having female priests is not inherently problematic or unbiblical. Indeed, the New Testament reaffirms this: with the death and resurrection of Jesus, a new Israel—the church—was created; it is a holy priesthood and a kingdom of priests who offer up spiritual sacrifices to God (1 Peter 2:5, 9; Rev. 1:6; 5:10; 20:6).

Why then no females in the Old Testament tabernacle/temple? The reason is this: to prevent the contamination of pure worship in Israel. In ancient Near Eastern religions, the gods (and goddesses) themselves partook in grotesque sex acts. They engaged in incest (e.g., Baal with his sister Anat). They participated in bestiality (e.g., Baal having sex with a heifer, which gives birth to a son). And they engaged in sexual orgies and seductions. And all this without a hint of condemnation![13]

The religions of the ancient Near East commonly included fertility cult rituals, goddess worship, and priestesses (who served as the wife of the god). Temple prostitutes abounded, and sexual immorality was carried out in the name of religion. To have sex with priestesses meant union with the goddess you worshiped. In fact, sex with a temple prostitute would prompt Baal and his consort Asherah to have sex in heaven, which in turn would result in fertility all the way around—more kids, more cattle, more crops. Sex was deified in Canaan and other ancient Near Eastern cultures. Adultery was fine as long as sex was "religious."[14] If we become what we worship, then it's not surprising that Canaanite religion and society became corrupted by "sacred sex." Therefore, Canaanite female and male cult prostitutes were forbidden (cf. Gen. 38:15, 22–30; Deut. 23:18–19; also Hosea 4:14). Israel wasn't to imitate the nations whose deities engaged in sexual immorality.

Were these religions tolerant? Yes, in all the wrong ways! From the gods downward, all kinds of sexual deviations were tolerated, but to the detriment of society and family. Indeed, many ancient Near Eastern law codes permitted activities that undermined family integrity and stability. For example, men were permitted to engage in adulterous relations with slaves and prostitutes. The laws of Lipit-Ishtar of Lower Mesopotamia (1930 BC) take for granted the practice of prostitution.[15] In Hittite law (1650–1500 BC), "If a father and son sleep with the same female slave or prostitute, it is not an offence."[16] As an aside, Hittite law even permitted bestiality: "If a man has sexual relations with either a horse or a mule, it is not an offence."[17]

The law of Moses sought to prevent Israelites from glorifying adultery (or worse) in the name of religious devotion. Keeping an all-male priesthood, then, helped create this kind of religious distinction as well as preserved the sanctity of marriage. It wasn't a slam against women. It was a matter of preserving religious purity and the sanctity of sex within marriage.

Keep in mind that in Israel priests carried out three kinds of duties:

1. teaching, judicial, administrative
2. prophetic (e.g., discerning God's will through the casting of lots, known as the Urim and Thummim)
3. cultic (religious ceremonies/rituals)

In Old Testament Israel, women like Miriam (Exod. 15:20), Deborah (Judg. 4–5, esp. 4:4), and Huldah (2 Kings 22:14) fulfilled the first two roles as teachers, judges, and prophetesses. The third area was prohibited to women—*and most other males*. In fact, even Israel's kings couldn't carry out various cultic duties (2 Chron. 26:16–21). So while patriarchalism was embedded in Israelite attitudes, that wasn't what kept women from being priests; rather, it was a matter of Israel's religious identity and moral well-being.

We could cover more territory than this, but hopefully these responses to the critics' arguments will help put these passages in context—and put some of the contentiousness to rest.

Further Reading

Davidson, Richard M. *Flame of Yahweh: Sexuality in the Old Testament.* Peabody, MA: Hendrickson, 2007.

Jones, Clay. "Why We Don't Hate Sin so We Don't Understand What Happened to the Canaanites: An Addendum to 'Divine Genocide' Arguments." *Philosophia Christi* n.s. 11 (2009): 53–72.

11

Bride-Price?

Polygamy, Concubinage, and Other Such Questions

Since the time of Thomas Jefferson, rumors have been swirling regarding his fathering a child through his slave girl Sally Hemings. During the 1990s, the discussion was ramped up, and President Jefferson was allegedly exposed as a hypocritical founding father. Further research, though, has shown that the likely culprit was Thomas's younger brother Randolph, who was at Monticello around the very time Hemings conceived and who was known to spend time with the slaves. On the other hand, Thomas, who was sixty-four at this time, was battling severe health problems, including intense migraines. Randolph, though given to drunkenness, was in better health, and his character wasn't nearly as refined as Thomas's.[1]

Now, if Thomas were the father of Hemings's child, then so much the worse for him! And his having slaves (with conflicted feelings, we should add) still wouldn't undermine the Declaration of Independence's affirmation that all humans are "created equal" and are "endowed by their Creator with certain unalienable rights." The same is true in the Old Testament. Even if prominent Old Testament figures had more than one wife or had concubines, this still doesn't overturn the standard of monogamy in Genesis 2:24. But was polygamy legally permitted? Or did Israel's laws prohibit this practice, even if Elkanah, David, Solomon, and others disregarded the prohibition?

In the ancient Near East, a married man could take a concubine—or second-class wife—when his situation was "inconceivable," that is, if his first wife was presumed to be infertile (or even if she became sick). In such cases, it wasn't unusual for a man to take another wife to produce offspring. When we look at Israel's history, we see the influence of this practice fairly early on. The family was central, and having children was vital to carrying on the family memory. To be childless—and therefore heirless—was considered a tragedy and even a disgrace. So a second-tier wife was often brought in to remedy the situation.

In the ancient Near East, polygamy was taken for granted and not officially prohibited. It was legally sanctioned in the Code of Hammurabi, which permitted the owner of a female slave, since she was property, to utilize her sexual and reproductive powers to bear children; if she produced children, she could go free on the death of her master.[2]

The earliest reference to polygamy (bigamy) in the Old Testament is the not-so-nice Lamech, who takes two wives (Gen. 4:19, 23–24)—the first of over thirty references to polygamy in the Old Testament. Later on in Genesis, Abraham couldn't produce a child with Sarah; so she gave him her servant Hagar as a "wife" (Gen. 16:3), and Ishmael came as a result. His birth produced conflict between Sarah and Hagar, with Abraham in the middle of it all. Hagar had apparently won in this game of one-upwomanship, until Sarah sent her away. (We'll look at the Sarah-Hagar story when we get to slavery and the New Testament.)

The same problems came to Jacob. Through trickery, he ended up with two wives instead of one. When Rachel and Leah realized they were infertile, in desperation they gave Jacob their handmaids in hopes of producing children in this honor-shame competition. One of these handmaids, Bilhah, is called both "concubine" and one of Jacob's "wives" (Gen. 35:22; 37:2), a second-string wife.

So there was apparently something official in this arrangement, even though the handmaids were second-tier wives. Concubines at times were simply second-class wives, though still officially married. Or the term can refer to a second wife who comes after the first one has died. For example, after Sarah died, the widower Abraham took another wife, Keturah. First Chronicles 1:32 refers to her as a "concubine [*pilegesh*]," but this term can be used of a legitimate wife, just not the original wife of a man.[3] Even the concubine mentioned in Judges 19 wasn't a mistress; she was considered married to a "husband" (v. 3). The text uses "father-in-law" and "son-in-law" to indicate genuine marital status (vv. 4–5, 7, etc.).

While polygamous marriages (including concubines) occurred in the Old Testament *without* God's stamp of approval, keep in mind that such marriages *still* brought with them a husband's commitment to protect and provide for his wife. By contrast, if a child came through a woman hired for sexual pleasure, this brought shame and no inheritance (e.g., Jephthah in Judg. 11:1–2).

When it came to Israel's rulers, political maneuvering—not simply sexual pleasure—was often involved in taking concubines. Things eventually get

ridiculous with Solomon having seven hundred wives and three hundred concubines (1 Kings 11:3), often taken from other nations for purposes of political
alliances. Yet Deuteronomy 17:17 strictly warned that Israel's future king(s)
shouldn't "multiply wives for himself, or else his heart will turn away; nor
shall he greatly increase silver and gold for himself"; nor should he accumulate
(chariot) horses or return to Egypt.

As it turns out, Solomon did *all* of these things, which were his downfall
(1 Kings 11:1). In 1 Kings, the biblical narrator uses irony to denounce Solomon's leadership and spiritual qualifications. From the very start of his reign,
he violated all of these prohibitions: (1) marrying Pharaoh's daughter and
other foreign wives (3:1; 11:1–8); (2) accumulating (chariot) horses (10:26);
(3) hoarding silver and gold (10:27); (4) making an alliance with Egypt through
marriage (3:1).[4] Solomon was also a tyrant who, according to his son Reho-
boam, put a "heavy yoke" on Israel and "scourged [them] with whips" (12:4,
14 NIV). Solomon's disobedience and heavy-handedness eventually led to
Israel's divided kingdom. Solomon squandered the potential and the gifts
God had given him. He failed to meet God's conditions: if Solomon would
obey, God would establish his kingdom; if he worshiped false gods, then Israel would be cut off from the land God had given them (1 Kings 9:4–8). The
appointed moral, spiritual example in Israel failed spectacularly, especially in
the area of marriage.

Endorsements of Polygamy?

There's the joke: "I treat both my wives equally. Isn't that bigamy?" We see a
good deal of bigamy (two wives) in the Old Testament, and it's not unusual
to hear critics say, based on certain Old Testament texts, that God actually
endorses polygamy/bigamy. However, if God commended or commanded
such a practice, this would be a deviation from the assumed standard of
heterosexual monogamy in Genesis 2:24 and elsewhere. We'll look at several
key texts on this topic.

No Polygamy: Leviticus 18:18

An excellent case can be made that Leviticus 18:18 prohibits polygamy: "Do
not take your wife's sister [literally, 'a woman to her sister'] as a rival wife and
have sexual relations with her while your wife is living" (NIV).[5] This text is
regularly overlooked in discussions of polygamy in the Old Testament. Part
of the reason for this oversight is where this verse happens to be found. This
verse's significance is obscured because it's preceded by various anti-incest
laws (vv. 6–17). We'll see, however, that Leviticus 18:18 is a transitional verse
and shouldn't be included in the anti-incest section. A major break occurs
between verses 17 and 18.

Each verse in 7–17 begins identically, starting with the noun "the nakedness (of) ['erwat]," and it leads up to the command, "You shall not uncover ____'s nakedness." Also, in each of these verses (except v. 9) an explanation is given for the prohibition (e.g., "she is your mother"); this explanation isn't found in verse 18, which we would expect if it were an incest prohibition.

By contrast, each verse in 18–23 begins with a different construction. Even if you don't read Hebrew, you can truly just glance at the text and immediately see the difference in structure starting with verse 18. Verses 18–23 each begin with what's called the *waw* conjunctive (like our word "and") followed by a different word than "nakedness" (*'erwat*); also, instead of the consistent use of the negative (*lo*) plus the verb "uncover" (*tegalleh*, from the root *galah*), as in 7–17, here the negative particles are used before verbs other than *uncover*. Why are these contrasts important? In verses 6–17, we're dealing with *kinship bonds* while verses 18–23 address prohibited sexual relations *outside of kinship bonds*.

Furthermore, the key word in 18:18 is *sarar*—that is, "to make a rival wife." The same word in noun form (*sarah*) is also found in 1 Samuel 1:6, the story of Elkanah and his wife Hannah and the "rival" wife Peninnah. Hannah and Peninnah weren't biological sisters, just two female Israelite citizens (or "sisters"). This fits what we find in the non-kinship section of Leviticus 18. So this law in 18:18, then, explicitly prohibits the taking of a second (rival) wife in addition to the first—the interpretation taken by the Qumran (Dead Sea scrolls) community, established in the second century BC.[6]

One final point here: the wording of 18:18 (literally, "a woman to her sister") itself indicates that this is not a literal sister. This phrase "a woman to her sister" and its counterpart, "a man to his brother," are used twenty times in the Hebrew Scriptures, and never do they refer to a literal sister or brother. Rather, they are idioms for "one in addition to another." So this verse doesn't refer to incest; rather, it refers to the addition of another wife to the first (i.e., polygamy).

What then about other instances in Scripture that seem to endorse polygamy? God forbids it in Leviticus 18:18, yet people practiced it in Israel. Of course, the same could be said about many prohibited practices: idolatry, infant sacrifice, oppressing the poor, and so on. Yet some will argue that polygamy is implied or even divinely encouraged in certain passages. So let's explore some of these texts.

Servant Girl as Prospective Wife: Exodus 21:7–11

If a man sells his daughter as a servant ['amah], she is not to go free as menservants do. If she does not please the master who has selected her for himself [i.e., he refuses to go through with a possible engagement], he must let her be redeemed. He has no right to sell her to foreigners, because he has broken faith with her. If he selects her for his son, he must grant her the rights of a daughter. If he marries another woman, he must not deprive the first one of her food, clothing and marital rights. (Exod. 21:7–11 NIV)

As we've seen earlier, this is another example of case law (casuistic law).[7] Such regulations don't assume that the described states of affairs are ideal. Case law begins with specific examples that don't necessarily present best-case scenarios: "if two men quarrel" or "if someone strikes a man" are examples of case law. So the law here instructs Israelites about what should be done under certain inferior conditions ("*If* a man sells his daughter . . . "). But we'll see that even if conditions are less than ideal, the goal is to protect women in unfortunate circumstances. Later on, we'll come back to this passage in the context of Israelite servanthood (slavery).

We're left to wonder: "What kind of father would *sell* his daughter?" Actually, when a father sells his daughter, he's doing so out of economic desperation, as we'll see later on in the chapters on servanthood, which is more like contracted employment. In fact, the father is doing this out of concern for his family, and Israel's laws provided a safety net for its very poorest. Voluntary selling was a matter of survival in harsh financial circumstances. Temporarily contracting out family members to employers, who also provided room and board, was the most suitable alternative during hard times. Safety nets shouldn't become hammocks, and a typical servant tried to work off the terms of his contract and become debt free.

As far as the marriageable daughter goes, a father would do his best to care for her as well. Here, he is trying to help his daughter find security in marriage; the father would arrange for a man with means to marry her.

Some people will argue, "Look, the man has a *son*. Therefore, he must be married, and so he's looking into the possibility of getting a *second* wife, maybe to produce children if his first wife is barren. So we have implicit support of polygamy here, don't we?"

This conclusion is too quick, however. It goes beyond the evidence. Two obvious options present themselves: (1) the man's first wife died; or (2) the man and his first wife divorced. Let's not forget that the son was of marriageable age—typically, in his twenties (as was the girl). So whether the man takes this young servant woman to be his wife or the wife of his son, we still have no polygamy either way.

Furthermore, this particular passage involves some issues in translation. The Hebrew text of verse 8 indicates that the man decides not to take the servant girl as his wife. In verses 9–10, two other possibilities arise: (1) the man (whether widowed or divorced) might give her to his son, or—and this is the tricky part—(2) he "marries another woman." Some suggest that this is an endorsement of polygamy: the man takes the servant girl *and* marries another woman in addition. But this is a misreading. We're already told in verse 8 that the man doesn't choose to take the servant woman as his wife. In that case, we should understand verse 10 to mean that he marries another *instead of* the servant woman.

Then what of the "marital rights" the man owes her? Doesn't this also sound like polygamy here? The problem with the translation "marital rights" ('onah) is this: it's a stab in the dark with a term *used only once* in the Old Testament. Words occurring once can often be tricky to handle, and translators should tread carefully. Some scholars have suggested more likely possibilities. For example, this word could be related to a word for oil (or possibly ointments); the servant girl should be sent out with three basic necessities: food, clothing, and oil.

However, an even more plausible rendering is available. The root of the word is associated with the idea of habitation or dwelling (*ma'on, me'onah*); for example, "God is a dwelling place," or heaven is God's holy "dwelling place" (Deut. 33:27; 2 Chron. 30:27). We can more confidently conclude that quarters or shelter (though possibly oil) are in view here, not conjugal rights. So the servant girl should be guaranteed the basic necessities: food, clothing, and lodging/shelter. So we're not even talking about polygamy here, let alone some implied support of it.

To review, the three issues here are:

1. If the man rejects the servant woman as a wife, she is to be given her freedom (redeemed/bought back).
2. If his son wants to marry her, she's to be taken in as a family member and treated as a daughter.
3. If the man marries another woman, the servant woman is to receive food, clothing, and lodging.

Although we'll touch on this passage again (in light of Deut. 15), I think we can set aside the polygamy question as far as Exodus 21 is concerned.

David: 2 Samuel 12:8

Allegedly, God's own commentary here (through Nathan the prophet) suggests an endorsement of polygamy. After David's power-rape of Bathsheba and the murder of her husband, Uriah, God tells David, "I also gave you your master's house and your master's wives into your care . . . ; and if that had been too little, I would have added to you many more things like these" (2 Sam. 12:8). Isn't God graciously providing multiple wives for David?

We should be careful about reading too much into the word *gave*. After all, the same word is used in 2 Samuel 12:11: "Behold, I will raise up evil against you from your own household; I will even take your wives before your eyes, and *give* them to your companion." Certainly God didn't demonstrate his approval of polygamy by "giving" David's wives over to his treacherous son Absalom.

Furthermore, the "master" mentioned in 12:8 is Saul. The sentence indicating that God "gave" Saul's "house" and "wives" to David is probably a general reference to the transfer of Saul's estate to the new monarch, David. If David took Saul's wife Ahinoam (1 Sam. 14:50) to be his own, this would be in violation of levitical law: Ahinoam was the mother of Michal, whom Saul gave to David as a wife, and Leviticus 18:17 forbids marrying one's mother-in-law. So this passage hardly lends support to God's endorsement of polygamy.

The Unloved Wife: Deuteronomy 21:15–17

If a man has two wives, the one loved and the other unloved, and both the loved and the unloved have borne him sons, if the firstborn son belongs to the unloved, then it shall be in the day he wills what he has to his sons, he cannot make the son of the loved the firstborn before the son of the unloved, who is the firstborn. But he shall acknowledge the firstborn, the son of the unloved, by giving him a double portion of all that he has, for he is the beginning of his strength; to him belongs the right of the firstborn. (Deut. 21:15–17)

What does this legislation do? It helps protect against favoritism. The firstborn's inheritance shouldn't be withdrawn just because his mother happens to be the unfavored wife.

Does this passage slyly endorse polygamy? Not at all. "If a man has two wives . . ." is an example of case law. It doesn't necessarily endorse a practice but gives guidance for when a particular situation arises. For example, Exodus 22:1 states, "If a man steals an ox or a sheep and slaughters it or sells it, he shall pay five oxen for the ox and four sheep for the sheep." This law isn't advocating stealing! It offers guidance in unfortunate circumstances—namely, when a theft takes place.

Similarly, in Matthew 19, Jesus is questioned about Deuteronomy 24:1, which begins, "When [if] a man takes a wife and marries her, and it happens that she finds no favor in his eyes because he has found some indecency in her, and he writes her a certificate of divorce and puts it in her hand and sends her out from his house . . ." Jesus tells his questioners that Moses didn't *command* this legislation (which was to protect a divorced woman from the whim of her husband, who later decides he wants her back); rather, he *permitted* it because of human hard-heartedness (Matt. 19:8).

Also, some scholars suggest that Deuteronomy 21:15–17 doesn't state that both wives are living and in the same house. The verb form of "has" suggests that the man may have remarried after his first wife's death.[8]

Let's try to wrap up the polygamy question by summarizing the appropriate response to polygamy in the Old Testament:

- The Old Testament makes clear the ideal built into creation. In Genesis 2:24, note the singular "wife" as well as "father and mother."
- Leviticus 18:18 expresses strong disapproval for polygamy, even if this law wasn't always carried out.
- The biblical writers hoped for better behavior.

- Some scholars have suggested that polygamy may have been tolerated for the practical reason that its prohibition would have been difficult to enforce.
- From Lamech's wives to those of Abraham, Esau, Jacob, David, and Solomon, wherever we see God's ideal of monogamy ignored, we witness strife, competition, and disharmony. The Old Testament presents polygamy as not only undesirable but also a violation of God's standards. Old Testament narratives subtly critique this marital arrangement.
- God warns the one most likely to be polygamous—Israel's king: "He shall not multiply wives for himself, or else his heart will turn away" (Deut. 17:17).
- God himself models covenant love for his people; this ideal union of marital faithfulness between husband and wife is one without competition.

The advice of Proverbs 5:15–18 is the presumed standard. A man should find delight and sexual satisfaction with his wife in monogamous marriage: "Drink . . . fresh water from your own well" (v. 15).

The Bride-Price

The idea of bride-price is presented by the New Atheists as though it's a matter of buying a wife like you would a horse or a mule. In actual fact, the bride-price was the way a man showed his serious intentions toward his bride-to-be, and it was a way of bringing two families together to discuss a serious, holy, and lifelong matter. Having sex with a young woman without the necessary preparations and formal ceremony cheapened the woman and sexuality. The process surrounding the bride-price reflected the honorable state of marriage.

Think of the dowry system used in places like India. In this case, the family of the bride-to-be gives money to the future husband's family. Such a transaction hardly means that the groom-to-be is mere property! Why automatically conclude that a *woman* is property because this marriage gift is given in the Old Testament but that a *man* isn't property under the dowry system?

The bride-price was more like a deposit from the groom's father to the bride's father. The Hebrew word for this deposit (*mohar*) is better translated "marriage gift." It not only helped create closer family ties between the two families but also provided economic stability for a marriage. This gift given to the bride's father (often several years' worth of wages) compensated him for the work his daughter would otherwise have contributed to the family. The marriage gift—preserved by the husband throughout the marriage—also served as security for the wife in case of divorce or her husband's death.[9] In fact, the bride's father would often give an even larger gift of property when the couple married. Hitchens's complaint about the Old Testament's bride-price is misguided.

Was Rape Allowed?

Some critics say that the law of Moses permits the rape of women or may condemn rape but with little concern for the victim's well-being. We should note two related passages. The first is Exodus 22:16–17:

> If a man seduces [*patah*] a virgin who is not engaged, and lies with her, he must pay a dowry for her to be his wife. If her father absolutely refuses to give her to him, he shall pay money equal to the dowry for virgins.

Extending and expanding on the discussion of Exodus 22:16–17, Deuteronomy 22:23–29 (which can be divided into three portions) reads this way:

> If there is a girl who is a virgin engaged to a man, and another man finds her in the city and lies with her, then you shall bring them both out to the gate of that city, and you shall stone them to death; the girl, because she did not cry out in the city [i.e., where her screams could be heard], and the man, because he has violated his neighbor's wife. Thus you shall purge the evil from among you. (vv. 23–24)

> But if in the field [i.e., where the girl doesn't have much chance to be heard] the man finds the girl who is engaged, and the man forces [*chazaq*] her and lies with her, then only the man who lies with her shall die. But you shall do nothing to the girl; there is no sin in the girl worthy of death, for just as a man rises against his neighbor and murders him, so is this case. When he found her in the field, the engaged girl cried out, but there was no one to save her. (vv. 25–27)

> If a man finds a girl who is a virgin, who is not engaged, and seizes [*tapas*— "takes/catches"—a weaker verb than "forces" in v. 25] her and lies with her and they are discovered, then the man who lay with her shall give to the girl's father fifty shekels of silver, and she shall become his wife because he has violated her; he cannot divorce her all his days. (vv. 28–29)

Upon closer inspection, the context emphasizes the *protection* of women, not the insignificance of women. We should first distinguish among three scenarios in the Deuteronomy 22 passage:

1. adultery between two consenting adults—a man and an engaged woman (v. 23), which is a violation of marriage ("he has violated his neighbor's wife")
2. the forcible rape of an engaged woman (v. 25), whose innocence is assumed
3. the seduction of an unengaged woman (v. 28), an expansion on the seduction passage of Exodus 22:16–17

In each case, the *man* is guilty. However, the critics' argument focuses on verses 28–29: the rape victim is being treated like she is her father's property. She's been violated, and the rapist gets off by paying a bridal fee. No concern is shown for the girl at all. In fact, she's apparently forced to marry the man who raped her! Are these charges warranted?

Regarding verses 28–29, various scholars see Exodus 22:16–17 as the backdrop to this scenario. Both passages are variations on the same theme. Even if there is some pressure from the man, the young woman is complicit; though initially pressured (seduced), she doesn't act against her will. The text says "*they* are discovered" (v. 28), not "*he* is discovered."[10] Both are culpable. Technically, this pressure/seduction could not be called forcible rape, falling under our contemporary category of statutory rape. Though the woman gave in, the man here would bear the brunt of the responsibility.

As it would have been more difficult for a woman to find a husband had she been sexually involved with another before marriage, her bride-price—a kind of economic security for her future—would have been in jeopardy. The man guilty of statutory rape *seduced* the unengaged woman; he wasn't a dark-alley rapist whom the young woman tried to fight off or from whom she tried to run away. This passage is far from being demeaning to women.

Both passages suggest two courses of action:

1. If the father and daughter agree to it, the seducer must marry the woman and provide for her all her life, without the possibility of divorce. The father (in conjunction with the daughter) has the final say-so in the arrangement. The girl isn't required to marry the seducer.
2. The girl's father (the legal point person) has the right to refuse any such permanent arrangement as well as the right to demand the payment that would be given for a bride, even though the seducer doesn't marry his daughter (since she has been sexually compromised, marriage to another man would be difficult if not impossible). The girl has to agree with this arrangement, and she isn't required to marry the seducer. In this arrangement, she is still treated as a virgin.[11]

Again, we don't see a lack of concern for the woman. Her well-being is actually the underlying theme of this legislation.

Women POWs as War Booty?

How amazing it would be to live in a war-free world. Although lately many Western democracies have been fairly free from the traumas and devastation of war, warfare in the ancient Near East was a way of life. (We'll say more on this in future chapters.) War brought with it certain unavoidable realities in the ancient world, and ancient Near Eastern peoples had different ways of "minimizing" the effects of war. One concern was prisoners of war (POWs). In the wake of battle, the problem arose: What was to be done with survivors?

Let's look at two texts that deal with foreign female POWs: Deuteronomy 20 and 21. We'll deal with them in reverse order.

Deuteronomy 21:10–14

When you go out to battle against your enemies, and the LORD your God delivers them into your hands and you take them away captive, and see among the captives a beautiful woman, and have a desire for her and would take her as a wife for yourself, then you shall bring her home to your house, and she shall shave her head and trim her nails. She shall also remove the clothes of her captivity and shall remain in your house, and mourn her father and mother a full month; and after that you may go in to her and be her husband and she shall be your wife. It shall be, if you are not pleased with her, then you shall let her go wherever she wishes; but you shall certainly not sell her for money, you shall not mistreat her, because you have humbled her. (Deut. 21:10–14)

In this scenario, the law served as a protective measure for the woman POW. She was the one who benefited from this legislation. The law defended her rights and personhood. For one thing, she wasn't raped, which was common practice in other ancient Near Eastern cultures. The would-be Israelite husband couldn't simply marry—let alone have sex with—her immediately. No, she was to be treated as a full-fledged wife. Unlike many Las Vegas weddings or the phenomenon of mail-order brides, the matter of marriage in Israel was not entered into lightly (motivated by, say, lust). That point is strongly reinforced in this passage.

The separation process allowed for a period of reflection. Before a woman POW was taken as a wife by the victorious Israelite soldier, she was allowed a transition period to make an outer and inner break from her past way of life. Only after this could she be taken as a wife. Given the seriousness of marital commitment, the time period allowed for the man to change his mind. The line "if you are not pleased with her" doesn't suggest something trivial, however, since the Mosaic law took seriously the sanctity of marriage.[12] If, for some reason, the man's attitude changed, the woman had to be set free.

Deuteronomy 20:13–14

When the Lord your God gives it [i.e., the city which has rejected Israel's terms of peace] into your hand, you shall strike all the men in it with the edge of the sword. Only the women and the children and the animals and all that is in the city, all its spoil, you shall take as booty for yourself. (Deut. 20:13–14)

We'll discuss warfare later. For now, the concern is the well-being of captured women and children. Although rape was a common feature in ancient

Near Eastern warfare, Israelite soldiers were prohibited from raping women, contrary to what some crassly argue. Sex was permitted only within the bounds of marital commitment, a repeated theme laid out in the Mosaic law. Rape in warfare wasn't a grand exception to the requirement of sexual fidelity.

As with Deuteronomy 21:10–14, the scenario is the same—namely, a soldier's taking a wife. Rather than being outcasts or the low woman on the totem pole, women captured in war could become integrated into Israelite society through marriage. Understandably, it was far less likely that *men* would have been as readily integrated into Israel's life and ways.[13]

Deuteronomy 25:11–12: An Offhanded Excursus

> If two men, a man and his countryman, are struggling together, and the wife of one comes near to deliver her husband from the hand of the one who is striking him, and puts out her hand and seizes his genitals, then you shall cut off her hand; you shall not show pity. (Deut. 25:11–12)

This passage refers to "the immodest lady wrestler," as one scholar humorously put it. Her action was considered a shameful act, and, what's worse, the man could possibly be permanently injured and thus deprived of future children. At first blush, this passage apparently requires that a woman's hand be cut off if she seizes the genitals of a man fighting with her husband.

Now, if this *were* the case, it would be the *only* biblical instance of punishment by mutilation; beyond this, where ancient Near Eastern laws call for bodily mutilation for various offenses, the Mosaic law does not. Before we explore the text in more detail, we should compare this to other fearsome punishments in the ancient Near East. As we've seen, the Babylonian Code of Hammurabi insisted that certain crimes be punished by cutting off the tongue, breast, hand, or ear—or the accused being dragged around a field by cattle. The law of Moses, though not ideal, presents a remarkable improvement when it comes to punishments.

A more plausible interpretation of this passage is the punishment of *depilation* ("you shall shave [the hair of] her groin"), not *mutilation*. The word commonly translated "hand" (*kaph*) can refer to the "palm" of a hand or some rounded concave object like a dish, bowl, or spoon, or even the arch of a foot. The commonly used word for "hand" (*yad*) isn't used here. It would be strange to cut off the palm of a hand!

Furthermore, in certain places in the Old Testament, the word *kaph* is clearly used for the pelvic area—either the concave hip socket (Gen. 32:26, 32) or the curve of the woman's groin area: "I arose to open for my lover, and my hands dripped with myrrh, my fingers with flowing myrrh, on the handles [plural: *kaphot*] of the lock" (Song of Songs 5:5 NIV). This language alludes back to the "locked garden" in 4:12: "You are a locked garden, my sister, my bride;

you are an enclosed spring, a sealed-up fountain" (NET). Scholars generally agree that the garden language is a metaphor for a woman's sexual organs, and its being "locked" implies her purity/virginity.[14]

Also, in the Deuteronomy 25 text, there is no indication of physical harm to the man (as some commentators commonly assume). For those who assume a literal "hand for a hand" punishment, remember that the man's hand *hasn't* been injured or cut off (if so, then the idea of cutting off her hand would make slightly more sense). In addition, shaving hair—including pubic hair—as a humiliating punishment was practiced in Babylon and Sumer (see also 2 Sam. 10:4–5; Isa. 7:20). This isn't mutilation for mutilation, but humiliation for humiliation.

In addition, the specific Hebrew *qal* verb form (in Deut. 25:12) has a milder connotation than the stronger, intensified *piel* verb form, meaning "cut off" or "(physically) sever [*qatsats*]." Whenever it appears in this milder form (Jer. 9:26; 25:23; 49:32), it means "clip/cut/shave [hair]." There's just no linguistic reason to translate the weaker verb form ("shave") as a stronger form (i.e., amputation). In this particular case, we're talking about the open concave region of the groin, and thus a shaving of pubic hair. In short, the woman's punishment is public humiliation for publicly humiliating the man—something still very severe and for which no mercy was to be shown. From a textual point of view, the superior view is clearly the "shaving" view, not the mutilation view.[15]

Is this an ideal punishment for all time? Not at all! However, it does stand out in marked contrast to the severe and excessive mutilation punishments common in the ancient Near East. In fact, Middle Assyrian laws (around 1100 BC) present a similar scenario (in the case of injury to the man), though with far more drastic consequences. If a woman in a quarrel injured a man's testicle, her finger was cut off. If the other testicle was injured, both of her eyes were gouged out.[16] Again, even if Deuteronomy 25 *were* dealing with an actual mutilation punishment, this would be (1) the only such punishment in the Mosaic law and (2) a dramatic contrast to the frequent mutilation punishments in the rest of the ancient Near East. But as we've seen, the language simply does not allow for this "amputation" rendering.

Israel's laws weren't perfect, to be sure. But when we compare them with various ancient Near Eastern law codes (whether regarding sexuality or other matters), the general impression noted by scholars is a range of dramatic— even radical—moral improvements in Israel.

Further Reading

Davidson, Richard M. *Flame of Yahweh: Sexuality in the Old Testament.* Peabody, MA: Hendrickson, 2007.

Jones, Clay. "Why We Don't Hate Sin so We Don't Understand What Happened to the Canaanites: An Addendum to 'Divine Genocide' Arguments." *Philosophia Christi* n.s. 11 (2009): 53–72.

Wenham, Gordon J. *Story as Torah: Reading Old Testament Narratives Ethically*. Grand Rapids: Baker Academic, 2000.

12

Warrant for Trafficking in Humans as Farm Equipment? (I)

Slavery in Israel

The runaway slave and abolitionist Frederick Douglass (1817–95) wrote in his autobiography about his first slaveowner, Captain Anthony.

> He was a cruel man, hardened by a long life of slave-holding. He would at times seem to take great pleasure in whipping a slave. I have often been awakened at the dawn of day by the most heart-rending shrieks of an own aunt of mine, whom he used to tie up to a joist, and whip upon her naked back till she was literally covered with blood. No words, no tears, no prayers, from his gory victim, seemed to move his iron heart from its bloody purpose. The louder she screamed, the harder he whipped; and where the blood ran fastest, there he whipped longest. He would whip her to make her scream, and whip her to make her hush; and not until overcome by fatigue, would he cease to swing the blood-clotted cowskin. I remember the first time I ever witnessed this horrible exhibition. I was quite a child, but I well remember it. I never shall forget it whilst I remember any thing. It was the first of a long series of such outrages, of which I was doomed to be a witness and a participant. It struck me with awful force. It was the blood-stained gate, the entrance to the hell of slavery, through which I was about to pass. It was a most terrible spectacle. I wish I could commit to paper the feelings with which I beheld it.[1]

Harriet Beecher Stowe (1811–96), author of the powerful bestseller *Uncle Tom's Cabin*, wrote that Southern masters had absolute control over every facet of their slaves' lives: "The legal power of the master amounts to an absolute despotism over body and soul," and "there is no protection for the slave's life."[2]

Biblical Indentured Service

A mistake critics make is associating *servanthood* in the Old Testament with antebellum (prewar) *slavery* in the South—like the kind of scenario Douglass described. By contrast, Hebrew (debt) servanthood could be compared to similar conditions in colonial America. Paying fares for passage to America was too costly for many individuals to afford. So they'd contract themselves out, working in the households—often in apprentice-like positions—until they paid back their debts. One-half to two-thirds of white immigrants to Britain's colonies were indentured servants.[3]

Likewise, an Israelite strapped for shekels might become an indentured servant to pay off his debt to a "boss" or "employer" (*'adon*). Calling him a "master" is often way too strong a term, just as the term *'ebed* ("servant, employee") typically shouldn't be translated "slave." John Goldingay comments that "there is nothing inherently lowly or undignified about being an *'ebed*." Indeed, it is an honorable, dignified term.[4] Even when the terms *buy, sell,* or *acquire* are used of servants/employees, they don't mean the person in question is "just property." Think of a sports player today who gets "traded" to another team, to which he "belongs." Yes, teams have "owners," but we're hardly talking about slavery here! Rather, these are formal contractual agreements, which is what we find in Old Testament servanthood/employee arrangements.[5] One example of this contracted employer/employee relationship was Jacob's working for Laban for seven years so that he might marry his daughter Rachel. In Israel, becoming a voluntary servant was commonly a starvation-prevention measure; a person had no collateral other than himself, which meant either service or death. While most people worked in the family business, servants would contribute to it as domestic workers. Contrary to the critics, this servanthood wasn't much different *experientially* from paid employment in a cash economy like ours.[6]

Now, debt tended to come to families, not just individuals. Whether because of failed crops or serious indebtedness, a father could *voluntarily* enter into a contractual agreement ("sell" himself) to work in the household of another: "one of your countrymen becomes poor and sells himself" (Lev. 25:47 NIV). Perhaps his wife or children might "be sold" to help sustain the family through economically unbearable times. If his kinfolk didn't "redeem" him (pay off his debt), then he would work as a debt-servant until he was released after six years.[7] Family land would have to be mortgaged until the year of Jubilee every fifty years (see Leviticus 25, which actually spells out successive stages of destitution in Israel in vv. 25–54).[8] In other words, this servanthood wasn't imposed by an outsider, as it was by slave traders and plantation owners in the antebellum South.[9] What's more, this indentured service wasn't unusual in other parts of the ancient Near East either (though conditions were often worse). And later on, when inhabitants of Judah took back Hebrew servants they had released, God condemned them for violating the law of Moses and for forgetting that they were once slaves in Egypt whom God had delivered. God told the Judahites that because of their actions they were going to be exiled in the land of their enemies (Jer. 34:12–22).

Once a servant was released, he was free to pursue his own livelihood without any further obligations within that household. He returned to being a full participant in Israelite society. Becoming an indentured servant meant a slight step down the social ladder, but a person could step back up as a full citizen once the debt was paid or he was released in the seventh year (or in the fiftieth year). Nevertheless, the law was concerned that indentured servants were to be treated as a man "hired from year to year" and were not to be "rule[d] over . . . ruthlessly" (Lev. 25:53–54 NIV). In fact, servants in Israel weren't cut off from society during their servitude but were thoroughly embedded within it. As I mentioned earlier, Israel's forgiveness of debts every seven years was fixed and thus intended to be far more consistent than that of Israel's ancient Near Eastern counterparts, for whom debt-release (if it occurred) was typically much more sporadic.

So unavoidable lifelong servanthood was prohibited, unless someone loved the head of the household and wanted to attach himself to him (Exod. 21:5). Servants—even if they hadn't paid off their debts—were granted release every seventh year with all debts forgiven (Deut. 15). As we'll see, their legal status was unique and a dramatic improvement over law codes in the ancient Near East. One scholar writes that "Hebrew has no vocabulary of slavery, only of servanthood."[10]

An Israelite servant's guaranteed release within seven years was a control or regulation to prevent the abuse and institutionalizing of such positions. The release year reminded the Israelites that poverty-induced servanthood wasn't an ideal social arrangement. On the other hand, servanthood existed in Israel precisely because poverty existed: no poverty, no servants in Israel. And if servants lived in Israel, it was a voluntary (poverty-induced) arrangement and not forced.

Means to Help the Poor

In the ancient world (and beyond), chattel (or property) slavery had three characteristics:

1. A slave was property.
2. The slave owner's rights over the slave's person and work were total and absolute.
3. The slave was stripped of his identity—racial, familial, social, marital.[11]

From what we've seen, this doesn't describe the Hebrew servant at all, nor does it (as we'll see in the next chapter) fit the non-Israelite "slave" in Israel.

Israel's servant laws were concerned about *controlling* or *regulating*—not *idealizing*—an inferior work arrangement. Israelite servitude was induced by poverty, was entered into voluntarily, and was far from optimal. The intent of these laws was to combat potential abuses, not to institutionalize servitude.

When we compare Israel's servant system with the ancient Near East in general, what we have is a fairly tame and, in many ways, very attractive arrangement for impoverished Israelites. The servant laws aimed to benefit and protect the poor—that is, those most likely to enter indentured service. Servanthood was *voluntary*: a person who (for whatever reason) doesn't have any land "sells himself" (Lev. 25:39, 47; compare Deut. 15:12). Someone might also sell a family member as an indentured servant in another's household to work until a debt is paid off. Once a person was freed from his servant obligations, he had the "status of full and unencumbered citizenship."[12]

Old Testament legislation sought to prevent voluntary debt-servitude. A good deal of Mosaic legislation was given to protect the poor from even temporary indentured service. The poor were given opportunities to glean the edges of fields or pick lingering fruit on trees after their fellow Israelites harvested the land (Lev. 19:9–10; 23:22; Deut. 24:20–21). Also, fellow Israelites were commanded to lend freely to the poor (Deut. 15:7–8), who weren't to be charged interest (Exod. 22:25; Lev. 25:36–37). And if the poor couldn't afford high-end sacrificial animals, they could sacrifice smaller, less-expensive ones (Lev. 5:7, 11). Also, debts were to be automatically canceled every seven years. In fact, when debt-servants were released, they were to be generously provided for without a "grudging heart" (Deut. 15:10 NIV). The bottom line: God didn't want there to be any poverty in Israel (Deut. 15:4). Therefore, servant laws existed to help the poor, not harm them or keep them down.

The Ultimate Goal: No Poverty, No Servanthood (Deut. 15:1–18)

At the end of every seven years you shall grant a remission of debts. This is the manner of remission: every creditor shall release what he has loaned to his neighbor; he shall not exact it of his neighbor and his brother, because the LORD's remission has been proclaimed. From a foreigner you may exact it [which was typically for business transactions, as we'll see later], but your hand shall release whatever of yours is with your brother. However, there will be no poor among you, since the LORD will surely bless you in the land which the LORD your God is giving you as an inheritance to possess, if only you listen obediently to the voice of the LORD your God, to observe carefully all this commandment which I am commanding you today. For the LORD your God will bless you as He has promised you, and you will lend to many nations, but you will not borrow; and you will rule over many nations, but they will not rule over you.

If there is a poor man with you, one of your brothers, in any of your towns in your land which the LORD your God is giving you, you shall not harden your heart, nor close your hand from your poor brother; but you shall freely open your hand to him, and shall generously lend him sufficient for his need in whatever he lacks. Beware that there is no base thought in your heart, saying, "The seventh year, the year of remission, is near," and your eye is hostile toward your poor brother, and you give him nothing; then he may cry to the LORD against you, and it will be a sin in you. You shall generously give to him, and your heart shall not be grieved when you give to him, because for this thing the LORD your God will bless you in all your work and in all your undertakings. For the poor will never cease to be in the land; therefore I command you, saying, "You shall freely open your hand to your brother, to your needy and poor in your land."

If your kinsman, a Hebrew man or woman, is sold to you, then he shall serve you six years, but in the seventh year you shall set him free. When you set him free, you shall not send him away empty-handed. You shall furnish him liberally from your flock and from your threshing floor and from your wine vat; you shall give to him as the LORD your God has blessed you. You shall remember that you were a slave in the land of Egypt, and the LORD your God redeemed you; therefore I command you this today. It shall come about if he says to you, "I will not go out from you," because he loves you and your household, since he fares well with you; then you shall take an awl and pierce it through his ear into the door, and he shall be your servant forever. Also you shall do likewise to your maidservant. It shall not seem hard to you when you set him free, for he has given you six years with double the service of a hired man; so the LORD your God will bless you in whatever you do. (Deut. 15:1–18)

This legislation commands the forgiveness of the poor person's (i.e., servant's) accumulated debt; this debt remission was to take place every seven years, which shows God's remarkable concern for the impoverished in the land. Now some will point to various Mesopotamian kings during the second millennium BC who released slaves and debtors during the first or second year of their reign—and another time or more beyond that. But such releases were typically sporadic, unlike the fixed intervals required in Israel every seventh and fiftieth year.[13]

If you just glanced over the Deuteronomy 15 text and didn't catch its significance, go back and *really* read it. The overriding, revolutionary goal expressed in this text is to totally eradicate debt-servanthood in the land: "there will be no poor [and therefore no debt servanthood] among you" (v. 4).[14] Being a realist, however, God was aware that inferior conditions would exist and that poverty (and thus servanthood) would continue in the land (v. 11). Even so, this undesirable situation was to be battled rather than institutionalized.

In keeping with this "eradicate poverty/eradicate servitude" spirit, a servant's release was to be accompanied with generous provisions and a gracious spirit. The "master" was to have no wicked thought toward his servant; instead, he was to generously load him up with provisions (vv. 13–14). The motivating reason for this kindness and goodwill was that "you were a slave in the land of Egypt, and the LORD your God redeemed you; therefore I command you this today" (v. 15). Even if poverty (and therefore servitude) couldn't be eradicated, Israel was to strive toward this goal.

The Dignity of Debt-Servants

Rather than relegating treatment of servants (slaves) to the end of the law code (commonly done in other ancient Near Eastern law codes), Israel's law code put the matter front and center in Exodus 21. For the first time in the ancient Near East, legislation required treating servants as persons, not property.

In other ancient Near Eastern cultures, it was the *king* who was the image of their god on earth—and certainly not the slave. By contrast, Genesis 1:26–27 affirms that all human beings are God's image-bearers. This doctrine serves as the basis for affirming the dignity and rights of every human. Likewise, Job 31:13–15 clearly reveals the inescapable humanity—and thus equality—of master and servant alike: "If I have denied justice to my menservants and maidservants when they had a grievance against me, what will I do when God confronts me? What will I answer when called to account? Did not he who made me in the womb make them? Did not the same one form us both within our mothers?" (NIV).

Servants (slaves) in Israel, unlike their ancient Near Eastern contemporaries, were given radical, unprecedented legal/human rights, even if not equaling that of free persons (who could, if unfortunate circumstances prevailed, find themselves needing to place themselves into indentured servitude).[15] As the *Anchor Bible Dictionary*'s essay on "Slavery" observes, "We have in the Bible the first appeals in world literature to treat slaves as human beings for their own sake and not just in the interests of their masters."[16] By comparison, "the idea of a slave as exclusively the object of rights and as a person outside regular society was apparently alien to the laws of the [rest of the] ANE," where slaves were forcibly branded or tattooed for identification (contrast this with Exod. 21:5–6). Indeed, in "contrast to many ancient doctrines, the Hebrew law was relatively mild toward the slaves and recognized them as human beings subject to defense from intolerable acts, although not to the same extent as free persons."[17] As we'll see, the protection of runaway slaves who fled to Israel was strikingly different from the slave laws in surrounding ancient Near

Eastern cultures, and this was due to Israel's own history as slaves in Egypt. This fact would in effect turn slavery into a "voluntary institution."[18]

Some will argue at this point that Hittite laws were softened when they were upgraded; they became more humanizing. True enough, but the results weren't always as positive as one might think. For example, murder no longer carried with it the death sentence—*except for slaves*. Free persons were punished by fining and by mutilation. The improvements were at best a mixed bag!

In the rest of this chapter, we'll see not only how three key laws in Israel were distinct in the ancient Near East but also how if they had been heeded by "Bible-believing" Southerners in the U.S. and "Christian" Europeans, slavery would not have been an issue. Let's look at these more closely.

Release of Injured Servants

Another marked improvement of Israel's laws over other ancient Near Eastern law codes is the release of injured servants (Exod. 21:26–27). When an employer (master) accidentally gouged out the eye or knocked out the tooth of his male or female servant/employee, he or she was to go free. No bodily abuse of servants was permitted. And as we'll discuss in the next chapter, if an employer's discipline resulted in the immediate death of his servant, that employer (master) himself was to be put to death (Exod. 21:20; note that the word for "punished" is very strong, always connoting the death penalty).

By contrast, Hammurabi's Code permitted the master to cut off his disobedient slave's ear.[19] Typically in ancient Near Eastern law codes, masters— not slaves—were merely financially compensated for injuries to their slaves. The Mosaic law, however, held masters accountable for their treatment of their own servants, not simply another person's servants. As we'll see shortly, if the servant died because of an employer's physical abuses, this was considered murder. All of this was unparalleled in other ancient Near Eastern codes.[20]

Some might ask whether releasing a servant for gouging out an eye or a tooth is a better reason for freeing servants than in other ancient Near Eastern cultures. After all, Hammurabi allowed for the release of a slave woman and her children (sired by the master) if the master decided not to adopt them.[21] Of course, the question itself is skewed.[22] As we've seen, Israelites were to release their servants every seven years, unless they wanted to stay on. In 1 Chronicles 2:34–35, Caleb's descendant Sheshan gave his daughter in marriage to his Egyptian servant Jarha—not a bad move up the social ladder!

As an aside, keep in mind that many—perhaps most—servants were young people who were parceled out by destitute parents to more prosperous families who would feed, clothe, and shelter them. Other adults served *in loco parentis*—in the place of parents—which typically included discipline of servant children. As Proverbs 29:19 puts it: "A servant cannot be corrected by mere words; though he understands, he will not respond" (NIV). The downside of this was that sometimes the head of the household would likely overdo the punishment, possibly resulting in injury.[23]

Anti-Kidnapping Laws

Another unique feature of the Mosaic law is its condemnation of kidnapping a person to sell as a slave, an act punishable by death:

> He who kidnaps a man, whether he sells him or he is found in his possession, shall surely be put to death. (Exod. 21:16)

> If a man is caught kidnapping any of his countrymen of the sons of Israel, and he deals with him violently or sells him, then that thief shall die; so you shall purge the evil from among you. (Deut. 24:7) (Note the prohibition of kidnapping in 1 Tim. 1:10.)

This ban against kidnapping is a point lost on, or ignored by, those who compare servanthood in Israel with slavery in the antebellum South, let alone the ancient Near East.

Helping Runaway Slaves

Up to this point, we've primarily referred to Israelite servants, not foreign ones. But this particular law reveals just how different Israel's laws were from the antebellum South—despite the Confederacy's claims of following the Bible faithfully. Also, this fugitive-harboring law would have applied to Israelite servants who left harsh employers for refuge. Another unique feature in Israel's "slave laws" was this: Israel was commanded to offer safe harbor to foreign runaway slaves (Deut. 23:15–16). The Southern states' Fugitive Slave Law legally required runaway slaves to be returned to their masters. This sounds more like the Code of Hammurabi than the Bible. Hammurabi even demanded the death penalty for those helping runaway slaves.[24]

In other less-severe cases—in the Lipit-Ishtar, Eshunna, and Hittite laws—*fines* were exacted for sheltering fugitive slaves.[25] Some claim that this was an improvement. Well, sort of. In these "improved" scenarios, the slave was still merely property, and ancient Near Eastern extradition arrangements still required that a slave be returned to his master. And not only this, but the slave was going back to the harsh conditions that prompted him to run away in the first place. Even upgraded laws in first millennium BC Babylon included compensation to the owner (or perhaps something more severe) for harboring a runaway slave. Yet the returned slaves themselves were disfigured, including having their ears slit and being branded.[26] This isn't the kind of improvement to publicize too widely! Yes, positive trends and moral improvements took place in ancient Near Eastern laws. But repeatedly we see a general, noteworthy moral difference between the law of Moses and other ancient Near Eastern law codes.

One more matter: although some claim that the runaway slave in Deuteronomy 23 isn't a foreigner but an Israelite, we have plenty of reason to reject that idea. For one thing, no mention of the word *brother* or *neighbor* is used. In addition, according to Leviticus 25, Israelites weren't allowed to enslave fellow Israelites. Also, the foreign fugitive slave could freely choose a place to live in Israel ("in your midst," "in one of your towns" [Deut. 23:16]), unlike the rest of the Israelites, who had to stay put on the land allotted to clans (cf. Numbers, Joshua). Thus, those who benefited weren't society's elite but vulnerable, marginalized foreign persons in the midst of a completely different society. Furthermore, Israelites entered servitude voluntarily whereas runaway slaves would likely have become slaves against their will. So if *alien* slaves received protection from harsh masters, how much more would this be so for *Israelites*.[27]

Summary Comments

In Abraham Lincoln's Second Inaugural Address (March 4, 1865) we find these familiar words regarding the North and the South:

> Both read the same Bible and pray to the same God, and each invokes His aid against the other. It may seem strange that any men should dare to ask a just God's assistance in wringing their bread from the sweat of other men's faces, but let us judge not, that we be not judged. The prayers of both could not be answered. That of neither has been answered fully. The Almighty has His own purposes.[28]

Yes, clearly both sides read from the same Bible and sought divine support to overcome their adversaries. However, the critics' common association of Israel's servant laws with those of the antebellum South is seriously misguided. We can plainly affirm that if the three clear laws of the Old Testament had been followed in the South—that is, the anti-kidnapping, anti-harm, and anti–slave-return regulations in Exodus 21:16, 20, 26–27 and Deuteronomy 23:15–16 and 24:7—then slavery wouldn't have arisen in America.

If you had to choose between servanthood in Israel and slavery in other ancient Near Eastern cultures, the sane person would pick Israel every time. The indentured servanthood model wasn't ideal, but Israel's laws reflected a greater moral sensitivity than their ancient Near Eastern counterparts.

In his classic *Theology of the Old Testament*, Walther Eichrodt summarizes the contrast well:

The norms given in the Book of the Covenant (Exod. 20–23) reveal, when compared with related law-books of the ancient Near East, radical alterations in legal practice. In the evaluation of offences against property, in the treatment of slaves, in the fixing of punishment for indirect offences, and in the rejection of punishment by mutilation, the value of human life is recognized as incomparably greater than all material values. The dominant feature throughout is respect for the rights of everything that has a human face; and this means that views which predominate universally elsewhere have been abandoned, and new principles introduced into legal practice. Ultimately this is possible only because of the profundity of insight hitherto undreamt of into *the nobility of Man*, which is now recognized as a binding consideration for moral conduct. Hence in Israel even the rights of the lowliest foreigner are placed under the protection of God; and if he is also dependent, without full legal rights, to oppress him is like oppressing the widow and orphan, a transgression worthy of punishment, which calls forth God's avenging retribution.[29]

In Israel, indentured servants (slaves) were to be treated as human beings—not as things—and they were protected from "inhuman abuse."[30] In Old Testament law, though there was a social distinction between a servant and a free person, a servant was certainly protected by the law. Abusing a servant would result in his going free. In the seventh year, a servant would be debt free and able to strike out on his own in his new status as a free person. Though there were some release laws in the ancient Near East, the contrasts between Israel's laws and other laws are more striking than the similarities. "The Israelites had six years of labor?" the critic asks. "Hammurabi allowed only three!" Generally speaking, though, in the ancient Near East, a "slave's right of manumission [gaining freedom] belonged exclusively to the slave's owner."[31]

The Code of Hammurabi and other ancient Near Eastern law codes stressed class distinctions and legislation corresponding to slaves, free persons, government officials, priests, and so on. These ancient Near Eastern laws were quite unlike the fairly nonhierarchical Old Testament. In Israel, even kings like David or Ahab weren't above the law. Indeed, when they were guilty of murdering Uriah and Naboth (respectively), God's prophets confronted them for taking the innocent lives of two ordinary citizens. (Though Canaanite kings assumed that the land belonged to them and their royal families, Naboth knew that the land belonged to God, which he graciously gave for Israelite families to use.)[32] Although God didn't use Israel's judicial system on kings, he certainly didn't give these kings a pass. God repeatedly brought severe judgments directly on the royal perpetrators of heinous crimes and acts of covenant disloyalty. God divided the kingdom because of Solomon's idolatry (1 Kings 11:13); he sent leprosy on Uzziah (2 Chron. 26:19); he sent Manasseh into exile (2 Chron. 33:10–11); and the list goes on. These incidents illustrate what Leviticus 19:15 commands: "You shall do no injustice in judgment; you shall not be partial to the poor nor defer to the great, but you are to judge your neighbor fairly," whether king or ordinary citizen.

Yes, Israel's treatment of servants (slaves) was unparalleled in the ancient Near East:

> No other ancient near Eastern law has been found that holds a master to account for the treatment of his own slaves (as distinct from injury done to the slave of another master), and the otherwise universal law regarding runaway slaves was that they must be sent back, with severe penalties for those who failed to comply.[33]

Though Israel's laws on servitude weren't the moral ideal, they show far greater moral sensitivity than other ancient Near Eastern texts. In doing so, they point us back to God's ideal at the beginning: all humans are God's image-bearers (Gen. 1:26–27). Contrary to what Christopher Hitchens and Sam Harris say, servanthood in Israel can hardly be called "a warrant for trafficking in humans" or a means of treating people "like farm equipment." No, God's ultimate intention wasn't for humans to "keep slaves."[34] In fact, the Genesis ideal is that all humans are equal and that they do not work for another; rather, each person under God's care is to be his own "master," sitting under his own vine and fig tree (1 Kings 4:25; Micah 4:4; Zech. 3:10).[35]

Further Reading

Chirichigno, Gregory C. *Debt-Slavery in Israel and the Ancient Near East*. JSOT Supplement Series 141. Sheffield: University of Sheffield Press, 1993.

Goldingay, John. *Old Testament Theology III: Israel's Life*. Downers Grove, IL: InterVarsity, 2009. See esp. pp. 458–75.

Wright, Christopher J. H. *Old Testament Ethics for the People of God*. Downers Grove, IL: InterVarsity, 2004.

13

Warrant for Trafficking in Humans as Farm Equipment? (II)

Challenging Texts on Slavery

We've given context and background regarding servitude in Israel—a noteworthy improvement on the slavery laws in other ancient Near Eastern texts. Yet there are still some challenging texts to consider.

Beating Slaves to Death (Exod. 21:20–21)

> If a man strikes his male servant or his female servant with a staff so that he or she dies as a result of the blow, he will surely be punished [*naqam*]. However, if the injured servant survives one or two days, the owner will not be punished [*naqam*], for he has suffered the loss. (Exod. 21:20–21 NET)

Allegedly, this treatment of the servant (the word *slave* is misleading) suggests to some that he's owned as a possession by another. This impression is reinforced by various translations that render the word *loss* as "property." Now, the word literally means "money"; so is this person is a commodity to exchange rather than a person to value?

The Old Testament affirms the full personhood of these debt-servants (e.g., Gen. 1:26–27; Job 31:13–15; Deut. 15:1–18), and this passage is no exception. It affirms the servant's full personhood. If the master struck a servant so that he immediately died, the master would be tried for capital punishment: "he shall be avenged" (Exod. 21:20 ESV). This verb *naqam* always involves the death penalty in the Old Testament—the implication is that judicial vengeance is the result.[1]

This theme is reinforced by the mention of taking "life for life" (Exod. 21:23–24), which follows on the heels of the servant-beating passage. This confirms that the servant was to be treated as a human being with dignity, not as property.

The staff or rod wasn't a lethal weapon, nothing like a spear or a sword. What if the servant *didn't* die immediately from the rod beating? What if he died after "a day or two"? In this case, the master was given the benefit of the doubt that the servant was likely being disciplined and that there was no murderous intent. Of course, if the slave died immediately, no further proof was needed. And if any permanent injury resulted (e.g., losing an eye or a tooth), then the servant was to be released debt free. This is an extraordinarily different treatment compared to other ancient Near Eastern laws in this regard. For example, Hammurabi insisted that payment went *to the master* for such injuries to a slave.[2] In the ancient Near East, where masters could treat slaves as they pleased, this passage upholds the dignity of debt-servants.[3]

Why then does the passage say that the slave is the master's "money" or "property"? The suggestion here isn't that servants were chattel or property. The servant/employee came into the master's/employer's house to get out of debt. So the employer stood to lose money if he mistreated his employee; his harsh treatment toward an employee could impact his money bag. And if he killed his employee/servant, then he was to be executed. Whether of a servant or a free person, murder was murder in Israel.

Let's go a bit deeper, though. Ancient Near Eastern scholar Harry Hoffner (a Hittitologist at the University of Chicago) rejects the common rendering "he [the servant] is his money" in favor of this one: "that [fee] is his money/silver." This "fee" reading is based on the context of Exodus 21:18–19 (part of a section on punishments dealing with quarrels and accidental killing): "If men have a quarrel and one strikes the other with a stone or with his fist, and he does not die but remains in bed, if he gets up and walks around outside on his staff, then he who struck him shall go unpunished; he shall only pay for his loss of time, and shall take care of him until he is completely healed." Like the modified Hittite law that required masters who had harmed their slaves to pay a physician to provide medical treatment, so here the employer had to pay the medical bills for the servant he had wounded. In verse 21, the Hebrew pronoun *hu* refers not to the servant ("he") but to the fee ("that") paid to the doctor tending to the wounded servant. Hoffner writes, "The fact that the master provided care at his own expense would be a significant factor when the judges respond to a charge of intentional homicide."[4]

Are these Exodus laws perfect, universal ones for all people? No, but in this and other aspects, we continually come across improved legislation for Israelite society in contrast to surrounding ancient Near Eastern cultures. As the Jewish scholar Nahum Sarna observes about this passage, "This law—the protection of slaves from maltreatment by their masters—is found nowhere else in the entire existing corpus of ancient Near Eastern legislation."[5]

Leaving Wife and Children Behind (Exod. 21:2–6)

> If you buy a Hebrew servant, he is to serve you for six years, but in the seventh year he will go out free without paying anything. If he came in by himself he will go out by himself; if he had a wife when he came in, then his wife will go out with him. If his master gave him a wife, and she bore sons or daughters, the wife and the children will belong to her master, and he will go out by himself. But if the servant should declare, "I love my master, my wife, and my children; I will not go out free," then his master must bring him to the judges, and he will bring him to the door or the doorposts, and his master will pierce his ear with an awl, and he shall serve him forever. (Exod. 21:2–6 NET)

Nuzi was located near Kirkuk, Iraq, close to the Tigris River.[6] Thousands of tablets—the Akkadian Nuzi texts—from the second millennium BC were found there. They mention legislation similar to this: if a slave entered a master's home single, he left single. If he entered with a spouse, then he left on his marry way! Now, if a wife had been given to him by his master, then she (and any children from this union) belonged to the master.

According to this Exodus passage, if a man was given a wife by his master/employer and they had children, then he had a choice: he could either leave by himself when the seventh year of debt release came, or he could continue as a permanent servant to be with his wife and children. It's a less-than-ideal setting to be sure, but let's probe the text more deeply.

At first glance, this text seems to treat females (and children) unfairly. The (apparently) favored male can come into a service arrangement and then go out of it. Yet the wife he married while serving his employer and any children who came while he served were (so it seems) "stuck" in the master's home and couldn't leave. That's not only male favoring; it strikes us as criminal! Wasn't this an earlier version of slave families during the antebellum South (like Frederick Douglass's) who were broken up and scattered by insensitive slaveowners?

Our first point in response is this: we're not told specifically that this scenario could also apply to a woman, but we have good reason to think this situation wasn't gender specific. (We'll see shortly that Deuteronomy 15 makes explicit that this scenario applied to a woman as well.) This is another example of case law: "if such and such a scenario arises, then this is how to proceed." Case law typically wasn't gender specific. Furthermore, Israelite judges were quite capable of applying the law to male and female alike. An impoverished woman, who wasn't given by her father as a prospective wife to a (widowed or divorced) man or his son (Exod. 21:7–11), could perform standard household tasks. And she could go free by this same law, just as a male servant could.[7] Various scholars suggest that the Scripture text could be applied to females quite readily: "If you buy a Hebrew servant, she is to serve you for six years. But in the seventh year, she will go out free. . . . If her master gives her a husband, and they have sons or daughters, the husband and the children will belong to her master, and she will go out by herself." The law makes perfect sense in light of this shift; its spirit isn't violated by doing so.

Some critics, though, would rather fight than shift. Rather than applying these case-law scenarios to both men and women, they'd rather put up resistance in order to make this law look its very worst. But we have no compelling reason to do so. Again, Israel's judges would have looked to this general passage for guidance regarding female servants. Simply because many verses in the law happen to use a masculine gender pronoun rather than alternating between "he" and "she" hardly means that women are thereby being excluded.

As an aside, the term *Hebrew* (at this stage in Israel's history) was broader than the term *Israelite*; the two terms would later be equated. The *habiru* were people not formally attached to established states like Egypt or Babylon; they were considered foreigners and noncitizens from the speaker's perspective. So this passage may well refer to a non-Israelite. That means this servant—possibly a foreigner—was to be released after six years unless he preferred the security of his employer's household. In this case, he could make the arrangement permanent. For now, we'll assume that this passage refers to an Israelite servant, but we'll revisit this issue when discussing Leviticus 25.

For our second point, let's (for the moment) stick with a *male* servant/employee scenario. Let's say his employer arranges for a marriage between him and a female employee. (In this case of debt-servitude, the employer's family would now engage in marriage negotiations.) By taking the male servant into his home to work off a debt, the boss has made an investment. He would stand to suffer loss if someone walked out on the contract. Think in terms of military service. When someone signs up to serve for three or four years, he still owes the military, even if he gets married during this time. Likewise in Israel, for debts to be paid off, the male servant couldn't just leave with his wife once he was married. He was still under contract, and he needed to honor this. And even when his contract was completed, he wasn't allowed simply to walk away with his wife and kids. After all, they were still economic assets to his boss.

What could the released man do? He had three options.

1. He could wait for his wife and kids to finish their term of service while he worked elsewhere. His wife and kids weren't stuck in the employer's home the rest of their lives. They could be released when the wife worked off her debt. Yet if the now-free man worked elsewhere, this would mean (a) he would be separated from his family, and (b) his boss would no longer supply him with food, clothing, and shelter. On the other hand, if he lived *with* his family after release, he'd still have to pay for room and board. So this scenario created its own set of financial challenges.
2. He could get a decent job elsewhere and save his shekels to pay his boss to release his wife and kids from contractual obligations. What a great option! Why not take this route? Because it would have been very dif-

ficult for the man to support himself *and* earn enough money for his family's debt release.

3. He could commit himself to working permanently for his employer—a life contract (Exod. 21:5–6). He could stay with his family and remain in fairly stable economic circumstances. He would formalize this arrangement in a legal ceremony before the judges (God) by having his ear pierced with an awl.

Before coming up with all sorts of modern Western solutions to solve these ancient Near Eastern problems, we should make greater efforts to better grasp the nature of Israelite servitude and the social and economic circumstances surrounding it. We're talking about unfortunate circumstances during bleak economic times. Israel's laws provided safety nets for *protection*, not oppression. It's obvious that this arrangement was far different from the South's chattel slavery, in which a slave wasn't a temporarily indentured servant who voluntarily sold himself to live in another's household to pay off his debts.

The Engaged Servant Girl (Lev. 19:20–21)

> Now if a man lies carnally with a woman who is a slave [i.e., servant] acquired for another man, but who has in no way been redeemed nor given her freedom, there shall be punishment; they shall not, however, be put to death, because she was not free. He shall bring his guilt offering to the LORD to the doorway of the tent of meeting, a ram for a guilt offering. (Lev. 19:20–21)

This passage is different from Deuteronomy 22:23–27, which we addressed earlier and which deals with an engaged *free* woman. Here the situation involves a free man and a *servant* girl promised to another man. The man is clearly guilty of adultery; he seems to be a seducer who is taking advantage of his position over a servant girl, something like what King David did with Bathsheba. We're dealing with statutory rape between the seducer and the servant girl, who was pressured to consent (see our discussion of Deut. 22:28–29).

In this murky and oft-debated passage, two issues are highlighted. First, the girl was *engaged* and not married. Second, she was a *servant girl* and not free; she hadn't yet been redeemed by a family member or liberated by her master. (This is the reason given for not punishing the girl or the seducer.) So her master wouldn't have had the typical claim on her, nor could he be compensated because she was engaged. This presents a kind of gray area in Israel's legislation with a mixture of a free person and an engaged servant (see the immediately preceding passage on mixtures in Lev. 19:19).[8]

As with other laws regarding women, the goal of this law was to protect those who were more vulnerable. We know that it's easier for persons in vulnerable situations to be taken advantage of and even sexually harassed.

In this case, the girl was taken advantage of, and she isn't punished. Notice too that, though she has a diminished social status, this status is viewed as temporary. It doesn't prevent her from being "given her freedom" (Lev. 19:20). Now, there's no death penalty for the man here (and we've seen that only murder *requires* the death penalty, while for adultery and other potential capital offenses, other compensation could be made). The offense is still very serious, and expensive reparations are required (i.e., a sacrificial ram).[9] Yet clearly the law protects girls who are taken as servants for their parents' debt.[10]

Based on Leviticus 19 (and a surface reading of Exod. 21), it may seem that women were treated as property. However, we've observed that, despite Israel's inherited and imperfect patriarchal structure, these laws actually served to protect women as well as the family structure, which was central to Israelite society. Rather than viewing these law texts as demeaning women, we should actually see them as protecting the vulnerable.

To get further perspective, however, consider again other ancient Near Eastern cultures in this regard. Punishments were often of the vicarious sort. For committing certain crimes, men would have to give up their wife, daughter, ox, or slave—a clear indication that a woman was often deemed the property of a man. Middle Assyrian laws punished not a rapist but a rapist's wife and even allowed her to be gang-raped. In other ancient Near Eastern laws, men could freely whip their wives, pull out their hair, mutilate their ears, or strike them—a dramatic contrast to Israel's laws, which gave no such permissions.[11] Again, despite some of Israel's problematic social structures and corresponding laws, Israel's legal system—if faithfully followed—created a morally preferable environment to other societies in the ancient Near East. (The operative words are "faithfully followed," which Israel wasn't very good at doing.)

Foreign Slaves

For they [Israelites] are My servants whom I brought out from the land of Egypt; they are not to be sold in a slave sale. You shall not rule over him with severity, but are to revere your God. As for your male and female slaves whom you may have—you may acquire male and female slaves from the pagan nations that are around you. Then, too, it is out of the sons of the sojourners [*toshabim*] who live as aliens [*ger*] among you that you may gain acquisition, and out of their families who are with you, whom they will have produced in your land; they also may become your possession. You may even bequeath them to your sons after you, to receive as a possession; you can use them as permanent slaves. But in respect to your countrymen, the sons of Israel, you shall not rule with severity over one another.

Now if the means of a stranger [*ger*] or of a sojourner [*toshab*] with you becomes sufficient, and a countryman of yours becomes so poor with regard to him as to sell himself to a stranger who is sojourning with you, or to the descendants of a stranger's family, then he shall have redemption right after he has been sold. One of his brothers may redeem him, or his uncle, or his uncle's son, may redeem him, or one of his blood relatives from his family may redeem him; or if he prospers, he may redeem himself. (Lev. 25:42–49)

Here we come across a jarring text, a significant distinction between *Israelite* servants/employees and *foreign* workers in Israel. Does this text regard foreign workers as nothing more than property?

Before we jump to this conclusion, we should look at what *precedes* this text—and at other scriptural considerations. When we do so, we'll continue to see that (1) these foreigners were still nowhere near the chattel slaves of the antebellum South; (2) a significant presence of apparently resentful foreigners required stricter measures than those for cooperative aliens who were willing to follow Israel's laws; (3) since only Israelites were allowed to own land (which ultimately belonged to Yahweh), foreigners who weren't in Israel just for business purposes were typically incorporated into Israelite homes to serve there, unless they chose to live elsewhere; and (4) strangers in the land could, if they chose, not only be released but potentially become persons of means. For poor foreigners wanting to live in Israel, voluntary servitude was pretty much the only option.

Being Nice to Strangers

In Leviticus 19:33–34, the Israelites were commanded to love the stranger in the land: "When a stranger [*ger*] resides with you in your land, you shall not do him wrong. The stranger who resides with you shall be to you as the native among you, and you shall love him as yourself, for you were aliens in the land of Egypt; I am the LORD your God." This is reinforced in Deuteronomy 10:19: "So show your love for the alien [*ger*], for you were aliens in the land of Egypt." So before we jump to conclusions about "harsh and oppressive" Old Testament laws regarding outsiders, we should take such texts seriously.

Since the land belonged to Yahweh (Lev. 25:23; Josh. 22:19), who graciously loaned it to the families of Israel, foreign settlers couldn't acquire it. Yet a foreigner (*nokri*) could become an alien (*ger*) if he embraced Israel's ways fully; he would no longer be a permanent outsider. Allowances were made for aliens in terms of gleaning laws and other provisions. The foreigner didn't need to feel excluded in the host country; presumably he wasn't forced to remain in Israel either. Though without land, he could share in the community life and religious celebrations of Israel with many improved economic and status perks; think of Rahab or Ruth here.

The Foreigner and the Alien

The established alien (*ger*) and the sojourner (*toshab*) were those who had embraced the worship of Yahweh, the covenant God of Israel. They had come from another land and had sought refuge in Israel for perhaps political or economic reasons—like Abraham in Hebron (Gen. 23:4), Moses in Midian (Exod. 2:22), Elimelech and his family in Moab (Ruth 1:1), or the Israelites in Egypt (Exod. 22:21). Perhaps the best term for such persons is *ethnic minorities*—persons with "distinctive racial or cultural traditions [who] are vulnerable to exploitation or discrimination by dominant groups in the population."[12] They had settled in the land for some time. They didn't have their own land but had come under the protection of Israel (Deut. 10:19). Furthermore, these resident aliens were proselytes or converts to the religion of Israel. (In fact, the term *ger* is typically translated *prosēlytos* in the Greek Old Testament.) Aliens (and foreigners [*nokrim*]), however, were permitted to eat nonkosher food (Deut. 14:21), but aliens couldn't eat food with blood in it (Lev. 17:10, 12–13). They kept the Sabbath laws, and they were circumcised, which meant they could celebrate Passover (Exod. 12:48–49; Num. 9:14). God is said to love the alien (Deut. 10:18), and the alien was not to be oppressed. However, the well-to-do alien (*ger*) was restricted from having an Israelite servant in his home (Lev. 25:47–49). An Israelite could not be a debt-servant of a non-Israelite alien—especially in light of God's delivering Israel from Egypt.

Foreigners (*nokrim* or sometimes *bene-nekar* [literally, "sons of a foreign land"]) were in a different category. Perhaps they came into Israel as prisoners of war, or they came voluntarily to engage in business transactions. They didn't embrace Yahweh worship and remained uncircumcised.[13] The foreigner didn't show concern for Israel's purity laws, and he was allowed to eat nonkosher foods. He likely didn't have a problem eating a dead animal not killed by a human. What's remarkable in Israel's legislation is the accommodation to the foreigner: if an Israelite saw an animal that had died by itself, he couldn't eat it (it would make him unclean), but he could give it to an alien (*ger*) or sell it to a foreigner (*nokri*) living in his town (Deut. 14:21). This was a way to show love to the alien and foreigner alike, even if the foreigner didn't embrace Israel's purity laws and didn't identify as fully as possible with God's people.[14]

Further, we've already noted that in a postwar situation (Deut. 21:10–14), a foreign woman could follow certain requirements to separate from her former culture and embrace her new one. After this, she could be elevated to the status of Israelite wife, a far cry from acquiring chattel.

Just because an outsider to Israel came to live in the land didn't mean he would necessarily become a household servant. The stranger (*ger*) or sojourner (*toshab*)—often used synonymously—could become a person of means (e.g., Lev. 25:47). The foreigner (*nokri*)—the word typically, though not always, has a negative connotation—often came to Israel for business transactions: "foreigners were normally present in a country for purposes of trade," which meant that "goods or money given to them on credit were usually investments or advance payments on goods, not loans because of poverty."[15] We should factor all of the above into our discussion of foreigners before looking at the downside of foreigners as servants.

There's more to the word *foreigner* than first meets the eye. In the Old Testament, the term is associated with someone who is dangerous or hostile to what is good and to God's purposes for Israel. The foreigner is frequently associated with idolatry (cf. Josh. 24:20; Jer. 5:19; Mal. 2:11), hostility (Neh. 9:2; 13:30),[16] or the enemy (2 Sam. 22:45–46). Solomon married foreign wives who led him into idolatry (1 Kings 11:1; cf. Ezra 10:2). Proverbs warns against the strange or foreign woman, who is an adulteress (Prov. 2:16; 5:20; 7:5; 23:27, etc.). Because of difficulty of integrating into Israel, foreigners may have served as forced laborers (*mas*) who worked for the state (cf. Deut. 20:11). They performed public works such as construction and undertook agricultural work as well. Under kings David and Solomon, Ammonites and Canaanites engaged in such work (2 Sam. 12:31; 1 Kings 9:15, 20–22; cf. Judg. 1:28–35). We don't know if they served part-time or permanently.[17]

Overall, the alien or stranger/temporary resident in Israel wasn't to be oppressed but was to be dealt with fairly (e.g., Exod. 22:21). Repeatedly in the law of Moses, God showed concern that outsiders/foreigners be treated well.

Special Considerations

What about loan discrimination? For Israelites, loans were given at cost; no interest was permitted. However, loans with interest were allowed when it came to the foreigner (*nokri*) in Israel (Exod. 22:25; Lev. 25:36–37; Deut. 15:3). Wasn't this unfair? Some have argued so. But as we've seen, typically foreigners sought loans for *business/investment purposes*, not because they were destitute and needed money to relieve their debt, let alone to keep from starving.

In other instances, the presence of foreigners was tricky. If Israel fought against other nations, some POWs might need to be assimilated into Israelite society. Structures were needed to prevent them from rising up in rebellion against their new masters or remaining consolidated in their own land where they could muster forces and launch a counterattack. In cases where Israel's captured enemies (especially the males) didn't care for the "laws of the land" and posed an internal threat to Israel's safety (e.g., Num. 21–22; 25; 31), servanthood was one way of subduing or controlling this menace.

Certain economic, military, and social realities made things messy.[18] Even so, Israel couldn't oppress or exploit foreigners. Deuteronomy 23 shows concern for desperate, threatened foreign slaves, and this text sheds light on—or even improves on—previous legislation in Leviticus 25. And there's no hint of racism here, as though being a non-Israelite was justification for Israelite slave keeping. In fact, as Roy Gane argues, the laws of Exodus 21:20–21, 26–27 protect from abuse *all* persons in service to others, not just Jews.[19]

Notice something important in Leviticus 25:44–47, which is typically over-looked by the critics. We've seen that kidnapping and slave trading were clearly prohibited by the Mosaic law, but foreigners would come to Israel as prisoners of war and, given the dangers of an internal uprising, would be pressed into supervised construction or agricultural work. Yet the very sojourners and aliens who were at first pressed into service (v. 45) were the same ones who had the capability of saving up sufficient means (v. 47). Yes, in principle, *all* persons in servitude within Israel except criminals could be released.[20]

At this juncture, let's note several important points about the "foreign servitude" passage of Leviticus 25: First, the verb *acquire* [*qanah*] in Leviticus 25:39–51 need not involve selling or purchasing foreign servants. For example, the same word appears in Genesis 4:1 (Eve's having "gotten a manchild") and 14:19 (God is the "Possessor of heaven and earth").[21] Later, Boaz "acquired" Ruth as a wife (Ruth 4:10), although she was no inferior but rather a full partner in Boaz's eyes.

Second, in some cases, foreign servants could become elevated and apparently fully equal to Israelite citizens. For instance, a descendant of Caleb ended up marrying an Egyptian servant. "Now Sheshan had no sons, only daughters. And Sheshan had an Egyptian servant whose name was Jarha. Sheshan gave his daughter to Jarha his servant in marriage, and she bore him Attai" (1 Chron. 2:34–35). Not only do we have marriage between a foreign servant and an established freeperson with quite a pedigree, but the key implication is that inheritance rights would fall to the servant's offspring (the genealogy lists Jarha's son Attai, who had a son Nathan, whose son was Zabad, and so on).

Third, foreign runaway slaves were given protection within Israel's borders and not returned to their harsh masters (Deut. 23:15–16). Kidnapping slaves was also prohibited (Exod. 21:16; Deut. 24:7). So serving within Israelite households was to be a safe haven for any foreigner; it was not to be an oppressive setting, but offered economic and social stability.

Fourth, we've seen that the "Hebrew" servant in Exodus 21:2 could well have been an outsider who had come to be a resident alien and was to be released in the seventh year, presumably to go back to his country of origin. However, he could make the arrangement permanent if he loved his master/employer and wanted to stay under his care. Given the security and provision of room and board for landless aliens, this arrangement could apparently be extended into the next generation(s). This setup wasn't to be permanent, unless the servant chose to stay with his master. John Goldingay writes, "Perhaps many people would be reasonably happy to settle for being long-term or lifelong servants. Servants do count as part of the family." He adds, "One can even imagine people who started off as debt servants volunteering to become permanent servants because they love their master and his household" (cf. Deut. 15:16–17).[22]

Fifth, the text of Leviticus 25 makes clear that the alien/stranger could potentially work himself out of debt and become a person of means in Israel:

"if the means of a stranger or of a sojourner with you becomes sufficient" (v. 47). This is another indication that he wasn't stuck in lifelong servitude without a choice. The terms *stranger* (*ger*) and *sojourner* (*toshab*) are connected to the terms used in verse 45 "*sojourners* who live as *aliens/strangers* among you"). That is, these "acquired" servants could potentially better themselves to the point of hiring servants themselves (v. 47). Of course, an alien could not hire an Israelite.

As we've seen in other scenarios, these situations weren't ideal given the inferior social structures of the time. God instituted laws for Israel that began where the people were. But we see a remarkable humanization encoded in Israel's laws—for foreign and Israelite servants alike.

Membership Has Its Privileges

If a foreigner happened to be poor, this circumstance could help create an incentive for the foreigner to become part of the Israelite community and share in, say, the Passover, something the alien could celebrate (Exod. 12:48–49). The foreigner (*ben-nekar*) wasn't allowed to participate in this feast (12:43) since he didn't care to identify himself with Israel's covenant and with Yahweh. Again, why should loans be *at cost* for people who chose to live in (and off) Israel without entering into the corporate life and worship of Israel? We should expect some difference between them.

Think of America's illegal immigration situation, a complex matter that's often emotionally charged on both sides of the debate. We all know how this goes: illegals slip across the United States–Mexico border to benefit from the U.S.'s economic way of life. Meanwhile, many foreigners desiring to live in the U.S. may follow all the legal channels to acquire a U.S. green card (resident alien status) in order to (perhaps) eventually become naturalized citizens; they wait a long time for their applications to be processed. Even so, their applications may be rejected. Yet illegals completely bypass the legal channels and maneuver their way across the border.

Now, I'm not unsympathetic with the concerns of illegals looking for a better life in the United States, and we should extend kindness and personal concern to them. Perhaps churches can try to assist undocumented aliens in getting a fair trial and making sure they're treated respectfully as God's image-bearers; perhaps churches could even sponsor them in hopes of their becoming naturalized citizens. But for the sake of maintaining order and preserving the privilege and dignity of citizenship in a country (cf. Rom. 13), priority should be given to tax-paying citizens over illegals when it comes to health care, drivers' licenses, insurance, and the like. It's understandable that when legal protocols aren't followed, certain privileges are withheld.[23]

The same held true in ancient Israel. The foreigner (*nokri*) was more like an illegal immigrant. The resident alien/sojourner (*ger*), however, sought to play by Israel's rules. Unlike the resident alien, foreigners weren't willing to abide by Israel's covenant relationship with God, so they shouldn't expect to receive all the privileges of an Israelite citizen. Ruth the Moabitess embraced the God of Israel and of her mother-in-law, Naomi: "Your people shall be my people, and your God, my God" (Ruth 1:16). If Gentiles like Ruth or Rahab or Uriah the Hittite were willing to fully embrace Israel's God, people, and laws, then they could become more easily incorporated into mainstream life in Israel, even if they couldn't own land. And foreigners didn't have to come to Israel at all.

Like the credit card company (American Express) used to say, "Membership has its privileges." The same pertained to membership within Israel.

Final Considerations

Leviticus 25 reflected an attempt to regulate and control potential abuses that often come through greed and social status. This legislation created a safety net for vulnerable Israelites; its intent was to stop generational cycles of poverty. The story of Ruth and Naomi actually puts flesh and bones on the Sinai legislation. It brings us from the theoretical laws to the practical realm of everyday life in Israel. We see how the relevant laws were to be applied when death, poverty, and uncertainty came upon an Israelite. We also witness a Gentile who came to Israel with her mother-in-law. Both were vulnerable and seeking refuge with relatives who could assist them. They were provided for as Ruth was able to glean in the fields of Boaz, a kinsman-redeemer. Naomi was cared for in her old age.[24]

We should consider Leviticus 25:44 in light of the Ruth narrative: "You may acquire [*qanah*] male and female slaves from the pagan nations that are around you." Interestingly, Boaz announced to the elders in Bethlehem that he had "acquired" Ruth as his wife: "Moreover, I have acquired [*qanah*] Ruth the Moabitess, the widow of Mahlon" (Ruth 4:10). Does this mean that Boaz thought Ruth was property? Hardly! Boaz had the utmost respect for Ruth, and he viewed her as an equal partner.

Was a foreign worker of a lower social rank than an Israelite servant? Yes. Was this an ideal situation? No. Am I advocating this for contemporary society? Hardly. Let's not forget the negative, sometimes God-opposing association bound up with the Old Testament use of the term *foreigner*. We often detect in this term a refusal to assimilate with Israel's ways and covenant relationship with God, which conflicted with God's intentions for his people. Again, foreigners could settle in the land, embrace Israel's ways, and become aliens or sojourners, which would give them greater entry into Israelite social life and economic benefit. And, as I've emphasized, the foreigner could have chosen to live elsewhere rather than in Israel. So we have a lot of complicating factors to consider here.

Even so, if we pay attention to the biblical text, the underlying attitude toward foreigners is far better than that found in other Near Eastern cultures. God constantly reminded Israel that they were strangers and aliens in Egypt (Exod. 22:21; 23:9; Lev. 19:34; Deut. 5:15; 10:19; 15:15; 16:12; 24:18, 22). This memory was to shape Israel's treatment of strangers in the land. That's why God commanded the following: caring for the needy and the alien (Lev. 23:22); loving the alien (Deut. 10:19); providing for his basic need of food (Deut. 24:18–22); promptly paying for his labor (Deut. 24:14–15). In addition, the Old Testament looks to the ultimate salvation of, yes, the foreigner and his incorporation into the people of God (Isa. 56:3 ["the foreigner who has joined himself to the Lord"]).

Lest we think that a foreigner's permanent servitude (which could well be understood as voluntary in Lev. 25) meant that his master could take advantage of him, we should recall the pervasive theme throughout the law of Moses of protection and concern for those in servitude. They weren't to be taken advantage of. So if a foreign servant was being mistreated by his master so that he ran away, he could find his way into another Israelite home for shelter and protection: "You shall not hand over to his master a slave who has escaped from his master to you. He shall live with you in your midst, in the place which he shall choose in one of your towns where it pleases him; you shall not mistreat him" (Deut. 23:15–16). This provision wasn't simply for a foreign slave running *to Israel* but also for a foreign servant *within Israel* who was being mistreated. Israel's legislation regarding foreign slaves showed concern for their well-being, very much unlike the Code of Hammurabi, for example, which had no regard for an owner's treatment of his slaves.[25]

Comparing Servitude Texts

Let's try to tie up some loose ends here. We looked at Deuteronomy 15:1–18 in the last chapter; so we won't cite the text in full here. This is the famous release text where God commanded generosity and goodwill toward debt-servants who were being released. God expressed the desire that there be no poor in the land at all.

Scholars have claimed that this passage stands in tension with the earlier servitude laws of Exodus 21:1–11 and Leviticus 25:39–46 (and we could add here Lev. 19:20–21).[26] If so, the tension may not be as great as some have assumed. For example, Exodus 21:7 doesn't expressly say that *female* servants were to be set free after the seventh year. We've argued, though, that this is implied; this verse is an instance of case law. Tension exists if we assume that gender switching isn't allowed by the text. But that's not so. We could add that verses 26–27 mention that a male or *female* servant may be freed if injured; if he or she was killed by an employer's abuse, the employer was to be put to death.

At any rate, Deuteronomy 15:12 explicitly affirms that both *male and female* servants were in view. *Both* were to be given freedom in the seventh year, the sabbatical release. If a genuine tension exists, then this passage suggests that the arrangement for acquiring a wife in Exodus 21:7–10 had later been *dropped* in Israel.[27]

What about the law that a male servant couldn't leave with his wife and children if his wife were given by his master (Exod. 21:4)? This appears to change by Leviticus 25:40–42 (in the Jubilee year laws), where the children (and presumably the wife) were to go free with the husband/father. Also, in contrast to Exodus 21:2–6, Leviticus 25:41–42 doesn't distinguish between children born before and children born during indentured servanthood. Yet already in Leviticus 25:40–42, in the Jubilee year (every fiftieth year), the children (and presumably the wife) were released with their father (husband).

We do see some tensions between earlier texts (like Exod. 21) and Deuteronomy 15. We don't need to thrown up our hands in despair at hopelessly contradictory texts. Rather, what we have here is a dynamic adjustment and a moral upgrade taking place within a short span of time in national Israel's early life. Remember the daughters of Zelophehad, who petitioned Moses for adjustments of the law (Num. 27)? Moses took their case before Yahweh, who approved their request. This is another example of an adjustment in Israel's laws, a move from inferior legislation to improved legal status. This is a far cry from Christopher Hitchens's notion of "unalterable" Old Testament laws.

Christopher Wright points out that in the final editing of the Pentateuch (Genesis–Deuteronomy), the editor(s) would certainly have been aware of these differences and tensions yet kept all of these texts in place. The editorial hand shows remarkable skill in handling the text.[28] In fact, the majority of scholars see Exodus giving the oldest law and Deuteronomy later revising and expanding it (which could also apply to the Leviticus text).[29] So the fact that these texts coexist in the same body of work itself suggests a possible reconciliation or rationale for doing so. Wright sees Deuteronomy "modifying, extending, and to some extent reforming earlier laws, with additional explicit theological rationale and motivation."[30] Even the ancient Israelite would recognize that Exodus 21, which emphasizes the humanness of servants (slaves), stood in a certain tension with the later text of Deuteronomy 15 (and Lev. 25).

So to obey Deuteronomy, to a certain extent, "necessarily meant no longer complying with Exodus [or Leviticus]."[31] These texts were deliberately kept together, in part to reflect this adjustment. Apparently, these tensions didn't seem all that wildly contradictory to the final editor of this portion of the Bible. This point serves to illustrate the "living, historical and contextual nature of the growth of Scripture."[32]

By the time we get to the prophet Amos (whose ministry was in the Northern Kingdom of Israel), God levels harsh words against those who are "buying the poor with silver and the needy for a pair of sandals, selling even the sweepings with the wheat" (8:6 NIV; cf. 2:6). Corrupt judges were bribed by the rich to make slave labor available to them. The poor were heavily fined and, when unable to pay, sold into servitude at low prices—thrown in with the sweepings of wheat.[33] In Amos, the Israelite poor were being mistreated and even being traded for a pair of sandals. How much worse it must have been for aliens in Israel, whom God commanded Israel to protect.

Isaiah expresses similar concern for Gentile fugitives fleeing Moab. Notice the great concern shown for the vulnerable and those escaping dangerous situations: "'Hide the fugitives, do not betray the refugees. Let the Moabite fugitives stay with you; be their shelter from the destroyer.' The oppressor will come to an end, and destruction will cease; the aggressor will vanish from the land" (Isa. 16:3–4 NIV).

In the prophetic book of Joel (2:29), God made an egalitarian promise to pour out his Spirit on *all* mankind, young and old, male and female—including male and female *servants*. This same theme is found in Job 31:15, where master and slave alike come from the same place—the mother's womb. They are fundamentally equal.

Reflecting on the wider context of Scripture passages reminds us not to focus on a single text but to see how each passage fits into the broader whole. Furthermore, any deviations from ideal moral standards of human equality and dignity set down at creation are the result of human hard-heartedness. Over and over, we're reminded of Israel's superior legislation in contrast to the rest of the ancient Near East.

Further Reading

Chirichigno, Gregory C. *Debt-Slavery in Israel and the Ancient Near East*. JSOT Supplement Series 141. Sheffield: University of Sheffield Press, 1993.

Gane, Roy. *Leviticus, Numbers*. NIV Application Commentary. Grand Rapids: Zondervan, 2004.

Hoffmeier, James K. *The Immigration Crisis: Immigrants, Aliens, and the Bible*. Wheaton: Crossway, 2009.

14

Warrant for Trafficking in Humans as Farm Equipment? (III)

Slavery in the New Testament

The three-day Battle of Gettysburg in early July 1863 took the lives of approximately fifty thousand Confederate and Union soldiers. Abraham Lincoln was invited to commemorate their deaths, dedicating the cemetery where over thirty-five hundred Union soldiers are now buried. His brief but powerful Gettysburg Address (November 19, 1863) began with these immortalized words: "Fourscore and seven years ago our fathers brought forth on this continent a new nation, conceived in liberty and dedicated to the proposition that all men are created equal." Lincoln appealed to the Declaration of Independence in his argument against slavery, something he had done throughout the Lincoln-Douglas debates (1858) and well before.[1]

Lincoln regularly appropriated this founding document to reshape Americans' thinking regarding slavery and the alleged subhumanity of blacks. Although America had fallen short of this ideal—whether in its breaking of treaties with Native Americans or the mistreatment of blacks—Lincoln called on his fellow citizens to think through the implications of this document. So at Gettysburg, Lincoln urged his hearers "to be dedicated here to the unfinished work which they who fought here have thus far so nobly advanced"; he longed to see fulfilled the vision articulated in the 1776 declaration: a "new birth of freedom."

The declaration's role in Lincoln's presidency illustrates a similar phenomenon in the Old Testament. Genesis 1 was "dedicated to the proposition that all men are created equal"! In the Mosaic law, God was pointing back to this creational "founding document," affirming that treating humans as property or inferiors was fundamentally at odds with it. Despite human fallenness, Old Testament readers were continually pointed toward the ideal.

Though our focus has been on the Old Testament, we should say something about slavery in the New Testament. The New Testament presupposes not only a fundamental equality because all humans are created in God's image (James 3:9) but also an even deeper unity in Christ that transcends human boundaries and social structures: "There is neither Jew nor Greek, there is neither slave nor free man, there is neither male nor female; for you are all one in Christ Jesus" (Gal. 3:28). We'll look at the implications of this Christian manifesto.

A Little Background

We need to reorient our thinking away from the Old Testament situation of (primarily) Hebrew debt-servanthood (from which male and female were to be freed in the seventh year). The landscape of the Roman world was much different—namely, the existence of institutionalized chattel (property) slavery. Rome (unlike Old Testament legislation) sought to institutionalize not merely servanthood but (chattel) slavery.

During the first century AD, 85 to 90 percent of Rome's population consisted of slaves.[2] Although slaves were considered their masters' property and didn't have *legal* rights, they did have quite a range of other rights and privileges. These included (1) the possibility of starting a business to earn potentially large sums of money, (2) the capability of earning money to eventually purchase freedom (manumission) from their masters, or (3) the right to own property (known as the *peculium*).[3] The work of slaves covered the spectrum from horrid conditions in mines to artisans, business agents, and other positions of respect and prestige such as civil or imperial servants.[4] So slavery wasn't unkind to *all* slaves in the Roman Empire.

The New Testament's Affirmations of Slaves as Persons

You've probably heard the complaint, "Jesus never said anything about the wrongness of slavery." Not so! Jesus explicitly *opposed* every form of oppression. Citing Isaiah 61:1, Jesus clearly described his mission: "to proclaim release to the captives, . . . to set free those who are oppressed" (Luke 4:18). This, then, would mean Rome's oppression and its institutionalizing slavery. Now, Jesus didn't create an economic reform plan for Israel, but he addressed heart attitudes of greed, envy, contentment, and generosity to undermine oppressive economic social structures. Likewise, New Testament writers often addressed the underlying attitudes regarding slavery. How? By commanding Christian masters to call their slaves "brother" or "sister" and to show them compassion, justice, and patience. No longer did being a master mean privilege and status but rather responsibility and service. By doing so, the worm was already in the wood for altering the social structures.[5]

As faithful followers of Christ, Paul and other New Testament writers likewise opposed dehumanization and oppression of others. They, for instance, fully rejected the idea that slaves were mere property. The status of slave or free was irrelevant in Christ (cf. Gal. 3:28; Col. 3:11). In fact, Paul gave household rules in Ephesians 6 and Colossians 4 not only for Christian slaves but for Christian *masters* as well. Slaves were ultimately responsible to God, their heavenly Master. But *masters* were to "treat your slaves in the same way"—namely, as persons governed by a heavenly Master (Eph. 6:9 NIV). New Testament commentator P. T. O'Brien points out that "Paul's cryptic exhortation is outrageous" for his day.[6] Given the spiritual equality of slave and free, slaves could even take on leadership positions in churches.

Paul would have considered the seventeenth- and eighteenth-century slave trade an abomination, an utter violation of human dignity and an act of human theft. In a "vice list" of Paul's in 1 Timothy 1:9–10, he expounded on the fifth through the ninth commandments in Exodus 20 and Deuteronomy 5; there he condemned "slave traders" (v. 10 NIV) who steal what isn't rightfully theirs.[7]

Critics wonder why Paul (or Peter in 1 Peter 2:18–20) didn't condemn slavery outright and tell masters to release their slaves. Yet we should first separate this question from other considerations, even if the New Atheists aren't necessarily interested in nuance. Paul's position on the status of slavery was clear on various points: (1) he repudiated slave trading; (2) he affirmed the full human dignity and equal spiritual status of slaves; and (3) he encouraged slaves to acquire their freedom whenever possible (1 Cor. 7:20–22). Paul's revolutionary Christian affirmations helped to tear apart the fabric of the institution of slavery in Europe.

Paul reminded Christian masters that they, with their slaves, were *fellow slaves* of the same impartial Master; so they weren't to mistreat them but rather deal with them as brothers and sisters in Christ. Paul called on human masters to grant "justice and fairness" to their slaves (Col. 4:1). In unprecedented fashion, Paul treated slaves as morally responsible persons (Col. 3:22–25) who, like their Christian masters, were brothers and part of Christ's body (1 Tim. 6:2).[8] Christian slave and master alike belonged to Christ (Gal. 3:28; Col. 3:11). *Spiritual* status was more fundamental than *social* status.

Paul (and Peter) didn't call for an uprising to overthrow slavery in Rome. They didn't want the Christian faith to be perceived as opposed to social order and harmony. Hence, Christian slaves were told to do what was right; even if they were mistreated, their conscience would be clear (1 Peter 2:18–20). Obligations fell to these slaves, yes, without their prior agreement. So the path for early Christians to take was tricky, very much unlike the situation in Old Testament Israel. On the one hand, a slave uprising would do the gospel a disservice and prove a direct threat to an oppressive Roman establishment (e.g., "Masters, release your slaves!" or "Slaves, throw off your chains!"). Rome would meet any flagrant opposition with speedy, forceful, lethal opposition. So Peter's admonition to unjustly treated slaves implies a suffering endured *without retaliation*. No, suffering in itself is not good (which would be a sadistic attitude to adopt and certainly not the view of Scripture); rather, the *right* response in the midst of suffering is commendable.

On the other hand, the early Christians undermined slavery indirectly and certainly rejected many common Greco-Roman assumptions about it, such as Aristotle's (slaves were inherently inferior to masters, as were females to males). Just as Jesus bore unjust suffering for the redemption of others and entrusted himself to the One who judges justly (1 Peter 2:20–24), so Christian slaves could bear hardship to show others—including their masters—the way of Christ and redemption through him, all the while entrusting themselves to God.[9] Thus, like yeast, such Christlike living could have a gradual leavening effect on society so that oppressive institutions like slavery could finally fall away. This is, in fact, what took place throughout Europe, as we'll see in the final chapter.

This was also the type of incremental strategy taken by President Abraham Lincoln. Though he despised slavery and talked freely about this degrading institution, his first priority was to hold the Union together rather than try to abolish slavery immediately. Being an exceptional student of human nature, he recognized that political realities and predictable reactions required an incremental approach. The radical abolitionist route of John Brown and William Lloyd Garrison would (and did!) simply create a social backlash against hard-core abolitionists and make emancipation all the more difficult.[10]

Paul's ministry illustrated how in Christ there was neither slave nor free. He greeted people in his epistles by name. Most of these individuals had commonly used slave and freedman names. For example, in Romans 16:7 and 9, he refers to slaves like Andronicus and Urbanus (common slave names) as "kinsman," "fellow prisoner," and "fellow worker." The New Testament approach to slavery was utterly contrary to aristocrats and philosophers like Aristotle, who held that some humans were slaves by nature (*Politics* I.13). New Testament Christianity hardly endorsed slavery; it leveled all distinctions at the foot of the cross. In Revelation 18:11–13, doomed Babylon stands condemned because she had treated humans as "cargo," having trafficked in "slaves [literally 'bodies'] and human lives." This repudiation of treating humans as cargo reflects the doctrine of the image of God in all human beings. No wonder the Christian faith was particularly attractive to slaves and lower classes:[11] it was countercultural, revolutionary, and anti–status quo. No wonder slavery in Europe eventually fizzled: Europeans Christians had the mind-set that owning another human being was contrary to creation and the new creation in Christ.

The Question of Onesimus

Now it has been alleged that Paul's returning the "runaway slave" Onesimus to his owner Philemon was a step backward—toward the oppressive Code of Hammurabi! The Old Testament prohibited such an action (Deut. 23:15–16), but Babylon's laws required returning a slave. So here it looks like Paul is siding with Hammurabi *against* the Old Testament! Do such charges have any merit?

It's been said that reading a New Testament epistle is like listening to just one party in a phone conversation. This is certainly true of the letter to Philemon. We hear only Paul's voice, but plenty of gaps exist that we'd like to have filled in. What was Paul's relationship to Philemon ("dear friend and fellow worker" and "partner" [vv. 1, 17 NIV])? What debt did Philemon owe Paul? How had Onesimus wronged Philemon (if he even did)?[12] Many interpreters have taken the liberty to "help" us fill in the gaps. Yet a common result is that they can read too much into the text. The stock fugitive-slave hypothesis (that Onesimus was a runaway slave of Philemon's) dates back to the church father John Chrysostom (347–407). However, genuine scholarly disagreement exists about this interpretation. For one thing, the epistle contains no verbs of flight, as though Onesimus had suddenly gone AWOL. And Paul revealed no hint of fear that Philemon would brutally treat a returning Onesimus, as masters typically did when their runaway slaves were caught.

It's been plausibly suggested[13] that Onesimus and Philemon were estranged Christian (perhaps biological) brothers. Paul exhorts Philemon not to receive Onesimus as a slave (whose status in Roman society meant being alienated and without honor); rather Onesimus was to be welcomed as a beloved brother: "that you might have him back for good—no longer as a slave, but better than a slave, as a dear brother. He is very dear to me but even dearer to you, both as a man and as a brother in the Lord" (Philem. 1:15–16 NIV). Notice the similar-sounding language in Galatians 4:7: "Therefore you are no longer a slave, but a son; and if a son, then an heir through God." This may shed further light on how to interpret the epistle of Philemon: Paul wanted to help heal the rift so that Onesimus (not an actual slave) would be received back as a beloved brother in the Lord, not even simply as a biological brother. To do so would be to follow God's own example in receiving us as sons and daughters rather than as slaves.

Even if Onesimus *were* an actual slave in the Roman Empire, this still doesn't mean he was a fugitive. If a disagreement or misunderstanding had occurred between Onesimus and Philemon, and Onesimus had sought out

Paul to intervene somehow or to arbitrate the dispute, this wouldn't have made Onesimus a fugitive. And given Paul's knowledge of Philemon's character and track record of Christian dedication, the suggestion that Onesimus's return was "Hammurabi revisited" is way off the mark. Again, if Onesimus *were* a slave in Philemon's household, Paul's strategy was this: instead of forbidding slavery, impose fellowship![14] Indeed, the New Testament church showed itself to be a revolutionary, new community united by Christ—a people that transcended racial, social, and sexual barriers.

Hagar, Sarah, and Paul

We should probably bring up the Hagar-Sarah story here. In Galatians 4:30, Paul refers to Sarah's act of sending Hagar away (Gen. 21). Some caricature this allegorization by asserting Paul's endorsement of Sarah's cruel desire to cast her out—and God told Abraham to go along with this (21:12)! Let's keep this in context. We've already seen that both Hagar and Ishmael contributed their share of difficulty and tension within the household; they were hardly blameless. God had also assured Abraham (as he had told Hagar previously) that God would take care of them and would make Ishmael into a great nation.

Paul refers to this passage (Gen. 21:10) to give the Galatians a message: get rid of the slave woman (4:30)! That is, they were to stop adhering to and depending on the Mosaic law to gain/maintain acceptance before God. The critics' misportrayal of Paul—that Paul was actually encouraging the mistreatment of slaves—is actually quite humorous.[15] (This is typical of left-wing fundamentalism.) It completely misses the very thrust of the allegory and the tone of Paul's strong opposition to Judaizers. The point was that their heresy mustn't be tolerated in the church. This doesn't reflect Paul's endorsement of slavery. In fact, Paul's heart cry was that his Jewish brothers would find salvation (Rom. 10:1), and his opposition to the Judaizers was accompanied with tears (Phil. 3:18).

God's Ultimate Goal: Enslaving Everyone?

From the very beginning, Scripture affirms that all persons are made in God's image—essentially, "there is neither Jew nor Greek, slave nor free, male nor female." Though humanity deviated from this ideal, Scripture regularly undermines human institutions that exist because of hardened human hearts, pointing people back to the creational ideal as well as forward to the new creational ideal in Christ, the new Adam.

Some critics claim that God's far-reaching goal is to enslave all people, the ultimate tyranny and dehumanization. Look at Isaiah 14:1–2 as a prime example:

The LORD will have compassion on Jacob; once again he will choose Israel and will settle them in their own land. Aliens will join them and unite with the house of Jacob. Nations will take them and bring them to their own place. And the house of Israel will possess the nations as menservants and maidservants in the LORD's land. They will make captives of their captors and rule over their oppressors. (NIV)

The critic tends to make this slave analogy walk on all fours—that is, the slavery image is extended far beyond the intended point of comparison. A less-selective look at Scripture reveals that the slavery image is just one swatch taken from a larger tapestry. God ultimately sought to bring blessing to all the nations (Gen. 12:3). Biblical pictures of God's subduing his and his people's enemies suggest that God's opponents won't have the final word; their opposition to God will have to give way to acknowledging God's lordship over all. Those refusing to acknowledge God's rightful place in the end freely separate themselves from God, the source of joy, hope, and peace. They will receive their divorce from God.

What about those who belong to Christ? To describe those wholly dedicated to God, the New Testament uses the language of *slave* (*doulos*). A number of modern translations render this word "servant," but the servant's bond to his employer is often temporary and detachable. But rather than being a picture of oppression, the "slave of righteousness" is no longer in bondage to sin (John 8:34; Rom. 6:17–20). We've seen earlier that by nature humans are worshipers; they're slaves to what they worship, whether false gods or the true one. To worship the true God with full devotion is actually a picture of genuine freedom and abundant living rather than oppression; false worship actually oppresses (John 10:10).

So the slave image shouldn't dominate the spiritual picture. Abraham is called God's servant (*'ebed*) as well as God's friend (Isa. 41:9; James 2:23). Jesus told his disciples that he no longer called them slaves (*douloi*) but friends (*philoi*). Jesus himself would lay down his life for his friends (John 15:13–15). The Son of Man, who himself came to serve humankind (Mark 10:45), took on the form of a slave—God in the flesh serving and dying for humanity (Phil. 2:5–11).

So are we slaves? Yes and no—something along the lines of what Martin Luther famously said: the Christian is *both* free and subject to none of his fellow human beings as well as dutiful servant who is subject to all.[16] Likewise, God is concerned about removing oppression by enabling us to find true freedom in loving and obeying God, who is both Master and Father. The Scriptures use the imagery of slavery and fear that is transformed into adoption as God's children with full security in God's love (Rom. 8:14–16; Gal. 4:3–8). The Scriptures refer to the privileged status as God's people and God's dwelling in their midst (Rev. 21:3). God's people are also the bride of Christ (Rev. 21:2).

God's kingdom rule isn't intended to oppress. In Matthew 20:1–16, the landowner who hires workers throughout the day asks the one grousing about bearing the heat of the day while others worked only a short time, "Is it not lawful for me to do what I wish with what is my own?" (v. 15). This is hardly despotism, as some claim. After all, the landowner was generous and certainly did no wrong; indeed, the master *initiated* the opportunity to work, and the worker *agreed* to the wage of a denarius, just like everyone else did.

As we review the New Testament, slavery language is one part of the bigger picture. Christ's ultimate goal isn't to oppress and destroy but to give life, to redeem, and to release (Luke 4:18). And Paul in Galatians 3:28 (the "Christian manifesto") doesn't abolish slavery; rather, he makes it ultimately irrelevant! All the structures that separated Jew and Greek, male and female, slave and free were radically overturned by their sharing a common meal together to celebrate the Lord's death (see 1 Cor. 11:17–34). Indeed, this was a defiant, countercultural act against Rome's embedded social structures—a far cry from the critics' "passive resignation" argument (that Paul didn't speak out against slavery but accepted it). Furthermore, the Lord's Supper was also a culturally shameful act: not only did these Christians worship a shamefully crucified (yet risen!) Messiah, but those who were "dishonorable" or of lower social status—females, Gentiles, and slaves—were treated as equals with males, Jews, and free persons. This "meal of shame" actually symbolized the removal of all dishonor at the foot of the cross. In the early church, a social revolution had begun![17]

Further Reading

Harris, Murray. *Slave of Christ: A New Testament Metaphor for Total Devotion to Christ*. Downers Grove, IL: InterVarsity, 1999.

Wright, Christopher J. H. *Old Testament Ethics for the People of God*. Downers Grove, IL: InterVarsity, 2004.

15

Indiscriminate Massacre and Ethnic Cleansing?

The Killing of the Canaanites (I)

Probably the most difficult Old Testament ethical issue is the divine command to kill the Canaanites.[1] Theologian-turned-atheist Gerd Lüdemann wrote that "the command to exterminate is extremely offensive"—a far cry from the merciful God frequently proclaimed in Scripture.[2] Consider just one of these passages:

> Only in the cities of these peoples that the LORD your God is giving you as an inheritance, you shall not leave alive anything that breathes. But you shall utterly destroy them: the Hittite and the Amorite, the Canaanite and the Perizzite, the Hivite and the Jebusite, as the LORD your God has commanded you, so that they may not teach you to do according to all their detestable things which they have done for their gods, so that you would sin against the LORD your God. (Deut. 20:16–18)

This is a tough question, and we'll take four chapters to tackle this and related issues. First, we'll review some introductory matters, then we'll address two possible scenarios regarding the Canaanite issue, and finally we'll look at the question of religion (whatever that term means) and violence.

Were the Canaanites *That* Wicked?

According to the biblical text, Yahweh was willing to wait about 430 years because "the sin of the Amorite [a Canaanite people group] has not yet reached its limit" (Gen. 15:16 NET). In other words, in Abraham's day, the time wasn't ripe for judgment on the Canaanites; the moment wasn't right for them to be driven out and for the land to "vomit them out" (Lev. 18:25 NET). Sodom and Gomorrah, on the other hand, *were* ready; not even ten righteous people could be found there (Gen. 18–19). Even earlier, at the time of Noah, humans had similarly hit moral rock bottom (Gen. 6:11–13). Despite 120 years of Noah's preaching (Gen. 6:3; cf. 5:32; 7:6; 2 Peter 2:5), no one outside his family listened; his contemporaries were also ripe for judgment. But it was only after Israel's lengthy enslavement in Egypt that the time was finally ripe for the Israelites to enter Canaan—"because of the wickedness of these nations" (Deut. 9:4–5). Sometimes God simply gives up on nations, cities, or individuals when they've gone past a point of no return. Judgment—whether directly or indirectly—is the last resort.

What kind of wickedness are we talking about? We're familiar with the line, "The apple doesn't fall far from the tree." In the case of the Canaanites, the Canaanites' moral apples didn't fall far from the tree of their pantheon of immoral gods and goddesses. So if the Canaanite deities engaged in incest, then it's not surprising that incest wasn't treated as a serious moral wrong among the Canaanite people. As we've seen, adultery (temple sex), bestiality, homosexual acts (also temple sex), and child sacrifice were also permitted (cf. Lev. 18:20–30).

Humans are "imaging" beings, designed to reflect the likeness and glory of their Creator. If we worship the creaturely rather than the Creator, we'll come to resemble or image the idols of our own devising and that in which we place our security.[3] The sexual acts of the gods and goddesses were imitated by the Canaanites as a kind of magical act: the more sex on the Canaanite high places, the more this would stimulate the fertility god Baal to have sex with his consort, Anath, which meant more semen (rain) produced to water the earth.

Let's add to this the bloodlust and violence of the Canaanite deities. Anath, the patroness of both sex and war, reminds us of the bloodthirsty goddess Kali of Hinduism, who drank her victims' blood and sat surrounded by corpses; she is commonly depicted with a garland of skulls around her neck. The late archaeologist William Albright describes the Canaanite deity Anath's massacre in the following gory scene:

> The blood was so deep that she waded in it up to her knees—nay, up to her neck. Under her feet were human heads, above her her human hands flew like locusts. In her sensuous delight she decorated herself with suspended heads while she attached hands to her girdle. Her joy at the butchery is described in even more sadistic language: "Her liver swelled with laughter, her heart was full of joy, the liver of Anath (was full of) exultation (?)." Afterwards Anath "was satisfied" and washed her hands in human gore before proceeding to other occupations.[4]

Canaanite idolatry wasn't simply an abstract theology or personal interest carried out in the privacy of one's home. It was a worldview that profoundly influenced Canaanite society. Given this setting, it's no wonder God didn't want the Israelites to associate with the Canaanites and be led astray from obedience to the one true God. He wanted to have Israel morally and theologically separate from the peoples around them.

In other words, the land of Canaan was no paradise before the Israelites got there. Israel had no inherent right to inhabit the land (as an undeserved gift from God), and neither did the Canaanites have a right to remain in it. In fact, both the Canaanites and the Israelites would experience (partial) removal from the land because of their wickedness.

I'm not arguing that the Canaanites were the *worst* specimens of humanity that ever existed, nor am I arguing that the Canaanites won the immorality contest for worst-behaved peoples in all the ancient Near East. That said, the evidence for profound moral corruption was abundant. God considered them ripe for divine judgment, which would be carried out in keeping with God's saving purposes in history.

Some argue that God is intolerant, commanding people to have "no other gods before Me" (Exod. 20:3). They state that Israel's laws illustrate the denial of religious freedom at the heart of Israelite religion. And didn't other ancient Near Eastern religions value religious diversity? Couldn't non-Israelites worship whatever god they wanted? Israel had committed itself to be faithful to Yahweh; as in any good marriage, spouses shouldn't play the field in the name of marital freedom. As for the Canaanites, God judged them not only because they happened to worship idols but also because of the corrupting moral practices and influences bound up with this idolatry. Notice that God judges the nations listed in Amos 1–2 not because they don't worship Yahweh but because of outrageous moral acts. I've already addressed the topic of divine jealousy, but I'll come back to some of these themes later.

So was God just picking on the Canaanites but not other peoples? No, Yahweh frequently threatened many nations with judgment when they crossed a certain moral threshold. For example, in Amos 1–2, God promised to "send fire" on nations surrounding Israel for their treacheries and barbarities. And he promised the same to Israel and Judah. Later, Jesus himself pronounced final judgment on nationalistic Israel, which would face its doom in AD 70 at the hands of the Romans (Matt. 24).

What's more, we moderns shouldn't think that severe divine judgment was only for biblical times, as though God no longer judges nations today. Despite many gains over the centuries in the areas of human rights and religious liberty, due to the positive influence of biblical ideals in America and other Western nations, Westerners have their own share of decadence, and we may resemble the Canaanites more than we realize. We should proceed cautiously about what counts for direct divine judgment, as we may not be able to determine this precisely.[5] These sorts of acts serve as illustrations of a cosmic final judgment yet to come. Ultimately, God's judgment will come to all who refuse to submit to God's kingdom agenda and instead seek to set up their own little fiefdoms. God grants humans freedom to separate themselves from God. In the end, humans can have their final divorce from God both as a just judgment as well as the natural fruit borne out of a life lived without God. As a last resort, God says to them, "*Thy* will be done."

Who Determines the Point of No Return?

Israeli psychologist Georges Tamarin undertook a study in 1966 involving 1,066 schoolchildren ages eight to fourteen. Presented with the story of Jericho's destruction, they were asked, "Do you think Joshua and the Israelites acted rightly or not?" Two-thirds of the children approved. However, when Tamarin substituted General Lin for Joshua and a Chinese kingdom three thousand years ago for Israel, only 7 percent approved while 75 percent disapproved.[6] The critic is baffled at this: "We rightly condemn the killing of an ethnic group when carried out by Nazis or Hutus. But Israel seems to get a pass—indeed, a divine *order*—when doing the same thing to the Canaanites!"

What guidelines do we have to determine when a culture is irredeemable, beyond the point of no moral and spiritual return? Don't we need something more than mere mortals to assess a culture's ripeness for judgment? Aren't these considerations too weighty for humans to judge? Yes, they are! Any such determinations should be left up to God—namely, through special revelation. The Israelites, when they went into battle against the Philistines *with* the ark of the covenant but *without* divine approval, were roundly defeated (1 Sam. 4). The requirement of special revelation before any such undertaking is precisely what we have in Scripture. The one true God told his prophet Moses or Samuel when the time was right. Likewise, without such clear divine guidance, Israel *wouldn't* have been justified in attacking the Canaanite strongholds.

Some TV stunt shows warn children, "Kids, don't try this at home!" Likewise, we could say about Israel's "holy war" situation: "Don't try this without special revelation!" These matters aren't up to humans to decide. Yahweh-initiated battles were never intended for non-prophet organizations! Think of the disastrous results when Israel attempted to go into other battles without divine approval (e.g., Num. 14:41–45; Josh. 7). As we've seen already, God's call to battle was unique to Israel's situation. Such a call, though, isn't an enduring, universally binding standard for all time and all cultures.

Did the Canaanites Know Better?

Some scholars have questioned whether we can hold the Canaanites morally accountable. After all, weren't they just practicing *their* religion, which they received from *their* parents, who received it from *their* parents? Shouldn't God have enlightened them about himself and his requirements for humans?

As we look at history, we see that nations and civilizations have been capable of moral reforms and improvements. We shouldn't be surprised at this. After all, God reveals himself to humans through conscience, reason, human experience, and creation. This revelation opens the door for moral improvements from one generation to the next. People without the Scriptures can still have access to what is good and right.

For a little support, let me quote a notable theist and a notable atheist. The notable theist is the apostle Paul, who affirms that special revelation isn't necessary for people to know about God or to recognize right and wrong:

> That which is known about God is evident within them [human beings]; for God made it evident to them. For since the creation of the world His invisible attributes, His eternal power and divine nature, have been clearly seen, being understood through what has been made, so that they are without excuse. (Rom. 1:19–20)

The notable atheist is philosopher Kai Nielsen:

> It is more reasonable to believe such elemental things [as wife beating and child abuse] to be evil than to believe any skeptical theory that tells us we cannot know or reasonably believe any of these things to be evil. . . . I firmly believe that this is bedrock and right and that anyone who does not believe it cannot have probed deeply enough into the grounds of his moral beliefs.[7]

We've seen how Amos 1–2 illustrates these two quotations nicely. God had warned the morally accountable Gentile nations surrounding Israel. Although they knew their moral duties, they disregarded them. Knowing better, they stifled compassion, suppressed their conscience, and carried out terrible atrocities, such as ripping open pregnant women or betraying vulnerable, displaced populations into the hands of their enemies. The author of Hebrews called the Canaanites "disobedient" (11:31)—that is, having a moral awareness but disregarding it. In C. S. Lewis's *Abolition of Man*, he lists moral codes of many cultures across the ages. They are strikingly similar at key points: honoring parents, being faithful in marriage, not stealing, not murdering, not lying, and so on.[8] In other words, doing the right thing isn't as elusive as some may think.

Consider Rahab and her family (Josh. 2). Though immersed in Canaanite culture, they prove to be a clear sign that other Canaanites could potentially have been rescued as well. Israel's God had convincingly delivered his people from Egypt. He had supplied signs and wonders, revealing his reality and surpassing greatness, and the Canaanites were fully aware of this (Josh. 2:9–11; 9:9–10). Some charge that Rahab was selling out her people to save her own neck. But is that fair? For one thing, Rahab risked a lot by taking in the foreign spies and hiding them. And surely loyalty to one's race or ethnic group isn't the ultimate virtue, particularly when it goes against what's right and true. Many Afrikaners in South Africa who protested apartheid broke with the traditions of their racially prejudiced ancestors, which was the right thing to do.

Was It Genocide and Ethnic Cleansing?

According to Richard Dawkins, the killing of the Canaanites was an act of ethnic cleansing in which "bloodthirsty massacres" were carried out with "xenophobic relish." Were the Israelites truly xenophobic—fearful of strangers (non-Israelites)?

Terms like *genocide* and *ethnic cleansing* evoke negative emotions in all of us. Dawkins isn't exactly interested in accuracy; so he resorts to misleading rhetoric to sway the jury. Ethnic cleansing is fueled by racial hatred. The alleged in-group pronounces a pox on the out-group and then proceeds to destroy them. Does this scenario really mesh with the facts about the Israelites, though? As it turns out, xenophobic attitudes didn't prompt the Israelites to kill Canaanites.

From the beginning, God told Abraham "all the families of the earth" would be blessed through his offspring (Gen. 12:3). We're not off to a very xenophobic start. Then we read many positive things about foreigners in the chapters that follow. Abraham met and honored Melchizedek (Gen. 14). He encountered just and fair-minded foreign leaders among the Egyptians (Gen. 12) and the Philistines (Gen. 20) who proved to be more honorable than Abraham. A "mixed multitude" left with Israel from Egypt (Exod. 12:38). Moses married a dark-skinned Cushite/Ethiopian (Num. 12:1). The Gentile Rahab and her family joined Israel's ranks (Josh. 6:23), in ironic contrast to the Israelite Achan, who stole goods from Jericho and was put to death for his disobedience (Josh. 7). Also, the very language of "dedication to destruction/ the ban [*herem*]" could be applied equally to Israel as well as to a Canaanite city (Deut. 13:16). Later on, Israel's prophets would readily condemn Israel's wickedness, as they would that of the surrounding nations. In general, God's judgments fall on those practicing evil and wickedness—whether Jew or Gentile, as Paul makes clear in Romans 1–3.

Furthermore, God also repeatedly commanded Israel to show concern for (non-Israelite) aliens or sojourners in their midst (e.g., Lev. 19:34; Deut. 10:18–19). Why? Because the Israelites had been strangers in Egypt. God frequently reminded his people to learn the lessons of their history so that they wouldn't be doomed to repeat it with Gentiles in their midst.

Furthermore, according to Israel's civil law, the stranger living in Israel had the same legal rights as the native Israelite: "There shall be one standard for you; it shall be for the stranger as well as the native, for I am the LORD your God" (Lev. 24:22; cf. Num. 35:15). As we've seen, the alien (*ger*)—one who embraced Israel's covenant and Israel's God—could participate in events such as the Passover (Num. 9:14). Negative concerns regarding the foreigner (*nokri*) had to do with theological compromise and idolatry; such negativity wasn't assumed when a non-Israelite like Rahab or Ruth or Uriah embraced Yahweh, the God of Israel.[9] We could add that God exhorted Israelites to show concern even for their personal enemies: "If you come across your enemy's ox or donkey wandering off, be sure to take it back to him. If you see the donkey of someone who hates you fallen down under its load, do not leave it there; be sure you help him with it" (Exod. 23:4–5).

What about God allowing Israelites to take interest from foreigners but not from fellow citizens (Deut. 23:20)? We've seen that interest was charged to foreigners, who were temporary residents and not members of society. They typically borrowed money to invest in profit-making pursuits and trading ventures; these weren't loans given to help foreigners escape poverty.[10] This regulation had a built-in incentive: the outsider (who didn't *have* to live in Israel) could choose to become a part of Israel and embrace the one true God; if so, he could benefit from divinely commanded economic perks and displays of Israelite concern. Instead of hostility, God commanded the Israelites to love and show concern for the resident aliens in their midst. The command to love the resident alien and to treat her the same way as a citizen (Lev. 19:33–34) is remarkable and unique in the ancient Near East's religious thoughts and practices.[11]

Critics will point to Deuteronomy 23:3: "No Ammonite or Moabite shall enter the assembly of the LORD; none of their descendants, even to the tenth generation, shall ever enter the assembly of the LORD." *That* doesn't seem very kind. However, earlier (in Deut. 2) three nations were favorably mentioned: Edom, related to Israel through Esau, Jacob's brother; and Moab and Ammon, nations from the sons of Abraham's nephew Lot. Notice that Israel is prohibited from fighting against them (vv. 4–6, 9, 19). So let's not misread 23:3 as xenophobia. That said, God took treachery against Israel very seriously. Genesis 12:3 implies judgment on those who would mistreat Israel. And Deuteronomy 23:4 reveals the reason for the Ammonites' and Moabites' exclusion from the assembly: "because they did not meet you with food and water on the way when you came out of Egypt, and because they hired against you Balaam the son of Beor from Pethor of Mesopotamia, to curse you" (see Num. 22–25). Even so, remember that generations later Ruth the *Moabitess* was readily received into the midst of Israel. A lot depended on whether the alien from Moab (or Ammon) fully embraced Israel's covenant, which meant his acceptance into the assembly as a genuine worshiper of Yahweh.[12] As John Goldingay writes:

> Being of non-Israelite origin is not a disqualification for membership of the [Israelite] community in any period. The question is, what God do you serve? The reason for not marrying a Canaanite is that this will turn you away from following Yhwh and lead to your serving other deities (Deut 7:3–4). A Canaanite who has made a commitment to Yhwh is a different matter.[13]

So we should put to rest this idea of divinely inspired racism or ethnocentrism. In fact, God regularly reminded his people not to get so high and mighty. He frankly told Israel that possessing the land wasn't due to their righteousness and uprightness of heart. It was because of the wickedness of the Canaanites. What's more, God considered the Israelites "a stubborn people" (Deut. 9:4–6). The most-favored-nation status was given with the goal of inviting others to experience God's gracious favor—and God could revoke that status. Likewise, just as he would give the land to a group of wandering, landless Israelites as an inheritance (Exod. 12:25; Num. 34:2), he could revoke it as well (Deut. 4:26). Those in the land—whether Canaanites or Israelites—were only tenants, not owners (Pss. 24:1; 50:12).[14]

We'll explore the phrase "utterly destroy" (*haram*) below. Suffice it to say here that God's charge to Israel to "utterly destroy" the cities of the morally bankrupt Canaanites was turned on Israel when groups of Israelites were seduced into following false gods (Deut. 13:15; cf. 7:4; 28:63). God was concerned with *sin*, not *ethnicity*. In fact, as we read the Old Testament prophets, they (with God) were angered about Israel's disobedience, and they threatened divine judgment on Israel/Judah more often than they did on the pagan nations. If we read carefully, it's obvious God was opposed to *Israel's* sin just as much as he was to that of their oppressors.

Inefficient Means?

Some critics raise a potentially embarrassing question: if God wanted to destroy Canaanite religion by removing the Canaanite peoples, didn't he fail spectacularly in achieving this purpose? Wasn't Old Testament Israel continually getting sucked into pagan idolatry? Why not a more effective divine judgment—perhaps scorching fire and brimstone to clear the land of Canaanite idolatry so that Israel wouldn't get entangled spiritually and morally?

Many critics focus on efficiency, that it's somehow immoral or un-Godlike to be less than efficient. But what theological reason compels us to assume that God must operate with maximum efficiency? Are we too Western in our assumptions about what God *ought* to do? Is God obligated to expedite his purposes? Must God's purposes be less "clunky" to reveal his divinity? Don't such questions take for granted knowing God's purposes in detail?

God doesn't seem to think it's a problem that a small planetary speck is home to all the universe's inhabitants while the rest of the cosmos is (from all we can see) uninhabited and uninhabitable. Throughout Scripture, God took plenty of time and utilized seemingly inefficient means to accomplish his purposes. For instance, God didn't exactly jump-start the descendants-as-numerous-as-the-stars program. Rather, he began with a barren, elderly couple—Abraham and Sarah—and then continued to work through a stubborn and rebellious nation. Biblical categories such as grace, covenant faithfulness, relationship, obedience, perseverance, and love are the more relevant considerations. Efficiency doesn't seem to figure in all that prominently. As a friend of mine says, "God is always *almost* late."

The Scriptures reveal a *sufficient* God, not necessarily an *efficient* one. And the question of efficiency revolves around what the particular *goal* is: "efficient" to do what and to exclude what, exactly? Getting hot-house-grown tomatoes from your supermarket may be efficient, but if maximal satisfaction is uppermost in your mind, then growing tomatoes in your backyard and enjoying their vine-ripened taste would be the way to go. Yes, it's more work and time, but the results are far more enjoyable and tasty.

Why then didn't God make sure that *no* Canaanite was left in the land just to make sure that Israel wouldn't be lured by the lifestyle encouraged by Canaan's idolatry? The Scriptures reveal a God who works through messy, seemingly inefficient processes—including human choices and failures (Gen. 50:20)—to accomplish his redemptive purposes in history. That humans see God's grace, holiness, and love is more of a priority than efficiency. The route God chose didn't require the death of every last Canaanite. Not only were the Canaanites *sufficiently* driven out so as not to decisively undermine Israel's spiritual and moral integrity in the long run, but, as we'll see below, Canaanites participate in God's redemptive plan in both the Old and New Testaments (e.g., Zech. 9; Matt. 15:22; cf. Ps. 87:4–6; Isa. 19:23–25).[15]

Despite occasional spiritual revivals and moral successes in Israel's history, her failure to eradicate idolatry led to many troubles. She paid for her compromises with an Assyrian captivity of the Northern Kingdom (722 BC) and then a Babylonian captivity of the Southern Kingdom (587/6 BC; cf. 2 Kings 17:7–41; 2 Chron. 36:15–21). The theological and moral threat of foreign religion, however, didn't so damage Israel that its monotheism and covenantal awareness were totally eclipsed. By the first century AD, the theological stage had been sufficiently set: Israel's Scriptures were preserved, her national identity forged, her temple worship restored, her messianic expectations rekindled, and her monotheistic dedication secured. Despite Israel's compromises and rebellions over the centuries, Jesus's arrival on the scene came "in the fullness of time" (see Gal. 4:4). Was this efficient? Not in an obvious way. Was it sufficient? Very much so.

Cosmic Warfare

The worship of idols wasn't innocent or harmless. The Old Testament connects idolatry with the demonic—that is, with the cosmic enemies of God who rebelled against him: "goat demons" (Lev. 17:7); "strange gods . . . demons . . . gods" (Deut. 32:16–21); "demons . . . idols" (Ps. 106:37–38); "demons" (Isa. 65:3, Greek Septuagint). Even Pharaoh—the earthly representation of Egypt's gods—was a picture of this cosmic opposition. So in the exodus, Yahweh is the cosmic warrior who engages the evil powers of Egypt and the forces that inspire them. The New Testament picks up on this theme (e.g., 1 Cor. 10:19–22; 2 Cor. 6:14–16; Eph. 6:12–18). God's act of engaging in battle is not for the sake of violence or even victory as such but to establish peace and justice.[16]

God's commands to Israel to wipe out Canaan's idols and false, immoral worship illustrate the cosmic warfare between Yahweh and the dark powers opposed to his rule. This theme of spiritual warfare is certainly much more pronounced in the New Testament, which clearly exposes Satan and his hosts as the ultimate enemies of God and of his kingdom's advance. Yahweh—"the LORD of hosts" (cf. Ps. 24:7–10)—is a "warrior" (Exod. 15:3) who opposes all that mars the divine image in humans, all that threatens human flourishing, and all that sets itself in opposition to God's righteous reign. "Yahweh wars" aren't simply a clash between this and that deity; they represent a clash of two world orders: one rooted in reality and justice, the other in reality-denial and brute power; one representing creational order, the other anticreation.[17]

Israel's taking Canaan, then, is unlike the General Lin analogy, in which a stronger nation happens to invade and overpower a weaker nation. This would rightly draw the reaction, "What gives the stronger nation the right?" So perhaps we should think more along the lines of the Sicilian police invading a Mafia stronghold to remove a corrupting network of crime so that citizens can live in peace rather than in fear.

Just as the plagues in Egypt were a demonstration of Yahweh's judgment on her gods, so Israel's wars revealed God's sovereign rule over the presumed gods of the nations. In Israel's officially sanctioned wars, God's supernatural power and supremacy were revealed:[18]

- God didn't allow Israel to have a standing army (cf. David's unlawful census in 2 Sam. 24:1–17); Israel's wars weren't for professionals but for amateurs and volunteers. Fighting, however, wasn't for the fainthearted or for those distracted by other concerns. Those lacking courage or who had other reasons for not wanting to fight were allowed—even *invited*—to excuse themselves from battle (e.g., Deut. 20:5–8).

- Soldiers fighting in a Yahweh war weren't paid, nor could they take personal plunder, unlike warfare tactics elsewhere in the ancient Near East.
- Kings, tribal leaders, and high priests weren't authorized to call for a war, only a prophet through divine revelation.
- Victories for Israel's (mainly) ragtag army clearly signaled that God was fighting on their behalf (e.g., 2 Chron. 20).

In Old Testament Israel's physical battles, God wanted to show forth his greatness, not a display of sheer human power. And though the true Israel—the church—doesn't wage war against "flesh and blood" (Eph. 6:12) today, our warfare against Satan and his hosts has its roots in Yahweh wars in the Old Testament.

Further Reading

Boyd, Gregory. *God at War: The Bible and Spiritual Conflict*. Downers Grove, IL: InterVarsity, 1997.

Hess, Richard S. "War in the Hebrew Bible: An Overview." In *War in the Bible and Terrorism in the Twenty-First Century*, edited by Richard S. Hess and Elmer A. Martens. Winona Lake, IN: Eisenbrauns, 2008.

Stuart, Douglas K. *Exodus*. New American Commentary 2. Nashville: B & H Publishing, 2008. See esp. pp. 395–97.

16

Indiscriminate Massacre and Ethnic Cleansing?

The Killing of the Canaanites (II)

As we've said, the Old Testament's "holy wars"—or, more accurately, "Yahweh wars"—are the most emotionally charged biblical problem raised by the New Atheists and by critics generally. Like it or not, war is a common feature of our fallen world. Indeed, we know that warfare was a way of life—and often a matter of survival—in the ancient Near East. However, the problematic wars take place primarily during and shortly after Israel's second historical stage under Joshua, the theocratic stage of Israel's existence. As we've mentioned, this Yahweh warfare wasn't the standard for the other stages in Israel's history. It wasn't intended as a permanent fixture in Israel's story. It was unique to Israel at a particular point in time and was not to be repeated in later history by Israel or by other nations. Without God's explicit command (and thus his morally sufficient reasons), attacking the Canaanites would *not* have been justified.

Infiltration, Internal Struggle, and Conquest

How did the Promised Land come to be inhabited by the Israelites? Biblical scholars and archaeologists continue the effort to uncover the nature of Israel's relationship to the Canaanites, and they are finding something more complex than the traditional Sunday school version of the conquest model. The bigger picture includes not just conquest but rather a combination of other factors. Besides military engagement, some type of infiltration took place (e.g., Judg. 1:1–2:5). Internal struggle was another feature—that is, Israel often did a poor job staving off idolatry and distinguishing itself from surrounding pagan lifestyles. Scripture's realistic acknowledgment that the Canaanites continued to live in the land suggests that something more than a military campaign took place.[1]

The books of Joshua and Judges suggest that taking the land included less-than-dramatic processes of infiltration and internal struggle. Israel's entrance into Canaan included more than the military motif. Old Testament scholar Gordon McConville comments on Joshua: we don't have "a simple conquest model, but rather a mixed picture of success and failure, sudden victory and slow, compromised progress."[2] Likewise, Old Testament scholar David Howard firmly states that the conquest model needs modification. Why? Because "the stereotypical model of an all-consuming Israelite army descending upon Canaan and destroying everything in its wake cannot be accepted. The biblical data will not allow for this." He adds that the Israelites entered Canaan and did engage militarily "but without causing extensive material destruction."[3] We'll come back to this significant point.

Ancient Near Eastern Exaggeration Rhetoric

Most Christians read Joshua's conquest stories with the backdrop of Sunday school lessons via flannel graph or children's illustrated Bible stories. The impression that's left is a black-and-white rendition of a literal crush, kill, and destroy mission. A closer look at the biblical text reveals a lot more nuance—and a lot less bloodshed. In short, the conquest of Canaan was far less widespread and harsh than many people assume.

Like his ancient Near Eastern contemporaries, Joshua used the language of conventional warfare rhetoric. This language sounds like bragging and exaggeration to our ears. Notice first the sweeping language in Joshua 10:40: "Thus Joshua struck all the land, the hill country and the Negev and the lowland and the slopes and all their kings. He left no survivor, but he utterly destroyed all who breathed, just as the LORD, the God of Israel, had commanded." Joshua used the rhetorical bravado language of his day, asserting that *all* the land was captured, *all* the kings defeated, and *all* the Canaanites destroyed (cf. 10:40–42; 11:16–23: "Joshua took the whole land . . . and gave . . . it for an inheritance to Israel"). Yet, as we will see, Joshua himself acknowledged that this wasn't literally so.

Scholars readily agree that Judges is literarily linked to Joshua. Yet the early chapters of Judges (which, incidentally, repeat the death of Joshua) show that the task of taking over the land was far from complete. In Judges 2:3, God says, "I will not drive them out before you." Earlier, Judges 1:21, 27–28 asserted that "[they] did not drive out the Jebusites"; "[they] did not take possession"; "they did not drive them out completely." These nations remained "to this day" (Judg. 1:21). The peoples who had apparently been wiped out reappear in the story. Many Canaanite inhabitants simply stuck around.

Some might accuse Joshua of being misleading or of getting it wrong. Not at all. He was speaking the language that everyone in his day would have understood. Rather than trying to deceive, Joshua was just saying he had fairly well trounced the enemy. On the one hand, Joshua says, "There were no Anakim left in the land" (Josh. 11:22); indeed, they were "utterly destroyed [haram]" in the hill country (11:21). Literally? Not according to the very same Joshua! In fact, Caleb later asked permission to drive out the Anakites from the hill country (14:12–15; cf. 15:13–19). Again, Joshua wasn't being deceptive. Given the use of ancient Near Eastern hyperbole, he could say without contradiction that nations "remain among you"; he went on to warn Israel not to mention, swear by, serve, or bow down to their gods (Josh. 23:7, 12–13; cf. 15:63; 16:10; 17:13; Judg. 2:10–13). Again, though the land "had rest from war" (Josh. 11:23), chapters 13 and beyond tell us that much territory remained unpossessed (13:1). Tribe upon tribe failed to drive out the Canaanites (13:13; 15:63; 16:10; 17:12–13, 18), and Joshua tells seven of the tribes, "How long will you put off entering to take possession of the land which the LORD, the God of your fathers, has given you?" (18:3).

Furthermore, God told the Israelites that the process of driving out the Canaanites would be a gradual one, as Deuteronomy 7:22 anticipated and as Judges 2:20–23 reaffirmed. Whatever the reason behind Israel's failure to drive them out—whether disobedience and/or God's slow-but-sure approach—we're still told by Joshua in sweeping terms that Israel wiped out all of the Canaanites. Just as we might say that a sports team "blew their opponents away" or "slaughtered" or "annihilated" them, the author (editor) likewise followed the rhetoric of his day.

Joshua's conventional warfare rhetoric was common in many other ancient Near Eastern military accounts in the second and first millennia BC. The language is typically exaggerated and full of bravado, depicting total devastation. The knowing ancient Near Eastern reader recognized this as hyperbole; the accounts weren't understood to be literally true.[4] This language, Egyptologist Kenneth Kitchen observes, has misled many Old Testament scholars in their assessments of the book of Joshua; some have concluded that the language of wholesale slaughter and total occupation—which didn't (from all other indications) actually take place—proves that these accounts are falsehoods. But ancient Near Eastern accounts readily used "utterly/completely destroy" and other obliteration language even when the event didn't literally happen that way. Here's a sampling:[5]

- Egypt's Tuthmosis III (later fifteenth century) boasted that "the numerous army of Mitanni was overthrown within the hour, annihilated totally, like those (now) not existent." In fact, Mitanni's forces lived on to fight in the fifteenth and fourteenth centuries BC.

- Hittite king Mursilli II (who ruled from 1322–1295 BC) recorded making "Mt. Asharpaya empty (of humanity)" and the "mountains of Tarikar-imu empty (of humanity)."

- The "Bulletin" of Ramses II tells of Egypt's less-than-spectacular victories in Syria (around 1274 BC). Nevertheless, he announces that he slew "the entire force" of the Hittites, indeed "all the chiefs of all the countries," disregarding the "millions of foreigners," which he considered "chaff."

- In the Merneptah Stele (ca. 1230 BC), Rameses II's son Merneptah announced, "Israel is wasted, his seed is not," another premature declaration.

- Moab's king Mesha (840/830 BC) bragged that the Northern Kingdom of "Israel has utterly perished for always," which was over a century premature. The Assyrians devastated Israel in 722 BC.

- The Assyrian ruler Sennacherib (701–681 BC) used similar hyperbole: "The soldiers of Hirimme, dangerous enemies, I cut down with the sword; and not one escaped."

You get the idea. Let's now return to the Old Testament text to press this point further. It's true that Joshua 9–12 utilizes the typical ancient Near Eastern literary devices for warfare. But at the book's end, Joshua matter-of-factly assumes the continued existence of Canaanite peoples that could pose a threat to Israel. He warns Israel against idolatry and getting entangled in their ways: "For if you ever go back and cling to the rest of these nations, these which remain among you, and intermarry with them, so that you associate with them and they with you, know with certainty that the LORD your God will not continue to drive these nations out from before you" (Josh. 23:12–13).

Earlier in Deuteronomy 7:2–5, we find a similar tension. On the one hand, God tells Israel that they should "defeat" and "utterly destroy [*haram*]" the Canaanites (v. 2)—a holy consecration to destruction. On the other hand, he immediately goes on to say in the very next verses:

> Furthermore, you shall not intermarry with them; you shall not give your daughters to their sons, nor shall you take their daughters for your sons. For they will turn your sons away from following Me to serve other gods; then the anger of the LORD will be kindled against you and He will quickly destroy you. But thus you shall do to them: you shall tear down their altars, and smash their sacred pillars, and hew down their Asherim [figures of Asherah, who was the Canaanite goddess of sexuality/sensuality], and burn their graven images with fire. (vv. 3–5)

If the Canaanites were to be completely obliterated, why this discussion about intermarriage or treaties? The final verse emphasizes that the ultimate issue was religious: Israel was to destroy altars, images, and sacred pillars. In other words, destroying Canaanite religion was more important than destroying Canaanite people.[6] This point was made earlier in Exodus 34:12–13: "Watch yourself that you make no covenant with the inhabitants of the land into which you are going, or it will become a snare in your midst. But rather, you are to tear down their altars and smash their sacred pillars and cut down their Asherim." In Deuteronomy 12:2–3, we read the same emphasis on destroying Canaanite *religion*:

> You shall utterly destroy all the places where the nations whom you shall dispossess serve their gods, on the high mountains and on the hills and under every green tree. You shall tear down their altars and smash their sacred pillars and burn their Asherim with fire, and you shall cut down the engraved images of their gods and obliterate their name from that place.

As Gary Millar writes, the concern of this destruction (*herem*) was "to see Israel established in a land purged of Canaanite idolatry as painlessly as possible." The goal was to "remove what is subject to [*herem*] laws (the idols)." The root of the dilemma Israel faced wasn't "the people themselves, but their idolatrous way of life." Failure to remove the idolatry would put Israel in the position of the Canaanites and their idols before God. Israel would risk being consecrated to destruction.[7]

Even so, the Israelites didn't do an effective job removing the snare of idolatry from the land (Ps. 106:34–35). Many of the Canaanites, as already noted, were still around "until this day," and many of them became forced laborers in Israel (Josh. 15:63; 16:10; 17:12–13; Judg. 1:19, 21, 27–35).

The Amalekites

In 1 Samuel 15 we encounter the remaining set of "destruction" references—reserved for an enemy hell-bent on Israel's annihilation. Here, God tells Saul to "utterly destroy [*haram*]" and "not spare" the Amalekites: "put to death both man and woman, child and infant, ox and sheep, camel and donkey" (v. 3). By the end of the chapter, Saul has apparently killed all the Amalekites—except king Agag—and he has spared lots of livestock. Saul didn't obey God fully, and the prophet Samuel had to step in and finish off Agag himself. Because Saul didn't carry out God's command completely, God rejected him as king.

As with the stories in Joshua, the surface reading here is that Saul wiped out all the Amalekites. We'll come back to this point, but first let's ask: Who were the Amalekites? These nomadic people were Israel's enemies from day one after the Red Sea crossing (Exod. 17). Weary and unprepared to fight, Israel faced a fierce people who showed no concern for the vulnerable Israelite population. The Amalekites were relentless in their aim to destroy Israel, and they continued to be a thorn in Israel's side for generations (e.g., Judg. 3:13; 6:3–5, 33; 7:12; 10:12; etc.).

Again, the 1 Samuel 15 story appears to be a clear-cut case of complete obliteration. No Amalekites remaining, right? Wrong! In 1 Samuel 27:8, "David and his men went up and raided the Geshurites and the Girzites"—and the "utterly destroyed" Amalekites! But was that the end of them? No, they appear again in 1 Samuel 30: the Amalekites made one of their infamous raids (v. 1); David pursued them to get back the Israelites and the booty the Amalekites had taken (v. 18); and four hundred of them escaped (v. 17). So contrary to the common impression, Saul *didn't* wipe out all the Amalekites, something 1 Samuel itself makes clear. And even David didn't complete the job. The Amalekites were still around during King Hezekiah's time 250 years later (1 Chron. 4:43).

Then we get to the time of Esther, when the Jews were under the rule of the Persian king Ahasuerus/Xerxes (486–465 BC). Here we encounter "Haman . . . the Agagite" (Esther 3:1). Remember King Agag the Amalekite from 1 Samuel 15:8? Yes, Haman was an Amalekite who continued the Amalekite tradition of aggression against God's people. An "enemy of the Jews" (Esther 3:10), Haman mounted a campaign to destroy the Jews as a people (3:13).

Knowing that callous Amalekite hostility would continue for nearly a millennium of Israel's history, God reminded his people not to let up in their opposition to the Amalekites (Deut. 25:15–17). Otherwise, the hardened Amalekites would seek to destroy Israel. If the Amalekites had their way, Israel would have been wiped off the map. Unlike other Canaanites, the Amalekites just couldn't be assimilated into Israel.

The moral of the story? Don't simply adopt the surface reading about Saul "utterly destroying" the Amalekites. When we read phrases like the destruction of "everything that breathes," we should be more guarded. In fact, for all we know and based on what we've seen in Joshua (and what we'll see below), Saul could well have been engaging combatants in battle rather than noncombatants. The "city of Amalek" (1 Sam. 15:5) was probably a fortified (perhaps semipermanent) military encampment.[8] Yes, decisive defeat is certainly in view, but something more is going on here. We'll continue to explore this below.

One more related point, however: the *herem* ("ban" or "consecration to destruction") language connected to Israel's warring against other nations first focuses on the Canaanites (*herem* used thirty-seven times); the second cluster of *herem* warfare (*herem* used ten times) focuses on the Amalekites in 1 Samuel 15. The use of *herem* for the conquest period—with its additional application to Israel's longstanding Amalekite enemies—indicates that the language is *restricted*. The language is not applied to Israel's warfare with other nations, nor do Israel's "holy wars" with other nations go beyond this limited time period.[9]

Men, Women, and Children

Old Testament scholar Richard Hess has written in great detail about the Canaanite question, and he offers further important insights on this topic.[10] He argues persuasively that the Canaanites targeted for destruction were political leaders and their armies rather than noncombatants. For example, Deuteronomy 20:10–18 mentions the "ban" or "dedication to destruction" (*herem*, its verb form is *haram*), which refers to the complete destruction of all warriors in the battle rather than noncombatants.[11]

However, doesn't Joshua 6:21 mention the ban—every living thing in it—in connection with men and women, young and old, ox, sheep, and donkeys? This stock phrase "men and women" occurs seven times in the Old Testament in connection with Ai (Josh. 8:25); Amalek (1 Sam. 15:3); Saul at Nob (1 Sam. 22:19 [only here are children explicitly mentioned]); Jerusalem during Ezra's time (Neh. 8:2); and Israel (2 Sam. 6:19; 2 Chron. 16:3). Each time—except at Nob, where Saul killed the entire priestly family except one (1 Sam. 22:20)—the word "all" (*kol*) is used.

The same idea applies to earlier passages in Deuteronomy: "we captured all his cities at that time and utterly destroyed the men, women and children of every city. We left no survivor" (2:34); and again, "utterly destroying the men, women and children of every city" (3:6). The expression "men and women" or similar phrases appear to be *stereotypical* for describing all the inhabitants of a town or region, "without predisposing the reader to assume anything further about their ages or even their genders."[12] (This becomes clearer in the next section.)

Let's remember that mercy was always available to any Canaanite who responded positively to the God of Israel. Although the ban was applied in specific settings, this doesn't preclude the possibility of sparing people like Rahab and her relatives. The ban allowed—and hoped for—exceptions.

Jericho, Ai, and Other Canaanite Cities

Joshua's language concerning Jericho and Ai appears harsh at first glance: "They devoted the city to the Lord and destroyed with the sword every living thing in it—men and women, young and old, cattle, sheep and donkeys" (6:21 NIV); "twelve thousand men and women fell that day—all the people of Ai" (8:25 NIV).[13] The average person isn't going to pick up on the fact that this stereotypical ancient Near Eastern language actually describes attacks on military forts or garrisons, not general populations that included women and children. There is no archaeological evidence of civilian populations at Jericho or Ai.

Given what we know about Canaanite life in the Bronze Age, Jericho and Ai were military strongholds. In fact, Jericho guarded the travel routes from the Jordan Valley up to population centers in the hill country. It was the first line of defense at the junction of three roads leading to Jerusalem, Bethel, and Orpah. That means that Israel's wars here were directed toward government and military installments; this is where the king, the army, and the priesthood resided. The use of "women" and "young and old" was merely stock ancient Near Eastern language that could be used even if women and young and old weren't living there. The language of "all" ("men and women") at Jericho and Ai is a "stereotypical expression for the destruction of all human life in the fort, presumably composed entirely of combatants."[14] The text doesn't require that women and young and old must have been in these cities.

The term *city* [*'ir*] reinforces this idea.[15] Jericho, Ai, and many other Canaanite cities were mainly used for government buildings and operations, while the rest of the people (including women and children) lived in the surrounding countryside. The Amarna letters (fourteenth century BC)—correspondence between Egyptian pharaohs and leaders in Canaan and surrounding regions—reveal that citadel cities or fortresses such as Jerusalem and Shechem were distinct from (and under the control of) their population centers.[16] Again, all the archaeological evidence indicates that no civilian populations existed at Jericho, Ai, and other cities mentioned in Joshua. Other biblical evidence of various cities used as fortresses, citadels, or military outposts also exists (e.g., Rabbah in 2 Sam. 12:26; Zion in 2 Sam. 5:7 and 1 Chron. 11:5, 7).

This fact is made all the more clear by an associated term, *melek* ("king"). This word was commonly used in Canaan during this time for a military leader who was responsible to a higher ruler off-site. What's more, the battles in Joshua do not mention noncombatants—women and children (we'll get to Rahab later). According to the best calculations from Canaanite inscriptions and other archaeological evidence (i.e., no artifacts or "prestige" ceramics indicating wealth/social status, as one would expect in general population centers), Jericho was a small settlement of probably one hundred or fewer soldiers. This is why all of Israel could circle it seven times and then do battle against it on the same day.[17]

As a side note, we could add that translating the numbers used in warfare accounts in the Old Testament can be tricky. The numbers simply may not be as high as what typical translations indicate. The Hebrew word *'eleph* (commonly rendered "thousand") can also mean "unit" or "squad" without specifying an exact number.[18]

So if Jericho were a fort, then "all" those killed therein were warriors along with political and religious leaders. Rahab and her family would have been the exceptional noncombatants dwelling within this military outpost.[19] The same applies throughout the book of Joshua. While the biblical text mentions specific "kings" (military leaders) who were killed in battle with Israel, it does not mention specific noncombatants who were killed. The cumulative case suggests quite the opposite of what we were taught in Sunday school class.

In addition, Saul's destruction of the Amalekites could have been a similar scenario (1 Sam. 15:3). The target could simply have been fortified Amalekite strongholds, not population centers. Again, the sweeping words "all," "young and old," and "men and women" were stock expressions for totality, even if women and children weren't present. This point is further reinforced by the fact that the Amalekites were far from annihilated. As we've already seen, Amalekites appear within the very book of 1 Samuel and well beyond (27:8; 30:1; 1 Chron. 4:43; etc.).

Rahab the Tavern Keeper

Why did the two Israelite spies hang out at a harlot's place? Doesn't this sound just a little fishy? On closer inspection, we can safely conclude that Rahab was in charge of what was likely the fortress's tavern or hostel; she didn't run a brothel, though these taverns were sometimes run by prostitutes.[20] Traveling caravans and royal messengers would commonly stay overnight at such places during this period.[21] The Code of Hammurabi parallels what we see in Joshua 2, complete with a female innkeeper: "If conspirators meet in the house of a [*female*] tavern-keeper, and these conspirators are not captured and delivered to the court, the tavern-keeper shall be put to death."[22]

Furthermore, such reconnaissance missions were common in the East. An innkeeper's home would have been an ideal meeting place for spies and conspirators. Such places notoriously posed a threat to security; because of this, the Hittites (in Turkey and northern Syria) prohibited the building of an inn or tavern near fortress walls.[23]

What about the idea of a sexual liaison? The book of Joshua goes out of its way to state that no such activity took place. The text says the spies "stayed there" not that they "stayed *with her*" (2:1 NIV). And it says they "came *into the house of* . . . *Rahab*" (2:1) not that they "went *in to Rahab*," which *would* imply a sexual relationship. Consider Samson, by contrast, who "saw a harlot . . . and went in to her" (Judg. 16:1). The Old Testament doesn't recoil from using such language; we just don't have any sexual reference here. Instead, the book of Joshua depicts Rahab as a true God-fearer. Yes, such taverns in the ancient Near East would draw people seeking sexual pleasure, but this doesn't apply to the Israelite spies, who visited there because it was a public place where they could learn about the practical and military dispositions of the area and could solicit possible support.[24]

The Canaanites' Refusal to Acknowledge the One True God

Unlike Rahab and her family, her fellow Jerichoites (and most of the Canaanites) refused to acknowledge the one true God. The example of Rahab and her family (and to some extent Gibeon) reveals that consecration to the ban (*herem*) wasn't absolute and irreversible. God was, as we've seen, more concerned about the destruction of Canaanite religion and idols than Canaanite peoples. God repeatedly expresses a willingness to relent from punishment and preserve those who acknowledge his evident rule over the nations (cf. Jer. 18:8).

For those demanding, "If God exists, let him show himself," it doesn't get much more dramatic than the Red Sea parting. The Creator and the God of Israel had made the headlines in Canaan! In the words of Rahab, "We have heard how the LORD dried up the water of the Red Sea before you when you came out of Egypt. . . . When we heard of it, our hearts melted and no courage remained in any man any longer because of you; for the LORD your God, He is God in heaven above and on earth beneath" (Josh. 2:10–11). In the words of the Gibeonites, "Your servants have come from a very far country because of the fame of the LORD your God; for we have heard the report of Him and all that He did in Egypt" (9:9; cf. Exod. 15:14–17; Deut. 2:25). Just as a pagan Nineveh repented at the sight and message of the beached (and bleached!) prophet Jonah, the Canaanites also could have repented—unless, of course, they were too far gone morally and spiritually.

In the New Testament, Jesus asserts that without a willing heart, a person won't turn to God even if someone rises from the dead (Luke 16:31). The repeated, visible pounding of Egypt's gods could have prompted the Canaanites to turn to the one true God, given they had a "heart condition" like Rahab's. Even Israel's sevenfold march around Jericho exhibited a formal opportunity for its king, soldiers, and priests to relent. The Hebrew word *naqap* ("circle, march around" in Josh. 6:3) involves various ceremonial aspects, including rams' horns, sacred procession, and shouting (cf. 2 Sam. 6:15–16). The word is found in Psalm 48: "Walk about Zion and *go around* her; count her towers; consider her ramparts" (vv. 12–13; also 2 Kings 6:14). The word suggests the idea of conducting an inspection. In the case of Jericho, the inspection was conducted to see if the city would open its gates. The city, however, refused to do so.[25] Each time the Israelites circled the city meant an opportunity for Jericho to evade the ban; sadly, each opportunity was met with Jericho's refusal to relent and acknowledge Yahweh's rule.

Israel's Warfare Methods

We've discussed Richard Dawkins's flawed claim that Israel engaged in ethnic cleansing, those "bloodthirsty massacres" carried out with "xenophobic relish." A review of Israel's warfare methods reveals otherwise. Israel's army simply didn't act like a horde of bloodthirsty, maniacal warmongers.

For one thing, the aftermath of Joshua's victories are featherweight descriptions in comparison to those found in the annals of the ancient Near

East's major empires: Hittite and Egyptian (second millennium BC), Aramaean, Assyrian, Babylonian, Persian, or Greek (first millennium BC).[26] Unlike Joshua's brief, four-verse description of the treatment of the five kings (10:24–27), Assyrians exulted in all the details of their gory, brutal exploits.

The Neo-Assyrian annals of Ashurnasirpal II (883–859 BC) take pleasure in describing the flaying of live victims, the impaling of others on poles, and the heaped up bodies for show.[27] They boast of how the king mounded bodies and placed heads into piles; the king bragged of gouging out troops' eyes and cutting off their ears and limbs, followed by his displaying their heads all around a city.[28]

Second, a number of battles Israel fought on the way to and within Canaan were *defensive*: the Amalekites attacked the traveling Israelites (Exod. 17:8); the Canaanite king of Arad attacked and captured some Israelites (Num. 21:1); the Amorite king Sihon refused Israel's peaceful overtures and attacked instead (Num. 21:21–32; Deut. 2:26–30); Bashan's king Og came out to meet Israel in battle (Num. 21:33; Deut. 3:1); Israel responded to Midian's calculated attempts to lead Israel astray through idolatry and immorality (Num. 31:2–3; cf. 25; 31:16); five kings attacked Gibeon, which Joshua defended because of Israel's peace pact with the Gibeonites (Josh. 10:4).

Besides this, God prohibited Israel from conquering other neighboring nations. These nations were Moab and Ammon (Deut. 2:9, 19), as well as Edom (Deut. 2:4–5; 23:7), even though they had earlier refused to assist the Israelites (Num. 20:14–21; cf. Deut. 2:6–8). Land-grabbing wasn't permitted by God, and Israel had no right to conquer beyond what God had sanctioned.

Third, all sanctioned Yahweh battles beyond the time of Joshua were defensive ones, including Joshua's battle to defend Gibeon (Josh. 10–11). Of course, while certain offensive battles took place during the time of the Judges and under David and beyond, these are not commended as ideal or exemplary.[29] We've also seen that fighting in order to survive wasn't just an adventure; it was a way of life in the ancient Near East. Such circumstances weren't ideal by far, but that was the reality.

The Midianites (Numbers 31)

As with Israel's lifelong enemies, the Amalekites (cf. Deut. 25:17–19), the Midianites also posed a serious threat to Israel. Whereas Amalek endangered Israel's very existence, Midian profoundly threatened Israel's spiritual and moral integrity as the people of God. With the help of the devious pagan prophet Balaam, the Midianites devised a plan to lead Israel into pagan worship. This involved ritual sex, feasting before their Baal, and bowing and sacrificing to him (Num. 25:1–2; 31:16). When he couldn't bring a curse down on Israel (Num. 22–24), he sought another way.

This is why Moses gives the command, "Now kill all the boys. And kill every woman who has slept with a man, but save for yourselves every girl who has never slept with a man" (Num. 31:17–18 NIV). This command must be understood in the context of Numbers 25. At Peor, the Midianite women deliberately seduced the Israelite men into orgiastic adultery as well as Baal worship.

The death sentence for *all* males is unusual. However, males were the potential enemy army to rise up against Israel. (Keep in mind that *the Israelite males* who participated in the seduction were also put to death.) Midian's brazen, evil intent to lead Israel astray called for a severe judgment. The intent of Moses's command was to undermine any future Midianite threat to Israel's identity and integrity.

What about the taking of young virgins? Some critics have crassly suggested that Israelite men were free simply to grab and rape young virgins. Not so. They were saved precisely because they *hadn't* degraded themselves by seducing Israelite men. As a backdrop, have a look again at Deuteronomy 21:10–14. There, a Gentile female POW couldn't be used as a sex object. An Israelite male had to carefully follow proper procedures before she could be taken *as a wife*. In light of the highly sensitive nature of sexual purity in Israel and for Israel's soldiers, specific protocols had to be followed. Rape was most certainly excluded as an extracurricular activity in warfare.

Making Offers of Peace First

In light of Deuteronomy 20's warfare procedures, many scholars argue that Israel was to offer terms of peace to non-Canaanite cities but *not* to Canaanite cities. This is the majority view, to be sure. However, others (including traditional Jewish commentators) have argued that the destruction of Canaanite cities wasn't unconditional and that treaties could have been made under certain conditions. As with Gibeon (despite being sneaky treaty makers), a straightforward peace pact could have been available to any Canaanite city.[30] As we saw with Jericho, a sevenfold opportunity was given for Jericho to make peace with Israel, which it refused to do. Consider Joshua 11:19: "There was not a city which made peace with the sons of Israel except the Hivites living in Gibeon; they took them all in battle." Like Pharoah, who opposed Moses, these Canaanite cities were so far gone that God simply gave them up to their own hardened, resistant hearts (v. 20).

Again, the primary focus in passages like Deuteronomy 7 and 20 is on Israel's ridding the land of idols and false, destructive religious practices. The ultimate goal isn't eliminating persons, as the inspection march around Jericho also suggests.

Driving Them Out

What adds further interest to our discussion is the language of "driving out" and "thrusting out" the Canaanites. The Old Testament also uses the language of "dispossessing" the Canaanites of their land (Num. 21:32; Deut. 9:1; 11:23; 18:14; 19:1; etc.).

> I will send My terror ahead of you, and throw into confusion all the people among whom you come, and I will make all your enemies turn their backs to you. I will send hornets ahead of you so that they will drive out the Hivites, the Canaanites, and the Hittites before you. I will not drive them out before you in a single year, that the land may not become desolate and the beasts of the field become too numerous for you. I will drive them out before you little by little, until you become fruitful and take possession of the land. (Exod. 23:27–30)

Driving out or dispossessing is different from wiping out or destroying. Expulsion is in view, not annihilation (e.g., "dispossess [*yarash*]" in Exod. 34:24; Num. 32:21; Deut. 4:38 NET). Just as Adam and Eve were "driven out [*garash*]" of the garden (Gen. 3:24) or Cain into the wilderness (4:14) or David from Israel by Saul (1 Sam. 26:19), so the Israelites were to "dispossess" the Canaanites. The Old Testament uses another term as well—"send/cast out [*shalach*]"—that sheds light on the Canaanite question: just as Adam and Eve were "sent out" from the garden (Gen. 3:23), so God would "send out" (or "drive out," Lev. 18:24; 20:23) the Canaanites. And upon examination, the driving out references are considerably more numerous than the destroying and annihilating ones.

In fact, even the verbs "annihilate/perish ['*abad*]" and "destroy [*shamad*]" aren't all that the critics have made them out to be. For example, God threatened to destroy Israel as he did the Canaanites. How? Not by literal obliteration but by removing Israel from the land to another land. Both verbs are used in Deuteronomy 28:63: "it shall come about that as the Lord delighted over you to prosper you, and multiply you, so the Lord will delight over you to make you perish and destroy you; and you will be torn from the land where you are entering to possess it." Even when Babylon *destroyed* the city of Jerusalem, all cooperative Jews were spared (Jer. 38:2, 17).[31] In short, fleeing Canaanites would escape; only the resistant were at risk. This brief examination of terms connected to Yahweh wars provides yet further indication that utter annihilation wasn't intended and that escape from the land was encouraged.

How then does this dispossessing or driving out work? It's not hard to imagine. The threat of a foreign army would prompt women and children—not to mention the population at large—to remove themselves from harm's way. The noncombatants would be the first to flee. As John Goldingay writes, an attacked population wouldn't just wait around to be killed. Only the defenders, who don't get out, are the ones who would get killed.[32] Jeremiah 4:29

suggests such a scenario: "At the sound of the horseman and bowman every city flees; they go into the thickets and climb among the rocks; every city is forsaken, and no man dwells in them."

Again, the biblical text gives no indication that the justified wars of Joshua were against noncombatants.[33] We read in Joshua (and Judges) that, despite the obliteration language, plenty of Canaanite inhabitants who weren't driven out were still living in areas where Israel settled. Moreover, Canaanites (in general) were to be displaced or driven out, not annihilated.

Joshua Utterly Destroyed Them Just as Moses Commanded

In the following texts, Joshua's utter destruction of the Canaanites is exactly what "Moses the servant of the LORD had commanded":

- "Joshua captured all the cities of these kings, and all their kings, and he struck them with the edge of the sword, and utterly destroyed them; just as Moses the servant of the LORD had commanded" (Josh. 11:12).
- "All the spoil of these cities and the cattle, the sons of Israel took as their plunder; but they struck every man with the edge of the sword, until they had destroyed them. They left no one who breathed. Just as the LORD had commanded Moses his servant, so Moses commanded Joshua, and so Joshua did; he left nothing undone of all that the LORD had commanded Moses" (Josh. 11:14–15).
- "that he might destroy them, just as the LORD had commanded Moses" (Josh. 11:20).

Remember Moses's sweeping commands to "consume" and "utterly destroy" the Canaanites, not to "leave alive anything that breathes"? Joshua's comprehensive language echoes that of Moses; Scripture clearly indicates that Joshua fulfilled Moses's charge to him. So *if* Joshua did just as Moses commanded, and *if* Joshua's described destruction was really hyperbole common in ancient Near Eastern warfare language and familiar to Moses, *then* clearly Moses himself didn't intend a literal, comprehensive Canaanite destruction. He, like Joshua, was merely following the literary convention of the day.[34]

Scripture and Archaeology

With its mention of gradual infiltration and occupation (Josh. 13:1–7; 16:10; 17:12), the biblical text *leads us to expect* what archaeology has confirmed—namely, that widespread destruction of cities didn't take place and that gradual assimilation did.[35] Only three cities (citadels or fortresses, as we've seen) were burned—Jericho, Ai, and Hazor (Josh. 6:24; 8:28; 11:13). All tangible aspects of the Canaanites' culture—buildings and homes—would have remained very much intact (cf. Deut. 6:10–11: "cities which you did not build"). This makes a lot of sense if Israel was to settle down in the same region—a lot less clean-up!

Furthermore, if we had lived back in Israel in the Late Bronze Age (1400–1200 BC) and looked at an Israelite and a Canaanite standing next to each other, we wouldn't have detected any noticeable differences between them; they would have been virtually indistinguishable in dress, homes, tableware, pottery, and even language (cf. 2 Kings 18:26, 28; Isa. 19:18). This shouldn't be all that surprising, as the Egyptian influence on *both* these peoples was quite strong.

What's more, Israel itself wasn't a pure race. For example, Joseph married an Egyptian woman, Asenath, who gave birth to Manasseh and Ephraim (Gen. 41:50); a "mixed multitude" came out of Egypt with them (Exod. 12:23; Num. 11:4); and other Gentiles like Rahab could be readily incorporated into Israel by intermarrying if they were willing to embrace the God of Israel. So how might Israelites distinguish themselves? Typically, by identifying their tribal or village and regional connections—for example, "Ehud the son of Gera, the Benjamite" (Judg. 3:15), "Izban of Bethlehem" (Judg. 12:8), "Elon the Zebulunite" (Judg. 12:11).

On the religious front, again, the Scriptures lead us to expect what archaeology supports. Yes, like the Canaanites, the Israelites sacrificed, had priests, burned incense, and worshiped at a "shrine" (the tabernacle). And though the Israelites were called to remain distinct in their moral behavior, theology, and worship, they were often ensnared by the immorality and idolatry of the Canaanite peoples. For example, Israel mimicked the Phoenicians' notorious practice of ritual infant sacrifice to the Baals and Asherahs and to Molech (e.g., 2 Kings 23:10; cf. Lev. 18:21; Deut. 18:10).

However, archaeologists have discovered that by 1000 BC (during the Iron Age), Canaanites were no longer an identifiable entity in Israel. (I'm assuming that the exodus from Egypt took place sometime in the thirteenth century BC.)[36] Around this time also, Israelites were worshiping a national God, whose dominant personal name was Yahweh ("the Lord"). An additional significant change from the Late Bronze to Iron Age was that town shrines in Canaan had been abandoned but not relocated elsewhere—say, to the hill villages. This suggests that a new people with a distinct theological bent had migrated here, had gradually occupied the territory, and had eventually become dominant.

We could point to a well-supported parallel scenario in the ancient Near East. The same kind of gradual infiltration took place by the Amorites, who had moved into Babylonia decades before 2000 BC. (Hammurabi himself was an Amorite who ruled Babylon.) They eventually occupied and controlled key cities and exerted political influence, which is attested by changes in many personal names in the literature and inscriptions. Babylonia's culture didn't change in its buildings, clothing, and ceramics, but a significant social shift took place. Likewise, we see the same gradual transition taking place in Canaan based on the same kinds of evidence archaeologists typically utilize. We're reminded once again to avoid simplistic Sunday school versions of how Canaan came to be occupied by Israel.

Summary

Let's summarize some of the key ideas in this chapter.

- The language of the consecrated ban (*herem*) includes stereotypical language: "all," "young and old," and "men and women." The ban could be carried out even if women and children weren't present.
- As far as we can see, biblical *herem* was carried out in particular military or combatant settings (with "cities" and military "kings"). It turns out that the sweeping language of the ban is directed at combatants.
- The ban language allows and hopes for exceptions (e.g., Rahab); it isn't absolute.
- The destruction language of ancient Near Eastern warfare (and the Old Testament) is clearly exaggerated. Groups of Canaanite peoples who apparently were "totally destroyed" were still around when all was said and done (e.g., Judg. 1).
- The greater concern was to destroy Canaanite religion, not Canaanites per se, a point worthy of elaboration (see the next chapter).
- The preservation of Rahab and her family indicates that consecration to the ban wasn't absolute and irreversible. God had given ample indications of his power and greatness, and the Canaanites could have submitted to the one true God who trumped Egypt's and Canaan's gods, sparing their own lives.
- The biblical text, according to some scholars, suggests that peace treaties could be made with Canaanite cities if they chose to, but none (except Gibeon) did so (Josh. 11:19). The offer of peace was implicitly made to Jericho.
- The biblical text contains many references to "driving out" the Canaanites. To clear away the land for habitation didn't require killing; civilians fled when their military strongholds were destroyed and soldiers were no longer capable of protecting them.
- From the start, certain (more cooperative) Canaanites were subjected to forced labor, not annihilation (Judg. 1:27–36; 1 Kings 9:20–21; Josh. 15:63; 16:10; 17:12–13; cf. Ps. 106:34–35). This was another indication that the ban wasn't absolute.

- Joshua carried out what Moses commanded (Deut. 7 and 20), which means that Moses's language is also an example of ancient Near Eastern exaggeration. He did not intend a literal, all-encompassing extermination of the Canaanites.
- The archaeological evidence nicely supports the biblical text; both of these point to minimal observable material destruction in Canaan as well as Israel's gradual infiltration, assimilation, and eventual dominance there.

We have many good reasons to rethink our paradigm regarding the destruction of the Canaanites. On closer analysis, the biblical text suggests that much more is going on beneath the surface than obliterating all the Canaanites. Taking the destruction of anything that breathes at face value needs much reexamination.

Further Reading

Goldingay, John. *Old Testament Theology: Israel's Life.* Vol. 3. Downers Grove, IL: InterVarsity, 2009. See esp. chap. 5, "City and Nation."

Hess, Richard S. "The Jericho and Ai of the Book of Joshua." In *Critical Issues in Early Israelite History*, edited by Richard S. Hess, Gerald A. Klingbeil, and Paul J. Ray Jr. Winona Lake, IN: Eisenbrauns, 2008.

———. *Joshua.* Tyndale Old Testament Commentary 6. Downers Grove, IL: InterVarsity, 1996.

———. "War in the Hebrew Bible: An Overview." In *War in the Bible and Terrorism in the Twenty-First Century*, edited by Richard S. Hess and Elmer A. Martens. Winona Lake, IN: Eisenbrauns, 2008.

Wright, Christopher J. H. *The God I Don't Understand.* Grand Rapids: Zondervan, 2008.

17

Indiscriminate Massacre and Ethnic Cleansing?

The Killing of the Canaanites (III)

Critics argue that the killing of the Canaanites set a negative, brutal precedent for national Israel. Curiously, professing Christians (during the Crusades, for instance) who were inspired by the Canaanite-killing texts to justify their actions completely ignored Jesus's own kingdom teaching.[1] Jesus had informed Pilate, "My kingdom is not of this world. If My kingdom were of this world, then My servants would be fighting" (John 18:36). Again, "all those who take up the sword shall perish by the sword" (Matt. 26:52).

On the other hand, we can confidently say that, precisely because of their commitment to Christ's kingdom *not* being of this world, Amish and Mennonite communities would most certainly not appeal to Joshua to justify engaging in atrocities. The difference is that some professing Christians are far more consistent in applying Jesus's teaching than others. It's one thing to say that holy war is at the very heart of a religion and its theology and another to misuse a religion's texts to justify warfare.

Furthermore, national Israel itself didn't utilize these Joshua texts to justify attacking non-Canaanite peoples. They may have defended themselves against other enemies, but that's a different story. Israelites throughout their history have not sought to commit non-Canaanite peoples to destruction. To quote John Goldingay once more: "Saul does not seek to devote the Philistines and David does not seek to devote [to destruction] the surrounding peoples whom he did conquer. Neither Ephraim nor Judah took on Assyria, Babylon, Persia, or the local equivalents of the Canaanites in the Second Temple period." He adds that Deuteronomy and Joshua do not set a pattern that "invites later Israel to follow, or that later Israel does follow."[2]

The Canaanites as the Redeemed People of God

Another factor to include in our discussion is God's promise to bless all the nations through Israel, including the Canaanites! Israel's prophets after Solomon came to view the nations once singled out for judgment as the ultimate objects of Yahweh's salvation. Peoples who historically had been Israel's fiercest, most brutal enemies would partake in a new covenant as God's multiethnic people. For instance, in Zechariah 9, God begins with a promise to humble and judge the Philistines (vv. 1–6). And "then they also will be a remnant for our God, and be like a clan in Judah, and Ekron [a city in Philistia] like a Jebusite" (v. 7). In other words, the Philistines—Israel's longstanding enemies—will become a redeemed remnant and will be incorporated into God's people, like one of the tribes of Israel. They will be "like a Jebusite." The Jebusites were a *Canaanite* people (Deut. 7:1) that were eventually absorbed into the fold of Israel (1 Chron. 21:15, 18, 28). But beyond this, God's salvation extends to all peoples, even the Canaanites, some of whom ultimately become part of God's redeemed remnant.

This theme is reinforced in Psalm 87, which lists (among others) Israel's chief oppressors: Egypt, Babylon, and Philistia. These nations in Israel's Hall of Infamy will one day be incorporated into the people of God.[3]

> I will record Rahab [Egypt] and Babylon among those who acknowledge me— Philistia too, and Tyre, along with Cush [Ethiopia]—and will say, "This one was born in Zion." Indeed, of Zion it will be said, "This one and that one were born in her, and the Most High himself will establish her." The LORD will write in the register of the peoples: "This one was born in Zion." (vv. 4–6 NIV)

Isaiah prophesied that the Gentile nations of Egypt and Assyria would become incorporated into the people of God. These nearly topped the list of Israel's oppressors:

> In that day there will be a highway from Egypt to Assyria, and the Assyrians will come into Egypt and the Egyptians into Assyria, and the Egyptians will worship with the Assyrians. In that day Israel will be the third party with Egypt and Assyria, a blessing in the midst of the earth, whom the LORD of hosts has blessed, saying, "Blessed is Egypt My people, and Assyria the work of My hands, and Israel My inheritance." (19:23–25)

In the New Testament, we begin to see this prophecy fulfilled, as Gentiles become incorporated into the new Israel, the church (Eph. 3:1–11; cf. Acts 15:16–17). In fact, in Jesus's own ministry, he extended concern to a *Canaanite* woman in the region of Tyre and Sidon (Matt. 15:22). God's ultimate concern to save even his own (people's) enemies comes full circle with the redemption of the Canaanites.

The Canaanite Question and Noncombatants

We've given abundant evidence for claiming that approved Yahweh wars in the Old Testament were limited to a certain window of time in Israel's history, to a certain smallish geographical location, and to a specific grouping of people. (Indeed, these specific divinely given parameters and controls were in marked contrast to other ancient Near Eastern nations, which had no such limits.)[4] This act of judgment was a corporate capital punishment that could be carried out only with the guidance of special, divine revelation.

Some people might argue that this scenario is a stretch. It may require too many qualifications. For example, what if Canaanite and Amalekite women, children, and the elderly really were targeted? What if the "all" doesn't apply only to combatants in Canaanite fortresses (cities) but is much more sweeping than this? Don't too many contingencies have to be *just right* to arrive at a palatable moral conclusion regarding the Canaanite question? If this were the case, then we could imagine how critics might exclaim, "I can't trust that God's character is the standard of goodness if he commands the killing of innocent children!" or "If that's the kind of God you worship, I want nothing to do with him!"

For anyone who takes the Bible seriously, these Yahweh-war texts will certainly prove troubling. This issue is certainly the most weighty of all Old Testament ethical considerations. We shouldn't glibly dismiss or ignore such questions. On the other hand, we hope that critics won't do a surface reading of these Old Testament texts.

If our scenario doesn't cover *all* the bases, it still goes a long way in providing perspective on what happened and didn't happen in Canaan. Simply put, the damage to and death of noncombatants would have been far less serious and extensive than what critics and believers alike have maintained based on a traditional surface reading of the text. Just review the previous chapter for a summary of all the qualifications and exceptions (e.g., exaggerated ancient Near Eastern language, the meaning of "driving out," destruction of idolatry over people, and so on).

Second, let's assume that women weren't combatants, like Joan of Arc against the English (1412–31) or Budicca (d. AD 60) against the Romans. Even so, Canaanite women would have participated in immoral, degrading activities (which we've reviewed). Deviant morality wasn't just the domain of men. We've seen how temple prostitution was religiously justified adultery, and how Canaanite gods themselves modeled adultery, bestiality, incest, and a host of other activities that their devotees practiced. Even before we get to Canaan, notice how readily the Midianite women sought to seduce Israelite men (Num. 25). Women may not have been combatants, but they were hardly innocent. And we could add that elderly Canaanites clearly shared blame in the moral corruption of their culture.

Third, if the evidence doesn't offer a complete answer, the lingering crucial question is, Why kill Canaanite infants and children? Surely they were innocent. From a theological side, we can say a couple of things.

1. God is the author of life and has a rightful claim on it as Creator. Therefore, humans can make no demands on how long a person ought to live on earth (Job 1:21). If God is God and we aren't, then our rights will necessarily be limited to some degree.
2. If any infants and children were killed, they would have entered the presence of God. Though deprived of earthly life, these young ones wouldn't have been deprived of the greatest good—enjoying everlasting friendship with God.

Perhaps more could be said here, but we must address another aspect of the Canaanite problem. But keep in mind that this noncombatant, worst-case scenario isn't the position I'm taking.

Psychologically Damaging?

On March 16, 1968, American troops brutally slaughtered over three hundred Vietnamese civilians in a cluster of hamlets, now infamously known as My Lai. They disregarded all Geneva Convention protocols, which regard harming noncombatants or the sick and wounded as a crime.[5] Wasn't the killing of the Canaanites a brutal task comparable to the My Lai massacre? How could God command such an undertaking? The theologian John Stott admits, "It was a ghastly business; one shrinks from it in horror."[6] In the context of another war, Confederate general Robert E. Lee affirmed, "It is well that war is so terrible; otherwise we should grow too fond of it."[7]

In the ancient Near East, however, warfare was a way of life and a means of survival. Fighting was a much less grim reality back then. In the ancient Near East, combatants and noncombatants weren't always easily distinguished. We've also observed that the hardness of human hearts (Matt. 19:8), in conjunction with the existence of fallen, morally blunted social structures in the ancient Near East, likely means that such actions would have been considerably less psychologically damaging for the ancient Israelite than for a citizen of Western culture. There is no evidence that Israelite soldiers were internally damaged by killing the Canaanites.

Beyond this, we should ask, What if there are some tasks that we would shrink from and that could even psychologically harm us but that still need to be done? The apostle Paul willingly gave himself up to "fill up what was lacking in Christ's afflictions" (see Col. 1:24). These are the allotted afflictions, tribulations, or birth pangs all believers must endure; they could include even the horrors of death itself. All that Paul endured for the sake of the gospel is startling (e.g., 2 Cor. 11:23–33), but he willingly shouldered this heavy burden.

Jesus reminded his followers to take courage because "I have overcome the world" (John 16:33). Christ permits his own people to endure persecution and even death's terrors (Heb. 11:36–40), just as he himself did. Yet he reminds his people that he suffers with them and doesn't forsake them (Matt. 25:40; Acts 9:4).

The Lord of the Rings describes the harrowing journey Frodo Baggins must take to Mount Doom, accompanied by his faithful Hobbit friend Samwise Gamgee. Into Doom's fires Frodo must throw the odious ring that has brought trouble not only to its wearers but to all of Middle Earth. This harsh, even detestable task fell to Frodo. It was perilous and emotionally exhausting. To fulfill this mission was in many ways psychologically damaging for him, though character-shaping in others. He loathed the burden of carrying the ring, which seemed to tear him apart inside. Yet Gandalf the Wise reminded him, "We cannot choose the time we live in. We can only choose what we do with the time we are given."[8]

We may not understand the tasks God assigns to us (whether we are thinking of Abraham with Isaac or the killing of Canaanites), and a certain task or calling may bring its share of traumas and sorrows. Theologian Vernon Grounds's wise words are insightful and widely applicable:

> An individual, quite completely free from tension, anxiety, and conflict may be only a well-adjusted sinner who is dangerously maladjusted to God; and it is infinitely better to be a neurotic saint than a healthy-minded sinner. . . . Healthy-mindedness may be a spiritual hazard that keeps an individual from turning to God precisely because he has no acute sense of God. . . . Tension, conflict, and anxiety, even to the point of mental illness, may be a cross voluntarily carried in God's service.[9]

A grander context should also be considered, something that couldn't be fully understood by Joshua's generation. If the Israelites hadn't done serious damage to the Canaanite religious infrastructure, the result would have been incalculable damage to Israel's integrity and thus to God's entire plan to redeem humanity. Much was at stake in creating the necessary context—including a set-apart people in a set-apart land—in order to bring about redemption and an eventually restored creation. Just as Frodo's success was precarious from start to finish, so was the journey from God's promise to Abram (Gen. 12) to the coming of the Messiah. God's plan involved a certain mysterious messiness, but this shouldn't deter us from seeing God's ultimate purposes at work.

The Broader Picture

God's overarching goal was to bring blessing and salvation to all the nations, including the Canaanites, through Abraham (Gen. 12:3; 22:17–18; cf. 28:13–14). The covenant God made with Abraham is unique in its sweeping, outsider-oriented, universally directed nature. It is unlike any other ancient religious movement.[10] Yet, for a specific, relatively short, and strategic period, God sought to establish Israel in the land with a view to fulfilling this long-term, global (indeed, cosmic) plan of redemption. God would simultaneously punish a wicked people ripe for judgment. Not doing so would have erased humankind's only hope for redemption.

God's difficult command regarding the Canaanites is also a limited, unique, salvation-historical situation. We could compare it to God's difficult command to Abraham in Genesis 22. John Goldingay says it well: "the fate of the Canaanites is about as illuminating a starting point for understanding First Testament ethics as Gen 22 [Abraham's binding of Isaac] would be for an understanding of the family."[11] Behind both of these harsh commands is the clear context of God's loving intentions and faithful promises.

The first harsh command involved Abraham and the miracle child Isaac. God had promised Abraham that through Isaac he would become the father of many. Previously, Abraham had seen God's provision for Ishmael and Hagar when he reluctantly let them go into the wilderness. God had reassured Abraham that Ishmael would become a great nation. In light of Abraham's previous experience, he was confident that God would somehow fulfill his covenant promises through Isaac even as they headed toward Mount Moriah. He was convinced that God would keep his promises even if it meant that God would raise Isaac from the dead. Thus, Abraham informed his servants, "*We* will worship, and then *we* will come back to you" (Gen. 22:5 NRSV; cf. Heb. 11:19). Abraham knew that God's purposes wouldn't be thwarted, despite this difficult command.

With the second harsh command regarding the Canaanites, we can't ignore the context of God's universal blessing to all nations, including national Israel's ancient enemies. The troubling, exceptional commands regarding both Isaac and the Canaanites must be set against their historical and theological context—namely, the background of Yahweh's enemy-loving character and worldwide saving purposes.

This is illustrated in the book of Jonah. God didn't punish the Ninevites—to the great disappointment of Jonah, who knew that this is the sort of thing

Yahweh does: he loves his (and Israel's) enemies. "I knew that You are a gracious and compassionate God, slow to anger and abundant in lovingkindness, and one who relents concerning calamity" (Jonah 4:2; cf. Exod. 34:6).

An Untamable God

We sensitized Westerners wonder why God gets so angry with Israel. Why all the judgment and wrath? Why does the Old Testament seem so undemocratic? We live in a time when we're very alert to racial discrimination and intolerance, but we aren't as sensitized to sexual sin as past generations were. We live in a time that sees death as the ultimate evil. Perhaps we need to be more open to the fact that some of our moral intuitions aren't as finely tuned as they ought to be. The same may apply to our thoughts about what God should or shouldn't have done in Canaan.[12]

Yale theologian Miroslav Volf was born in Croatia and lived through the nightmare years of ethnic strife in the former Yugoslavia that included the destruction of churches, the raping of women, and the murdering of innocents. He once thought that wrath and anger were beneath God, but he came to realize that his view of God had been too low. Here Volf puts the New Atheists' complaints about divine wrath into proper perspective:

> I used to think that wrath was unworthy of God. Isn't God love? Shouldn't divine love be beyond wrath? God is love, and God loves every person and every creature. That's exactly why God is wrathful against some of them. My last resistance to the idea of God's wrath was a casualty of the war in the former Yugoslavia, the region from which I come. According to some estimates, 200,000 people were killed and over 3,000,000 were displaced. My villages and cities were destroyed, my people shelled day in and day out, some of them brutalized beyond imagination, and I could not imagine God not being angry. Or think of Rwanda in the last decade of the past century, where 800,000 people were hacked to death in one hundred days! How did God react to the carnage? By doting on the perpetrators in a grandfatherly fashion? By refusing to condemn the bloodbath but instead affirming the perpetrators' basic goodness? Wasn't God fiercely angry with them? Though I used to complain about the indecency of the idea of God's wrath, I came to think that I would have to rebel against a God who wasn't wrathful at the sight of the world's evil. God isn't wrathful in spite of being love. God is wrathful because God is love.[13]

The apostle Paul brings these features together: "Behold then the kindness and severity of God" (Rom. 11:22).

Maybe the ideal "God" in the Westerner's mind is just too nice. We've lost sight of good and just while focusing on nice, tame, and manageable. We've ignored sternness and severity (which make us squirm), latching on to our own ideals of comfort and convenience. We've gotten rid of the God who presents a cosmic authority problem and substituted controllable gods of our own devising. We've focused on divine love at the expense of God's anger at what ultimately destroys us or undermines our fundamental well-being.

Philosopher Paul Moser observes:

> It would be a strange, defective God who didn't pose a serious cosmic authority problem for humans. Part of the status of being *God*, after all, is that God has a unique authority, or lordship, over humans. Since we humans aren't God, the true God would have authority over us and would seek to correct our profoundly selfish ways.[14]

Unlike ancient Near Eastern deities, the Savior of Scripture (like Narnia's Aslan) is not safe. As a fellow church member, Ellie, recently put it, he is "a butt-kicking God."

Today's version of spirituality is tame and makes no demands on us. A mere impersonal force behind it all doesn't call us on the carpet for our actions. We can play games with a pantheon of these kinds of deities. By contrast, the living God—a "hunter, king, husband," C. S. Lewis says—is trying to get our attention by pulling from the other end at the cord of our lives.[15] Because life isn't about us as the center of reality, God becomes the "transcendental Interferer"[16] and the hound of heaven to help our restless souls ultimately find their rest in him.

If we take God seriously, he will most certainly mess up our lives, make us uncomfortable, and even disorient us. After all, we can easily get accustomed to our own self-serving agendas and idols. The atheist has it *almost* right: humans regularly *do* make gods in their image. Yet the biblical God isn't the kind we make up. He refuses to be manipulated by human schemes. He makes us all—including his true devotees—uncomfortable, which in the end is what we truly need to overcome our self-centeredness. "Whoever wishes to save his life will lose it; but whoever loses his life for My sake will find it" (Matt. 16:25).

Even so, this God also shows himself to be a promise-making God who is worthy of our tenacious trust, despite the puzzles, discomforts, storms, and even horrors we may endure. C. S. Lewis commends this "obstinacy of faith." He asserts that trust in a personal God (as opposed to a mere proposition) "could have no room to grow except where there is also room for doubt." Lewis goes so far as to say that love involves trusting a friend beyond the evidence, even, at times, against the evidence. He reminds us that we should give the benefit of the doubt to a friend, even if the friend may display seemingly puzzling and uncharacteristic behavior. For example, if a trusted friend pledges to meet us somewhere but fails to show up, which of us "would not feel slightly ashamed if, one moment after we had given him up, he arrived with a full explanation of his delay? We should feel that we ought to have known him better."[17]

The God Who Commands

Some critics argue that because God commands the killing of the Canaanites (a specific action in a specific historical context for a specific theological purpose), then we can generalize: "action X is always permissible." And, of course, if you allow this, then terrorism becomes permissible in the name of whatever authority: "Allah said it; I believe it; that settles it!" This isn't very good reasoning, of course, but it's all too common when it comes to the Canaanite question. The earlier discussion of Genesis 22 (see "Philosophical Reflections on God's Command to Abraham" in chapter 5) overlaps with the Canaanite question; you can revisit that chapter with the Canaanites in mind. However, here we'll look at things from another angle.

If infants are killed by God's command, they aren't wronged, for they will be compensated by God in the next life. So why not support infanticide? Why not kill *all* infants to make sure they are with God in the hereafter? This question commonly raised by critics doesn't follow, of course, for at least four reasons:

1. In the context of God's ongoing special revelation to Israel, God gave an unrepeatable command for a specific purpose, which the Scriptures themselves make clear; this command is not to be universalized.
2. Since life belongs to God, any harm caused due to specific purposes in a specific context would be overshadowed by divine benefits in the afterlife.
3. While the infant would go to God's presence, the killer has not only taken another's life but also sinned (primarily) against God (cf. Ps. 51:4).
4. The killer is responsible for the consequences of his own actions— namely, taking innocent life. He is not responsible for granting heavenly life. The giver of heavenly benefit cannot be the human agent but only God himself (another agent).

So when the killer takes matters into his own hands, he is acting presumptuously. The killer is not benefiting the infant; he is only harming the infant. The killer brings only death, not benefits; it is *God* who bestows the benefit of heavenly life. The killer isn't "responsible" for getting an infant to heaven; he isn't the one bestowing the highly valued benefit. The killer neither *causes* these benefits nor is *responsible for* them.[18]

By contrast, in this worst-case scenario, God commands the Israelite soldiers to take the lives of some civilians, including children. In this special circumstance, the soldiers *would be* instruments of bringing heavenly life to these young ones. Given God's specific purposes, this scenario would differ from the infanticide committed by, say, Susan Smith, who strapped her children into her car and let it roll into a lake. No, Smith *didn't* "give" her children a better life in heaven by drowning them. She defied God's purposes and sinned against God and her children.

Humans and the Worm's-Eye View

The book of Job sheds helpful light, reminding us that the full picture is not always available to us. We aren't necessarily in the best position to decipher God's purposes. Like Job, we may find ourselves left with a puzzling gap between what we clearly know of God and what seems to be a harsh exception. (Job's friends certainly thought they had the correct perspective regarding "when bad things happen to good people.") Though blameless yet severely afflicted, Job received no answers to his questions. And while he did eventually receive his audience with God, he still received no answer to his "why" question. Though baffled as ever, Job did obtain assurances of God's wisdom, which far surpasses ours. He learned that God's character is trustworthy and his presence sufficient, even when we remain stumped in the face of unanswered questions.

Back in 1997, my family was involved in a serious auto accident on a county highway in rural Wisconsin. The other driver tried to avoid a dog and struck our van instead. Peter, our second child, was five at the time. He was injured when his head struck the side window, resulting in a skull fracture and multi-layered lacerations to his forehead. He needed several surgeries—and daily applications of a sticky ointment called Kelo-cote—to get his forehead back to normal. Our last great task was removing Peter's postsurgical bandage from his crusted-over-but-healing forehead. (Previous experience told us this was at least a two-person operation.) We had talked up the event as a momentous occasion to celebrate. But Peter screamed, cried, resisted, and tried to run away, as though we were trying to harm him. An ignorant eavesdropper outside the bathroom door—no, the house!—could possibly have concluded that we were evil torturers.

No doubt, children may draw all sorts of faulty conclusions about their "immoral" parents simply because they don't understand what their parents are doing. Parents, in order to train their children, may seem overly strict when they insist that kids apologize even when they don't feel like it. Parents may appear tyrannical when they override the freedom of a child who happens to be making all the wrong decisions about friendships or dubious activities. Parents may do things that strike their young children as utterly out of character or even immoral, yet the problem will be resolved with further information or the maturity of years and experience.[19] Couldn't the Canaanite question fit into this category?

Think again of Frodo in *The Lord of the Rings*. He tells his faithful friend, "I can't do this, Sam." But Sam tries to put his task in proper perspective:

I know. It's all wrong. By rights we shouldn't even be here. But we are. It's like in the great stories, Mr. Frodo—the ones that really mattered. Full of darkness and danger, they were. And sometimes you didn't want to know the end. Because how could the end be happy? How could the world go back to the way it was when so much bad had happened? But in the end, it's only a passing thing, this shadow. Even darkness must pass. A new day will come. And when the sun shines, it will shine out the clearer. Those were the stories that stayed with you—that meant something—even if you were too small to understand why.[20]

Likewise, we may not be in the best position to understand the nature of God's commands regarding the Canaanites in light of his overarching purposes. Perhaps we have more of a worm's-eye view than we would like to think. As Isaiah 55:8–9 affirms: " 'For My thoughts are not your thoughts, nor are your ways My ways,' declares the LORD. 'For as the heavens are higher than the earth, so are My ways higher than your ways and My thoughts than your thoughts.' "

Several stanzas in William Cowper's hymn "God Moves in a Mysterious Way" express quite well the gap that exists between God and us—and how we may misperceive what God is doing:

> Judge not the Lord by feeble sense,
> But trust Him for His grace;
> Behind a frowning providence
> He hides a smiling face.
>
> His purposes will ripen fast,
> Unfolding every hour;
> The bud may have a bitter taste,
> But sweet will be the flower.
>
> Blind unbelief is sure to err
> And scan His work in vain;
> God is His own interpreter,
> And He will make it plain.[21]

Jesus and the Bigger Picture

As we grapple with difficult Old Testament questions, we can go beyond Job's limited perspective to glimpse God more clearly, as revealed in Jesus. In Christ's incarnation and atoning death, we see how the God of Abraham, Isaac, and Jacob brings his unfolding purposes to fulfillment. As the Israelites had hoped, God showed up on the scene, though not in the way they had anticipated. He stooped to share our lot, enduring life's temptations, injustices, sufferings, and cruelties. However we view the Canaanite question, God's heart is concerned with redemption. This becomes especially evident in how low God was willing to go for our salvation, dying naked on a cross, enduring scorn and shame, and suffering the fate of a criminal or slave. Michael Card's song "This Must Be the Lamb" depicts this powerfully. He writes that the religious leaders mocked Christ's true calling, laughing at his fate, "blind to the fact that it was God limping by."[22]

Since God was willing to go through all of this for our salvation, the Christian can reply to the critic, "While I can't tidily solve the problem of the Canaanites, I can trust a God who has proven his willingness to go to such excruciating lengths—and depths—to offer rebellious humans reconciliation and friendship." However we're to interpret and respond to some of the baffling questions raised by the Old Testament, we shouldn't stop with the Old Testament if we want a clearer revelation of the heart and character of God.

In the New Testament, God redeems his enemies through Christ's substitutionary, self-sacrificial, shame-bearing act of love (Rom. 5:10). Though a Canaanite-punishing God strikes us as incompatible with graciousness and compassion, we cannot escape a redeeming God who loves his enemies, not simply his friends (Matt. 5:43–48). Indeed, he allows himself to be crucified *by* his enemies in hopes of redeeming them: "Father, forgive them; for they do not know what they are doing" (Luke 23:34).

Further Reading

Goldingay, John. *Old Testament Theology: Israel's Life*. Vol. 3. Downers Grove, IL: InterVarsity, 2009. See esp. chap. 5, "City and Nation."

Hess, Richard S. "War in the Hebrew Bible: An Overview." In *War in the Bible and Terrorism in the Twenty-First Century*, edited by Richard S. Hess and Elmer A. Martens. Winona Lake, IN: Eisenbrauns, 2008.

Wright, Christopher J. H. *The God I Don't Understand*. Grand Rapids: Zondervan, 2008.

———. *Old Testament Ethics and the People of God*. Downers Grove, IL: InterVarsity, 2006.

18

The Root of All Evil?

Does Religion Cause Violence?

In Mark Juergensmeyer's book *Terror in the Mind of God*, he claims that religion is violent by nature. How so? It tends to "absolutize and to project images of cosmic war"—even if a religion's ultimate goal is peace and order. Juergensmeyer's recommendation? Injecting into religion the softening Enlightenment values of "rationality and fair play"; this will help stop the violence and killing to produce peace and harmony in this world.[1]

Three years earlier, Regina Schwartz wrote *The Curse of Cain*, challenging the "violent legacy of monotheism" (which includes Judaism, Islam, and Christianity). Belief in one God (monotheism) and exclusive truth claims go hand in hand, which allegedly leads to problems for everybody else. Those embracing the "one true God" will reject, hate, and remove all outsiders, who don't accept their God or their worldview.[2] Monotheism and exclusive truth claims create an us-them mentality: to preserve *our* identity and religious purity, *they* must be removed. This is what Richard Dawkins means about Israel's God being obsessed with "his own superiority over rival gods and with the exclusiveness of his chosen desert tribe."[3]

That's why Cain, whose offering was rejected by God in favor of his brother Abel's, rose up and murdered him. Likewise, God unfairly chose the younger Jacob over Esau, which produced conflict between them. For similar reasons, the chosen Israelites ended up killing the un-chosen Canaanites; God was on Israel's side, not the Canaanites'. Alienation and murder are the predictable results of monotheism. So we shouldn't be surprised by acts like the September 11 terrorist attacks—the very claim the New Atheists make.[4] The alternative to coercive religion would be Enlightenment values of tolerance favoring diversity and pluralism; these values generously welcome outsiders and don't stifle creativity.

Do We Just Need Enlightenment Values?

To the contrary, we could argue that we don't need less religion and more Enlightenment values. Ironically, the barbarity of the Enlightenment's French Revolution turned the pursuit of liberty, equality, and fraternity into inhumanity and a nightmare of cruelty. As many have argued, institutionalizing pluralism and diversity in society can have the effect of excluding and eliminating traditional religion from the conversation.

Properly understood, we actually need more religion, not less. But we need the right kind of religious values, not simply anything that calls itself religious (think Jim Jones, David Koresh, and jihadists). When given proper consideration, a truly biblical worldview should have a place at the table given its foundation for morality and its positive culture-shaping influence, a point we'll explore in the last chapters. The biblical faith actually supports tolerance: despite our disagreements, human beings are still God's image-bearers, and we are to seek to live at peace with all insofar as we're able (Rom. 12:18). It supports diversity: because of Christ's death, he has broken down dividing walls of race, class, and gender (Gal. 3:28; Eph. 2:11–22). While the apostle Paul talks about warfare, he refers to *spiritual* warfare in Ephesians 6. But while we can bracket the topic of fighting a just war (e.g., to stop Nazi aggression), the Christian's war doesn't require earthly weapons (2 Cor. 10:4). The kind of conquest Paul calls for is overcoming evil with good (Rom. 12:21).

So we're not talking about generic religion, as though all religions are alike and that any one religion is as harmful as the next. Also, we should ask if a religion is true. Does it square with and explain reality? We shouldn't make the mistake the conquering Assyrians did, who "spoke of the God of Jerusalem as of the gods of the peoples of the earth, the work of men's hands" (2 Chron. 32:19). So when we're talking about more religion, we're also talking about one that's true.

What about Schwartz's claim that monotheism leads to violence? It's hard to see how God's *oneness* could lead to violence in itself. For one thing, Schwartz ignores Old Testament references to God's grace, compassion, patience, and mercy (e.g., Exod. 34:6–7). Theologian Miroslav Volf argues that if one gets rid of monotheism, "the division and violence between 'us' and 'them' hardly disappears."[5] In the eyes of pagan, Roman, emperor-worshiping polytheists (i.e., worshipers of many gods), Christians were persecuted as atheists: belief in one God was close enough. Ironically, monotheistic Christians were singled out for attack by the diversity-affirming religionists in the Mediterranean world!

Beyond this, history (in addition to tomorrow's headlines) is littered with not-necessarily monotheistic tribes warring against each other or this communist government attacking that religious group. And why the focus on religion per se? Why not attack politics and political abuses of religion? What about ethnic tribalism that gives rise to hostility and violence, as in the former Yugoslavia? Why not consider complex sociological and historical factors that contribute to conflict? Alienation, poverty, disempowerment, racism/tribalism, power structures, historical feuding, and animosity may give rise to anger and then to violence. Religion often turns out to be the label used to justify violence between warring parties.

So why think that religion is the *sole* factor, the entire cause of blame? Rather than dragging God into the situation to cover over the root problem(s), we should resist the manipulation of God for our purposes. And what about the positive effects of a religion? What if more benefit than harm comes from a particular religion? The notion that religion *causes* violence or harm typically obscures a complexity of factors involved.

Raising Cain

What of Schwartz's problem of Cain? God didn't choose Abel *at the expense of Cain*. God had warned Cain of his sinful attitude, saying that he must master the sin that is "crouching at the door" (Gen. 4:7). Cain could have offered an acceptable sacrifice if his resentment had turned to humility. Though Cain was angry and his "countenance fell" (4:5–6), God reminded him that such a condition wasn't inevitable: "If you do well, will not your countenance be lifted up?" (v. 7). Plainly, God didn't favor Abel at Cain's expense. In fact, even after Cain killed Abel, God still granted a protective grace to Cain.

The same applies to Jacob and Esau. Though Esau didn't receive the inheritance rights, he was still reconciled to his trickster brother at story's end (Gen. 33:4). Esau succeeded while Cain failed. God shouldn't be blamed in either scenario. And when it comes to Israel and the nations, God's choosing Israel didn't exclude other nations from salvation (e.g., Rahab, Ruth, Nineveh in Jonah's day). Indeed, God's desire is to include all who will come to him.

Even within Israel, God chose the tribe of Judah, through which the Davidic Messiah would come. Again, this was a means of bringing salvation to the Jews but also to the Gentiles. Just because God chose to work through Judah, who had a besmirched reputation (Gen. 37:23–27; 38), didn't mean that Joseph (a man of faith and integrity) couldn't experience salvation or receive God's blessing through trust and obedience.

Besides this, consider how some persons are more intelligent, athletic, artistic, or pleasant looking than others. We don't have perfect equality here, except in the dignity and worth of each individual. Yes, those apparently less endowed can become resentful or jealous of those seemingly more endowed, *or* one can recognize the graces one has received and constructively deal with disappointments. In fact, some of the presumed assets of money, good looks, or intelligence can actually be spiritual hindrances and sources of pride and self-sufficiency.

Think of the blind hymn writer Fanny Crosby (1820–1915). When she was six weeks old, a doctor applied the wrong medicine—a hot poultice—on her inflamed eyes, which resulted in permanent blindness. Rather than becoming resentful, she vowed to be content with her lot in life. She wrote some of the most uplifting hymns sung by Christians such as "To God Be the Glory, Great Things He Hath Done" and "Jesus Keep Me Near the Cross." Reflecting on her blindness, she wrote these stanzas:

> Oh what a happy soul I am,
> Although I cannot see;
> I am resolved that in this world
> Contented I will be.
> How many blessings I enjoy,
> That other people don't;
> To weep and sigh because I'm blind,
> I cannot, and I won't.[6]

The Rights of Self-Exclusion

Schwartz's problem is that she hasn't taken the doctrine of the Trinity seriously enough. The Triune God—Father, Son, and Spirit—is not a self-enclosed deity. He graciously creates human beings to share in his life, joy, and goodness. God is indeed humble and other-centered, serving his creatures and showing kindness to all (Matt. 5:45). A central distinguishing feature of God—and of those who take his rule seriously—is love for one's enemies. This isn't the easy love of being good to those who are good to us but the tough, gritty, and most complete love over all other types of love (Matt. 5:46–48).

Someone may object: "Isn't there the doctrine of hell, the ultimate exclusion? Why doesn't God show absolute hospitality to all without exclusion? Isn't this the truly peaceful alternative?" Miroslav Volf astutely observes that "absolute hospitality" becomes difficult when the unrepentant perpetrators sit down with their unhealed, violated victims. Such a perverse view of hospitality would actually "enthrone violence because it would leave the violators unchanged and the consequences of violence unremedied."[7] The older brother in the prodigal son story (Luke 15) was left with a decision: would he stay outside to sulk and pout, or would he come in to celebrate the return of his younger brother and thus show honor to his gracious father?

Hell itself is the act of self-exclusion from God, the final act of self-assertion and control. If we want a divorce from God, he will grant it. Hell isn't a torture chamber of everlasting fire. Hell is ultimately a realm of self-separation and quarantine from God's presence (2 Thess. 1:9). Spirit beings (the devil and his angels) will have the final separation from God that they desire. C. S. Lewis puts it this way:

> I would pay any price to be able to say truthfully "All will be saved." But my reason retorts, "Without their will, or with it?" If I say "Without their will" I at once perceive a contradiction; how can the supreme voluntary act of self-surrender be involuntary? If I say "With their will," my reason replies "How if they *will not* give in?"[8]

No, the problem isn't religion, although many religiously inspired actions are certainly perverse and grotesque. In the Old Testament, we see that God desires to include Jew *and Gentile*, friend *and enemy* alike in his saving purposes. When we come to the New Testament, this vision of one people from all ethnic groups is finally being realized.

Properly understood, the Christian faith (and not some generic category called religion), with its doctrine of the self-giving and other-centered Trinity, is actually a beacon of hope for peacemaking and reconciliation (Rom. 5:6–11; Eph. 2:14–17). Some may refuse to participate and continue the conflict, but that is not the fault of the Christian faith.

What about the Crusades?

Critics mention the Crusades as evidence for the violence of Christianity. We can readily admit that the Crusades, the Inquisition, and Europe's religious wars were a tragedy, a blot on the history of Christendom. But do these events reflect the *essence* of Christianity? All this talk of religion causing war raises questions of its own. What do we mean by religion? Every religion that has ever existed? Confucianism, Buddhism, Baha'i, Christian Science, Jehovah's Witnesses? And the religion-war connection assumes that religion has little connection to truth. Any unique, authentic, honest-to-goodness divine revelation isn't even on the critics' radar screen. Nor is the question asked, Is violence imbedded in this particular religious tradition, or is it utterly inconsistent with that particular religion?

Those who (rightly) critique the Crusades as morally misguided will go further to lump the Crusades with Islamic jihad. Doing so is a mistake, and I can only sketch out the generalities here.[9] The Arabic term *jihad* means "struggle," which can encompass inner, intellectual, or moral struggle as well as militant, violent struggle. However, the more traditional Islamic understanding of jihad is the violent kind that has characterized the sweep of Islam's history; there's little support for jihad as mere spiritual/internal struggle.[10]

Even if we compare the Crusades with militant, aggressive Islamic jihad, the Crusades come out looking considerably better:

The Crusades (1095–1291)	Jihad in Islam
The Crusades lasted about two hundred years.	Jihad has been ongoing for more than thirteen hundred years.
The Crusades have been criticized as the beginning of imperialism.	Muhammad's imperialistic jihad expeditions began more than five hundred years prior to the Crusades.
The Crusades began as an effort to recapture from Muslims land once occupied by Christians.	Jihad began with the intent to take Christianized territory never occupied by Muslims, to establish the umma (Islamic community).
Jesus, in whose name the Crusades were fought, did not teach or exemplify violence against those who refused his message.	Muhammad not only preached violence against nonbelievers but also engaged in it himself in over sixty aggressive military campaigns.
The earliest followers of Jesus and those who wrote the New Testament didn't advocate violence. In its earliest centuries, the politically powerless Christian faith expanded through deeds of love and communicating the life-changing news of Christ.	The Qur'an includes many militant, aggressive texts. After Muhammad's death, Islam was extended far and wide through violence. It overran previously Christianized areas and regularly posed a threat to established Christendom (e.g., Spain, France, Vienna).

Consider the comments of Bernard Lewis, the leading Western scholar on Islam. He nicely summarizes the significant differences between Islamic jihad and the Crusades—despite both being waged as holy wars against infidel enemies for the true religion:

> The Crusade is a late development in Christian history and, in a sense, marks a radical departure from basic Christian values as expressed in the Gospels. Christendom had been under attack since the seventh century, and had lost vast territories to Muslim rule; the concept of holy war, more commonly a just war, was familiar since antiquity. Yet in the long struggle between Islam and Christendom, the Crusade was late, limited, and of relatively brief duration. Jihad is present from the beginning of Islamic history—in scripture, in the life of the Prophet, and in the actions of his companions and immediate successors. It has continued throughout Islamic history and retains its appeal to the present day. The word *crusade* derives of course from the cross [Latin, *crux*] and originally denoted a holy war for Christianity. But in the Christian world it has long since lost that meaning. . . . *Jihad* too is used in a variety of senses, but unlike *crusade* it has retained its original, primary meaning.[11]

Critics of the Crusades or the Inquisition are certainly correct that the Christian shouldn't advocate atrocities or execution for heresy in the name of Jesus. And we should ask the critics, "Why select these *anti*-Christian events as exhibits A and B for the Christian faith rather than looking to the example and teachings of Jesus himself, not to mention Francis of Assisi, Martin Luther King Jr., Mother Teresa, William Wilberforce, and other Christian peacemakers?" Indeed, atrocity and theological reigns of terror carried out in Jesus's name oppose all that Jesus stood for in his ministry.

Are Yahweh Wars in the Old Testament Just Like Islamic Jihad?

Though I address this topic in more detail elsewhere,[12] we should probably say something about the common accusation, "Aren't the Old Testament's Yahweh wars just like militant Islamic jihad?"

We should keep in mind that Islam traditionally has divided the world into two realms: "the abode of Islam/peace" (*dar al-Islam/salam*), where Islam dominates, and "the abode of war" (*dar al-harb*), where the rule of Islam should be extended—by war, if necessary. Islam is a dominant creed. Traditionally, the Muslim attitude toward non-Muslims has been ruler versus ruled, victor versus vanquished. Indeed, ancient Islam never gave thought to a Muslim living under a non-Muslim government.[13]

Offensive warfare and quashing the opposition has been the heart of Islam from the very beginning. (1) Its founder Muhammad engaged in over sixty military campaigns; (2) the Qur'an contains many harsh, aggressive, and militaristic passages; (3) ever since Muhammad's death, his followers have spread Islam by violent means, often taking over vast segments of Christianized territories; (4) most Muslim countries today (with the exception of Mali and Senegal) have a terrible human rights record, and if most Muslims from these countries are to find political freedom, ironically, they must move to the West rather than stay in their country of origin.

Jewish Egyptian scholar Bat Ye'or has thoroughly documented the history of dhimmitude (the condition of Christians, Jews, and other non-Muslims [*dhimmis*] under Islamic law) in Muslim-dominated areas. Any Muslim tolerance shown to non-Muslims could always give way to militant jihad if tribute (*jizya*) wasn't paid to Muslims. Ye'or thoroughly documents the oppression and even "open extermination of Christian populations and the disappearance of Eastern Christian culture."[14]

The "myth of Muslim toleration," she says, didn't exist before the twentieth century. That is a modern creation of the West. It was the result of political and cultural difficulties once colonizing powers like England and France withdrew from North Africa and the Middle East—without the will to protect Christian minorities there. A whole literature developed praising Muslim tolerance toward Jews and Christians; they emerged for economic (think oil!) and political reasons. Not wanting to rock the boat, the withdrawing powers preferred an economically profitable pro-Islamic policy.[15] And though the Qur'an declares, "Let there be no compulsion in religion" (2:256), compulsion has been part of the Muslim mind-set from the beginning. This isn't to deny the presence of many peace-loving Muslims throughout the world; I myself have come to befriend many of them over the years. We can be most grateful for such peace-oriented Muslims, though perhaps more of them could speak out more forcefully against violence carried out in the name of Islam.

What then should we make of the comparison between Islamic jihad and the approved Yahweh wars in the Old Testament? Here's a brief overview of the key differences:

	Yahweh War in the Old Testament	Islamic Jihad
Geography	War was geographically limited to the Promised Land.	There are no geographic limitations to jihad. The non-Muslim world is the "abode of war."
Historical Length/ Limit	Such war was limited primarily to one generation (around the time of Joshua), though minor conflicts continued with persistent enemies of Israel.	There are no historical/temporal limitations to jihad.
Objects of War	War was to punish a hopelessly corrupted culture (morally and theologically), not because they were non-Israelites or even because they didn't worship Yahweh. This punishment came after a period of over four hundred years when the Canaanites' sin had ripened fully (Gen. 15:16).	Aggression/war is directed toward non-Muslims (including Christians and Jews—"people of the book").
Objects of God's Love	Yahweh loves even his enemies/ those who don't love him (cf. Gen. 12:3; Jonah). His redemptive plan encompasses the traditional enemies of Israel (Babylon, Assyria, Egypt) and incorporates them into the people of God.	God loves only those who love and obey him.
Standard of Morality	God's compassionate and gracious nature is the source of God's commands.	The Qur'an stresses God as sheer will (as opposed to a morally good nature), who commands whatever he likes.

	Yahweh War in the Old Testament	Islamic Jihad
Fulfilling God's Plan	The Messiah's kingdom is to be characterized by peace (Isa. 9:6; 11:1–10). In the New Testament, Jesus's task is to undermine the true enemy—Satan and his hosts (John 14:30; Eph. 6:10–18; Col. 2:15)—not Israel's political enemies.	Muhammad's military aggression is viewed by many Muslims as normative (which sets back the clock on what the Messiah came to fulfill, undermining God's ultimate purposes). Note: As traditionally understood, the Qur'an's tolerant verses are earlier and thus outweighed by the later more militant verses.
Normativity of War	Fighting against Canaanites was not intended to be normative and ongoing (having the force of divine commands) but unique. God has a new nonnationalistic covenant in mind for his people (Jer. 31; Ezek. 36).	The military aggression of Muhammad (Islam's founder), supported by the Qur'an's militarism, Islam's aggressive history, and present political realities in the Muslim countries suggest an intrinsic pattern.

Does religion cause violence? Is religion dangerous? To say yes to these questions would be a crass generalization. For one thing, this view fails to account for many variations within all the world's traditional religions, some of which are fairly tame and nonthreatening. Second, those who support this notion fail to ask whether militant texts in certain holy books are normative and permanent or unique and nonrepeatable. Third, this assumption doesn't distinguish between the essence of a religion and tragic abuses by its practitioners. Fourth, it doesn't consider truth in religion—that some religious viewpoint may actually be true and therefore its competitors would be in error where they disagree with the truth. Finally, the view that religion is dangerous because it excludes other views is itself incoherent. It leaves us wondering, "Doesn't this mushy pluralism exclude or marginalize the very 'narrow' religious views of, say, monotheism?" To make *any* truth claim is to assert that its opposite is false.

Further Reading

Copan, Paul. *When God Goes to Starbucks: A Guide to Everyday Apologetics.* Grand Rapids: Baker, 2008.

Volf, Miroslav. "Christianity and Violence." In *War in the Bible and Violence in the Twenty-First Century*, edited by Richard S. Hess and Elmer A. Martens. Winona Lake, IN: Eisenbrauns, 2008.

Ye'or, Bat. *Islam and Dhimmitude: Where Civilizations Collide.* Teaneck, NJ: Farleigh Dickinson University Press, 2002.

PART 4

Sharpening the Moral Focus

19

Morality without a Lawgiving God?

The Divine Foundation of Goodness

Christopher Hitchens throws down the gauntlet: "I defy you, or anyone, to name one more deed that I would not do, unless I . . . became a Christian."[1] Sam Harris writes of the "myth of secular moral chaos"—that is, morality and social order don't need God or religion as their basis. After all, there are plenty of moral atheists and many immoral religious devotees. He rejects the notion that rape or killing children is wrong just because God says so.[2]

Likewise, Daniel Dennett challenges the notion that goodness is opposed to scientific materialism: "There is *no reason at all* why a disbelief in the immateriality or immortality of the soul should make a person less caring, less moral, less committed to the well-being of everybody on Earth than somebody who believes in 'the spirit.'" He adds that a "good scientific materialist" can be just as concerned about "whether there is plenty of justice, love, joy, beauty, political freedom, and yes, even religious freedom" as the "deeply spiritual." Indeed, those calling themselves spiritual can be "cruel, arrogant, self-centered, and utterly unconcerned about the moral problems of the world."[3]

In his BBC antireligious documentary *The Root of All Evil?* Richard Dawkins insists that kindness, generosity, and goodness can be found in human nature and that Darwinism explains this. How? We have altruistic genes. We're genetically wired to scratch another's back. In other words, genes create morality; God or religion doesn't. We humans have a moral conscience and a mutual empathy that are constantly evolving.[4]

The message from all of these atheists is loud and clear: people can be moral without believing in God. A more careful examination reveals that the New Atheists are right on one level but wrong on another.

A Matter of Consistency?

Though accusing Yahweh of being a moral monster, Dawkins has his own problem: he has gone on record *denying* the very existence of evil and goodness.

> If the universe were just electrons and selfish genes, meaningless tragedies . . . are exactly what we should expect, along with equally meaningless *good* fortune. Such a universe would be neither evil nor good in intention. . . . The universe we observe has precisely the properties we should expect if there is, at bottom, no design, no purpose, no evil and no good, nothing but blind pitiless indifference.[5]

In *A Devil's Chaplain*, he asserts, "Science has no methods for deciding what is ethical. That is a matter for individuals and for society."[6] If science alone gives us knowledge, as Dawkins claims, then how can he consider God's actions immoral or religion the root of all evil? As we'll see, Dawkins is helping himself to the metaphysical resources of a worldview he repudiates.

Knowing vs. Being

Let's be clear: the New Atheists *are* absolutely correct that we don't need to believe in God or follow the Bible to have a general knowledge of what's right and wrong. Like theists, atheists have been made in God's image, and they can recognize the same sorts of virtues and behaviors, as atheists themselves like to point out. Having been made in the divine image, we've been designed to function properly by living morally. So if we take our conscience seriously (as we see Gentiles should have done in Amos 1–2), we can get a lot right morally. Those denying that kindness is a virtue or that torturing babies for fun is wrong don't need an argument; they need psychological and spiritual help! They're suffering from moral malfunction. When people tell me, "Well, the 9/11 terrorists sincerely believed they were doing what was right," I reply, "A lot of people in psychiatric wards sincerely believe they're Alexander the Great, Julius Caesar, or Napoleon Bonaparte!" Sincerity isn't necessarily an indication of proper function.

Some atheists will say that we know rape is wrong because it violates the victim's rights and rips apart the social fabric. The problem with moral atheism, though, is that it doesn't go far enough. Notice how atheists who believe in real right and wrong make a massive intellectual leap of faith. They believe that somehow moral facts were eternally part of the "furniture" of reality but that from impersonal and valueless slime, human persons possessing rights, dignity, worth, and duties were eventually produced. These moral truths were "anticipating" the evolution of morally valuable human beings who would have duties to obey them. Yes, atheists can *know* that rape is wrong, but that's no surprise if they have been made in the image of God, whom they refuse to acknowledge. The more fundamental question that atheism seems unable to answer is: How did they come to *be* rights-bearing, valuable persons?[7] The problem isn't one of *knowing*; it's one of *being*.

Let's change the scenario from a rape on the street to the use of a date rape drug at a party. Wanting to get what he wants, a young man places this drug into the drink of an unsuspecting woman. Suppose he's nice enough to take certain precautions so that there are no obvious consequences to his actions. The woman wakes up later not knowing the difference. Why is this act still so repugnant? After all, the woman doesn't know anything, the guy had his pleasure, and no one is the wiser. And why should Dawkins be outraged at such an action? After all, as Dawkins says, human beings simply "dance" to the music of their DNA.[8] If there's a deviation from genetically produced kindness and generosity, it's not truly *immoral*; it's just a genetic glitch.

It's wrong to rape a girl—whether she knows what's happening or not—because she has intrinsic dignity and rights. For the same reason, it's wrong to mock and insult the mentally challenged even if they don't seem to be hurt by these verbal assaults. Where then do dignity and rights come from in a world of electrons and selfish genes? The doctrine of the image of God supports our strongest intuitions that humans aren't objects to use and abuse but persons who should be respected and treated fairly before the law.

Intrinsically valuable, thinking persons don't come from impersonal, nonconscious, unguided, valueless processes over time. A personal, self-aware, purposeful, good God provides the much-needed context that a God-less universe just can't. Personhood and morality are necessarily connected; moral values are rooted in personhood. Without God (a personal Being), no persons—and thus no moral values—would exist at all. Only if God exists can moral properties be realized.

Some atheists will claim that moral values are "just there"—necessary truths that are part of the furniture of the universe. If that's the case, as we just noted, then what a whopping cosmic coincidence that these moral laws were somehow *anticipating* the eventual emergence of moral creatures who would have duties to obey these laws. God's existence and creation of humans makes better sense of the connection between genuine, universal moral standards (rooted in God's nature) and human dignity and worth.

Even secular ethical systems—whether variations on the ethical views of the philosophers Aristotle or Kant or perhaps some social contract view—may affirm many truths that believers in God affirm. These systems may agree that we ought to carry out certain moral obligations or cultivate certain character qualities. Even so, these systems are still incomplete because they don't offer a basis for human dignity and worth.

The Hitchens Challenge

What about the Hitchens challenge? Can we name one moral virtue in a Christian that an atheist like Hitchens doesn't have? Yes! How about not honoring God or giving him thanks (Rom. 1:21)? What about the sin of human self-sufficiency and the refusal to submit to God's authority (Ps. 2)? What about Hitchens's despising God's offer of salvation or his refusal to depend on God's grace (Matt. 23:37)? If the two great commands are to love God fully and to love one's neighbor as oneself, and Hitchens is as good as he says he is, then he *still* flunks the test at 50 percent. He has rejected the "great and foremost command" (Matt. 22:38–39).

I wonder if Hitchens worries about things; he isn't interested in casting his cares on the One who cares for him (1 Peter 5:7). Does Hitchens love his enemies and do good to them (Matt. 5:44)? Does he take God's name in vain (Exod. 20:7)? Does he forgive others as he has been offered forgiveness (Eph. 4:32)?

Perhaps we can take things a step further. Guenter Lewy, the agnostic political scientist who taught at the University of Massachusetts, has observed that there are some moral virtues that atheism is unlikely to produce:

> Adherents of [a naturalistic] ethic are not likely to produce a Dorothy Day or a Mother Teresa. Many of these people love humanity but not individual human beings with all their failings and shortcomings. They will be found participating in demonstrations for causes such as nuclear disarmament but not sitting at the bedside of a dying person. An ethic of moral autonomy and individual rights, so important to secular liberals, is incapable of sustaining and nourishing values such as altruism and self-sacrifice.[9]

Along these lines, the Christian writer Malcolm Muggeridge wrote that he spent many years in India and Africa, where he witnessed "much righteous endeavor undertaken by Christians of all denominations." By contrast, however, "I never, as it happens, came across a hospital or orphanage run by the Fabian Society or a Humanist leper colony."[10] Even if we consider such undertakings of self-sacrifice morally praiseworthy and even heroic, they don't seem to be very biologically advantageous.

Can Naturalistic Evolution Explain Morality?

Dawkins claims that kindness and generosity are rooted in our genes. We've developed an awareness of morality that proves to be biologically beneficial. Although I go into more detail on this question elsewhere, let me offer a few responses here.

Why Trust Our Genes?

If we're nothing more than the products of naturalistic evolution trying to fight, feed, flee, and reproduce, why trust the convictions of our minds—whether about truth or morality? If we're just dancing to our DNA—over which we have absolutely no control—how do we know we're right about anything? We'd only be accidentally right, but this can't be called knowledge. As Charles Darwin mused, "With me the horrid doubt always arises whether the convictions of man's mind, which has been developed from the mind of the lower animals, are of any value or at all trustworthy. Would any one trust in the convictions of a monkey's mind, if there are any convictions in such a mind?"[11]

We could accidentally believe true things that help us to survive. But we could just as well have many *false* beliefs that help us to survive. For example, we might be hardwired to believe that humans are valuable and have rights or that we have moral duties to perform. Such beliefs might help us survive as a species, but they would be completely false.

The naturalistic evolutionary process is interested in fitness or survival, not in true belief. So not only is objective morality undermined, but so is rational thought. According to atheistic evolutionists Michael Ruse and E. O. Wilson, morality is a "corporate illusion" that has been "fobbed off on us by our genes to get us to cooperate."[12] We *think* we really ought to love little children, but we're wrong to conclude that right and wrong really exist. This illusion that we have moral duties is compelling and strong. Without it, we'd ignore or disobey our moral impulses. However, having moral *inclinations* is far different from having moral *duties*, which brings us to our next point.

Moving from "Is" to "Ought"

According to the skeptic Michael Shermer, whom Dawkins approvingly cites, asking "Why should we be moral?" is like wondering "Why should we be hungry or horny?" Shermer insists that "the answer is that it is as much a part of human nature to be moral as it is to be hungry, horny, jealous, and in love."[13] Such drives are hardwired into us by evolution. But as C. S. Lewis noted, moral impulses, given such hardwiring conditions, are no more true (or false) "than a vomit or a yawn."[14] Thinking "I ought" is on the same level of "I itch." Indeed, "my impulse to serve posterity is just the same sort of thing as my fondness for cheese" or preferring mild or bitter beer.[15]

In effect, all Shermer can do is describe how human beings *actually* function, but he can't prescribe how humans *ought* to behave. There's no difference between whether I ought to be moral and whether I ought to be hungry, since both are functions of evolutionary hardwiring. These states just *are*.

If, on the other hand, humans are made in the image of God and have value from the start, then we don't have to wonder about how to move from the "is" of nature to the "ought" of genuine moral obligation. A supremely valuable Being is at the heart of reality; no is-ought problem exists if theism is true.

Arbitrary Morality

Ruse and Wilson report that instead of evolving from "savannah-dwelling primates," we, like termites, could have evolved needing "to dwell in darkness, eat each other's [waste], and cannibalise the dead." If the latter were the case, we would "extol such acts as beautiful and moral" and "find it morally disgusting to live in the open air, dispose of body waste and bury the dead."[16] So our awareness of morality ("a sense of right and wrong and a feeling of obligation to be thus governed") is of "biological worth," serves as "an aid to survival," and "has no being beyond this."[17] Naturalistic morality is arbitrary and could have developed in opposite directions. We happen to admire the morality that evolution has passed on to us, but we could be singing the praises of the very opposite morality for the same reasons: we dance to our DNA.

To further illustrate, consider the book *A Natural History of Rape*, co-authored by a biologist and an anthropologist.[18] The upshot of the book is that rape can be explained biologically: when a male cannot find a mate, his subconscious drive to reproduce his own species makes him force himself upon a female. After all, such acts happen in the animal kingdom with, say, male mallards or scorpion flies. The authors don't advocate rape; in fact, they claim that rapists aren't excused for their (mis)behavior. But if the rape impulse happens to be embedded into human nature from antiquity and if it bestows biological advantage, how can the authors suggest that this behavior *ought* to be ended? The authors' resistance to rape, despite its naturalness, suggests objective moral values that transcend nature. An ethic rooted in nature appears to leave us with arbitrary morality. Theism, on the other hand, begins with value; the is-ought gulf is easily bridged.

Again, it's hard to see how the naturalist/atheist can move from material, valueless, nonconscious processes to the production of valuable, rights-bearing human beings. From valuelessness, valuelessness comes. Matter doesn't have the capacity to produce value. Physics textbooks don't include goodness or even consciousness in their attempted definitions of matter.

By contrast, the God hypothesis doesn't force us to make a huge leap from valuelessness to value. Rather, we begin with value (God's good character), and we end with value (divine image-bearing humans with moral responsibility and rights). A good God effectively bridges the chasm between is and ought. Value exists from the very beginning; it is rooted in a self-existent, good God. So for all their criticisms of religion, New Atheists still lack the moral foundations to justify genuine moral criticism of theism, nor can atheism truly ground moral value or human dignity and worth.

Further Reading

Copan, Paul. "God, Naturalism, and the Foundations of Morality." In *The Future of Atheism: Alister McGrath and Daniel Dennett in Dialogue*, edited by Robert Stewart. Minneapolis: Fortress Press, 2008.

————. "*True for You, but Not for Me*": *Overcoming Common Objections to Christian Faith*. 2nd ed. Minneapolis: Bethany House, 2009.

Copan, Paul, and Mark D. Linville. *The Moral Argument*. New York: Continuum Press, forthcoming.

Hare, John. *Why Bother Being Good? The Place of God in the Moral Life*. Downers Grove, IL: InterVarsity, 2002.

20

We Have Moved beyond This God (Haven't We?)

Jesus as the Fulfiller of the Old Testament

The Gifts of the Jews

On February 16, 1809, John Adams wrote a letter to F. A. Vanderkemp in which he insisted that "the Hebrews have done more to civilize man than any other nation." Not only did their laws help bring a civilizing influence to the nations, but they preserved and propagated to humankind "the doctrine of a supreme, intelligent, wise, almighty sovereign of the universe, which I believe to be the great essential principle of all morality, and consequently of all civilization."[1]

In his fascinating book *The Gifts of the Jews*, Thomas Cahill reinforces this argument. This ancient nomadic desert tribe helped introduce to humanity a sense of history—a past, present, and future—and the idea that history is going somewhere, that it has a point.[2] For the Mesopotamians, Egyptians, and other ancient peoples, time was cyclical—the same old same old. We could say the same about many Eastern philosophies and religions today; they espouse the doctrine of karma with its reincarnation cycles of birth, death, and rebirth.

What's more, the Old Testament reveals a God who has a global (cosmic) plan and who involves humans as history-shaping participants in that plan. Yes, humans matter. The Old Testament's genealogies reflect the important role that humans play in the unfolding of God's purposes.

On top of this, the Jews introduced a robust monotheism. Rather than being just one god in a pantheon of others or just a regional deity, Yahweh was/is the only deity who matters. Indeed, he is the only one who exists. Along with this, the Jews introduced a new way to experience reality. There is a divine being who regularly, personally engages humans, whose choices really make a difference. Human decision making has great significance, and God interweaves these choices into his overarching plans. We're not the pawns of fate or at the mercy of the whims of the gods. On the other hand, humans aren't so powerful that they can manipulate God to do their bidding. These themes are some of the gifts of the Jews to the rest of the world.

The Gifts of the Christians

Horrendous, anti-Christian actions have been carried out in the name of Christ: the Crusades, the Inquisition, witch-hunting, or fighting between Catholics and Protestants in Europe could be named. Not that Jesus wants to be identified with this kind of religious zealotry. Many things can be done in God's name that cause it to be "blasphemed among the Gentiles" (Rom. 2:24).

The problem with Christopher Hitchens's claim that "religion poisons everything" is that it's both vague and extreme. The term *religion* in the existing literature is notoriously vague and difficult to define. And if Dennett and Hitchens suggest that Stalin was somehow "religious," then at this point we throw up our hands in bewilderment. Hitchens's statement about religion's noxious influence is also extreme in its lopsidedness. Does religion poison everything and bring no benefits whatsoever? More thoughtful, sophisticated atheists would strongly disagree. As atheist philosopher Walter Sinnott-Armstrong responds, this religion-poisons-everything slogan is "inaccurate and insulting." He advises atheists not to cheer on or laugh at Hitchens's jokes, nor should they remain silent. To Sinnott-Armstrong, Hitchens's critique of religion is "like a senile relative" who is constantly making "bizarre statements"; his assessment is neither fair nor very illuminating.[3]

Ironically, the New Atheists' moral grenades lobbed against the Christian faith in the name of morality are actually historically founded upon the very faith they criticize. Historians have documented that the values of human rights, tolerance, social justice, and racial reconciliation are the legacy of the Christian faith, not some secular Enlightenment ideals. For all her flaws, the Christian church has played an important part in bringing huge benefits to civilization. This impact has often been inspired by devotion to Christ, which overflows to love for one's neighbor to the glory of God.

These documented achievements include the following:[4]

- Eradicating slavery: As the Christian faith spread into barbarian Europe after the fall of Rome, the practice of slavery dwindled. Slavery virtually died out in Europe by the Middle Ages, when Europe was well Christianized. When slavery reappeared, it was strongly opposed by dedicated believers among the Mennonites and Quakers as well as by Christian leaders such as theologian Richard Baxter, John Wesley, and William Wilberforce.

- Opposing infanticide and rescuing infants from exposure: This practice, common among the Greeks and Romans, was outlawed in the fourth century, under the influence of Christians.

- Eliminating gladiatorial games: These brutal games usually involved slaves and criminals. They were outlawed in the late fourth century in the East and the early fifth century in the West.

- Building hospitals and hospices: Unlike Greeks and Romans, early Christians were concerned about health care, looking after the sick and the dying. Once the Christian faith became official in the empire, this ministry expanded considerably. The Council of Nicea (AD 325) commissioned bishops to establish hospice care in every city where a church building existed. The first hospital was built under St. Basil in Caesarea (369). By the Middle Ages, hospitals existed throughout Europe. (Think too of Florence Nightingale, the founding of the Red Cross, and so on.)

- Elevating women's status/rights: Although feminists claim that the Christian faith puts women down and keeps them under, history shows the opposite. Though women have been routinely oppressed in most cultures, we see something different in Jesus's treatment of women (e.g., the Samaritan woman in John 4, or Mary and Martha in Luke 10:38–42). Luke's Gospel highlights the prominent place of women in Jesus's life and ministry. Early Christians routinely protected women and children from neglect and abuse.

- Founding Europe's and North America's great universities: The Sorbonne, Oxford, Harvard, Yale, and Princeton are some of the many notable universities established to God's glory. In Europe, many universities sprang forth from medieval monasteries; in America, the earliest and most notable universities began as institutions for training pastors and missionaries.

- Writing extraordinary works of literature: The remarkable literature of Christians inspired by their faith ranges from Augustine's *City of God* and Eusebius's *Ecclesiastical History* to Dante's *Comedy* and John

Milton's *Paradise Lost* to the works of J. R. R. Tolkein, C. S. Lewis, Flannery O'Connor, and Aleksandr Solzhenitsyn.

- Engaging in/writing about philosophy and theology and the life of reason: Some of the leading representatives include Augustine, Anselm, Thomas Aquinas, Blaise Pascal, Søren Kierkegaard, and Jonathan Edwards. Today, organizations such as the Society of Christian Philosophers and the Evangelical Philosophical Society attest to this ongoing tradition.

- Creating beautiful masterpieces of art, sculpture, and architecture: Think of Michelangelo, Rembrandt van Rijn, Peter Paul Rubens, or the Byzantine and gothic cathedrals.

- Establishing modern science: Modern science had its roots in the biblical conviction that the world was created by a rational God. For this reason, it was orderly and predictable, and it could be studied and understood by human minds. We could mention Isaac Newton, Galileo Galilei, Nicholas Copernicus, Johannes Kepler, Michael Faraday, William T. Kelvin, Robert Boyle, Anton Lavoisier, and many others.

- Composing brilliant music: The works of Johann Sebastian Bach, Georg F. Handel, Felix Mendelssohn, and Franz Joseph Haydn speak for themselves.

- Advocating human rights, democracy, political freedoms, concern for the poor: These themes are rooted in the biblical ideals that all humans are made in God's image, that they have dignity and worth, and that they are equal before the law.

It's difficult to exaggerate the impact that Jesus of Nazareth has had on history and the countless lives impacted by this one man's life and teaching—indeed, the transforming power of his cross and resurrection. The historian Jaroslav Pelikan remarked that by the changing of the calendar (to BC and AD according to "the year of our Lord") and other ways, "everyone is compelled to acknowledge that because of Jesus of Nazareth history will never be the same."[5]

Dawkins is quite wrong in asserting that the Christian faith—like Islam—was spread by the sword.[6] If he took an honest look at Christian history, he would have to acknowledge that the earliest Christian movement was one of the politically and socially disempowered. This movement was first called "the Way" (Acts 19:9, 23; 22:4; 24:14, 22) in honor of its Savior (John 14:6), and it often gathered to itself slaves and members of the lower classes. In the first three centuries, the church grew by deeds of love and mercy and the proclamation of the Good News of Jesus. Holy wars had no place in this nonviolent movement.

Rodney Stark—the respected eight-hundred-pound gorilla among sociologists—shows in his book *The Victory of Reason* how the "success of the West, including the rise of science, rested entirely on religious foundations, and the people who brought it about were devout Christians."[7] But don't just take a Christian sociologist's word for it. Jürgen Habermas is one of Europe's most prominent philosophers today. Another fact about Habermas: he's a dyed-in-the-wool atheist. Yet he highlights the inescapable historical fact that the biblical faith was *the* profound influence in shaping civilization. Consider carefully his assessment:

> Christianity has functioned for the normative self-understanding of modernity as more than just a precursor or a catalyst. Egalitarian universalism, from which sprang the ideas of freedom and a social solidarity, of an autonomous conduct of life and emancipation, the individual morality of conscience, human rights, and democracy, is the direct heir to the Judaic ethic of justice and the Christian ethic of love. This legacy, substantially unchanged, has been the object of continual critical appropriation and reinterpretation. To this day, there is no alternative to it. And in light of current challenges of a postnational constellation, we continue to draw on the substance of this heritage. Everything else is just idle postmodern talk.[8]

In the words of human rights scholar Max Stackhouse, "Intellectual honesty demands recognition of the fact that what passes as 'secular,' 'Western' principles of basic human rights developed nowhere else than out of key strands of the biblically-rooted religion."[9]

Consider three fundamental historical facts. (1) Talk of natural right(s) emerged in the Catholic theology of the Middle Ages, a language which itself was built on the biblical understanding of the image of God in all humans. (2) The chief movers who established the Universal Declaration on Human Rights of 1948 (which speaks of humans being "endowed with reason and conscience") were primarily church coalitions and individual Christian leaders who worked closely with some Jewish rabbis to create a "new world order" of human rights. (3) Even the allegedly secular Enlightenment's universal human rights emphasis has deep theological roots; this is quite obvious in the two leading documents of the eighteenth century: the Declaration of Independence (which speaks of humans being "endowed by their Creator with certain unalienable rights") and the French Declaration of the Rights of Man and Citizen (affirming human rights "in the presence and under the auspices" of God, "the Supreme Being"). In short, the Judeo-Christian imprint on human rights in the present is vital for correcting much secularist religion bashing.[10]

Even non-Westerners have come to recognize the remarkable impact of the Christian faith in the West. *Time* magazine's well-respected correspondent David Aikman reported the summary of one Chinese scholar's lecture to a group of eighteen American tourists:

> "One of the things we were asked to look into was what accounted for the success, in fact, the pre-eminence of the West all over the world," he said. "We studied

everything we could from the historical, political, economic, and cultural perspective. At first, we thought it was because you had more powerful guns than we had. Then we thought it was because you had the best political system. Next we focused on your economic system. But in the past twenty years, we have realized that the heart of your culture is your religion: Christianity. That is why the West has been so powerful. The Christian moral foundation of social and cultural life was what made possible the emergence of capitalism and then the successful transition to democratic politics. We don't have any doubt about this."[11]

This lecturer was not some ill-informed crackpot. To the contrary, he represented one of China's premier academic research organizations—the Chinese Academy of Social Sciences (CASS). We don't just find Western scholarly support for the Jewish-Christian worldview. We find it in the East as well!

Jesus as the Climax

The Scriptures begin with the creational affirmation that all humans are made in God's image. In many ways, the improvements of the Old Testament over a good deal of other ancient Near Eastern legislation were a significant move toward that ideal. The Old Testament provides us with enduring perspectives about human dignity and fallenness, not to mention moral insights regarding justice, faithfulness, mercy, generosity, and the like.

However, if we stop with the Old Testament, we won't see the entire story line as it's brought to completion in Jesus. The Old Testament was in many ways anticipatory of something far greater. So if Jesus truly brought a new covenant for the true Israel and has begun to renew the creation as the second Adam, then we ought to concern ourselves with how his incarnation, ministry, atoning death, and resurrection shed light backward on the Old Testament, with all its messiness. To stop with Old Testament texts without allowing Christ, the second Adam, and the new, true Israel to illuminate them, our reading and interpretation of the Old Testament will be greatly impoverished and, in certain ways, misrepresented.

One day we'll fully enjoy the realization of pristine goodness and *shalom*. In the new heaven and earth, no social or racial discrimination will exist. Swords will be beaten into plowshares. Peace will reign. In his own day, Jesus reaffirmed Old Testament texts about loving God and neighbor and called Israel back to live by God's creational designs. That was then, but hardened hearts are still with us today. Yet Jesus's approach to the Old Testament should instruct us Christians living in the already/not yet. We're living with many benefits of the cross of Christ (already), but we still live in a fallen world as we await the new heaven and earth and the receiving of our resurrection bodies (not yet).

Though the New Atheists don't intend it and though they often go about it in wrongheaded ways, they can serve as a proper challenge for us Christians.

How? By reminding us to be more thoughtful in our faith, to live kingdom-centered lives with greater Christian passion and consistency, to deepen our commitment to justice and opposing oppression, to think through contemporary obstacles to belief, and to offer a more compelling vision in word and deed to a watching world. We all need to take a fresh look at Jesus and let our gaze at him shape our devotion to him, our love for others (even our enemies), and our concern for the culture and world in which we find ourselves. Author and pastor Tim Keller gives us a start for our reflection:

> If your fundamental is a man dying on the cross for his enemies, if the very heart of your self-image and your religion is a man praying for his enemies as he died for them, sacrificing for them, loving them—if that sinks into your heart of hearts, it's going to produce the kind of life that the early Christians produced. The most inclusive possible life out of the most exclusive possible claim—and that is that this is the truth. But what is the truth? The truth is a God become weak, loving, and dying for the people who opposed him, dying forgiving them.[12]

While we may stumble or be troubled when reading certain Old Testament texts, we can put them in proper perspective by looking in the right places. The ultimate resolution is found in God's clarifying Word to us and the One who became flesh and lived among us, who died and rose again on our behalf. The God whom the New Atheists consider a monster is not just a holy God to be reckoned with but a loving, self-sacrificing God who invites us to be reconciled to him.

Further Reading

Hill, Jonathan. *What Has Christianity Ever Done for Us?* Downers Grove, IL: InterVarsity, 2005.

Schmidt, Alvin. *How Christianity Changed the World*. Grand Rapids: Zondervan, 2004.

Stark, Rodney. *The Victory of Reason*. New York: Random House, 2005.

Wright, N. T. *Evil and the Justice of God*. Downers Grove, IL: InterVarsity, 2006.

Discussion/Study Questions

Introduction

- In light of your reading of the Old Testament, have you come across any passages you've found troubling or perplexing? Discuss some of these.
- Do you think many Christians are unaware of some of the challenges and difficulties in the Old Testament? Why is this a problem? How should pastors or Christian leaders approach Old Testament difficulties?

Part 1: Neo-Atheism

1. Who Are the New Atheists?

- What have you read on the New Atheists? What are your impressions of them?
- Have you met people who have been influenced by their writings?
- From what you know of the New Atheists, do any of this chapter's comments about them ring true in your estimation?
- While exploring the internet, have you seen any other critiques about the New Atheists?
- Discuss Rodney Stark's comment about "angry and remarkably nasty atheists." What advice would you give about engaging in discussion with an "angry atheist"? Look at James 1:19; 1 Peter 3:15; Titus 2:10.
- What do you think of Michael Novak's claim that the New Atheists write with a certain defensiveness and desperation? In what ways is this so?

2. The New Atheists and the Old Testament God

- After reading this chapter, what do you find are the more challenging issues mentioned by the New Atheists?
- In your conversations with other Christians or non-Christians, what Old Testament ethical questions tend to come up?

- Do you think that certain Old Testament texts are not as problematic as some people claim? Do you have any insights that might help put these texts into proper perspective?
- How do you respond to the challenge, "The God of the Old Testament is a lot nastier than the God of the New Testament"?
- What do you think of Dawkins's claim that "religion" is "the root of all evil"?
- Does Dawkins have a point about the "ubiquitous weirdness of the Bible"? Is this a fair statement?

Part 2: God: Gracious Master or Moral Monster?

3. *Great Appetite for Praise and Sacrifices? Divine Arrogance or Humility?*

- What is pride? What is humility?
- In the past, what have your impressions been about divine pride? Did you take for granted that God was proud (or something like it)? Had you ever thought of God being humble? What do you think of the claim that God is humble?
- What is the point of God's act of making human beings in his image?
- What do you think of the New Atheists' claim that belief in God has its source in biology (being "wired" by evolution to believe to enhance survival)? Is this a big threat to the truth of the Christian faith? Why or why not?
- How is humility different in God as opposed to human beings?
- What is the point of worship? Of praise?
- In what ways does God show himself to be humble?

4. *Monumental Rage and Kinglike Jealousy? Understanding the Covenant-Making God*

- Describe the bad kind of jealousy and the good kind of jealousy. Why is divine jealousy so deeply misunderstood?
- How does the analogy of marriage help us better understand divine jealousy? What impressions do you get from the biblical language that portrays God's "marriage" to his people?
- Why is idolatry both seductive and dangerous?
- What do you think of the concept of "divine vulnerability"? Discuss what this means—and what it doesn't mean.
- When is anger appropriate? Discuss the point that anger is often the first indication that we care.
- Why is it helpful to think of jealousy as protective?

5. *Child Abuse and Bullying? God's Ways and the Binding of Isaac*

- Has anyone you know ever raised concerns over this passage in Genesis 22? How did the discussion go?
- Does the critic have a point on the moral problems raised by this narrative? In what way?
- What do you think of the Abraham vs. Moses comparison to illustrate faith vs. the lack thereof? How is Abraham's faith in relation to the law understood by Paul in Romans 4? In what way is this comparison about faith helpful in understanding Genesis 22?
- How does the context of Abraham's call and his experience with his son Ishmael prepare Abraham for God's command in Genesis 22?
- As you look more closely at the text of Genesis 22, what stands out to you as you grapple with the command of God to Abraham?
- Review the quotations by Elie Wiesel and Jürgen Moltmann and discuss their significance.
- How does the New Testament shed light on God's command to Abraham? In what ways does the New Testament bring helpful clarity to some of the moral questions raised by Genesis 22?
- What is problematic with the charge that Jesus's death on the cross was an instance of "divine child abuse"?

Part 3: Life in the Ancient Near East and in Israel

6. *God's Timeless Wisdom? Incremental Steps for Hardened Hearts*

- Discuss C. S. Lewis's mention of "chronological snobbery." Why is this relevant for a discussion on "strange" Old Testament passages?
- What do we mean by the law of Moses being inferior and provisional? How does this help us understand the Mosaic law's role in our thinking today?
- What ideals does God establish in Genesis 1–2 (at creation) that serve as a reference point as we work through Old Testament ethical questions?
- Is it useful to think of Israel's laws as realistic, "incremental" steps toward the ideal? Is this a serious problem? Why or why not?
- How does Matthew 19:8 (the law and hardened human hearts) give insight regarding the less-than-ideal legislation in the law of Moses?
- What do you think of the discussion regarding the redemptive movement across the sweep of Scripture?
- Israel's history called for different courses of action/living in light of the unfolding context. How do we avoid the problem of relativism as applied to the Old Testament? Why is it right to avoid the thinking that something was true or right for Israel back then (e.g.,

battling the Canaanites) but not so for Israel later on? How do we avoid charges of relativism?

- What do we mean by the is-ought problem? Why is it important to distinguish between *is* and *ought* as we read through the Old Testament?

7. *The Bible's Ubiquitous Weirdness? Kosher Foods, Kooky Laws? (I)*

- What is the significance of the triangle image of God-people-land?
- Why was the grace-gratitude ideal supposed to be central to Israel's existence? How was this to be lived out in her everyday life?
- Contrast the church-state issue for Christians today and ancient Israel in the Old Testament. Why should we keep this difference in mind? What are the dangers if we don't?
- Are certain Islamic states really theocracies? What is the biblical perspective on this?
- What does *holiness* mean? What is the relationship of God's holiness to Israel's?
- Why did Israel have so many holiness laws? Why all the food, clothing, and planting regulations?
- Summarize what is meant by *clean* and *unclean* in the law of Moses. What is the significance of these categories?
- What is the relationship of clean and unclean animals to the spheres they inhabit? What message was God sending to Israel?

8. *The Bible's Ubiquitous Weirdness? Kosher Foods, Kooky Laws? (II)*

- Why are (1) hygiene and (2) false Canaanite religion insufficient contexts to account for Israel's kosher laws?
- What is meant by the "angles" of creation as well as fall, death, and abnormality? In what ways do these help us better understand Israel's food laws?
- What is the connection between the unblemished priest and the unblemished animal (from Lev. 21 and 22)? How does this comparison give insight into God's own expectations for his people Israel?
- Why do various bodily discharges create conditions of uncleanness? Does this at all reflect Israel's symbolic separation from Canaanite religion? In what way(s)?
- What is meant by the holiness gap?

9. *Barbarisms, Crude Laws, and Other Imaginary Crimes? Punishments and Other Harsh Realities in Perspective*

- Besides the passages mentioned early in the chapter, what other passages in the Old Testament strike you as harsh or brutal?

- What are your impressions of the treatment of the Sabbath-breaker and the blasphemer?
- Discuss the significance of this passage: "By those who come near Me I will be treated as holy, and before all the people I will be honored" (Lev. 10:3).
- Discuss the passage of the "glutton and drunkard" son (Deut. 21:18–21). What are some important considerations as we approach this harsh text?
- Why were mediums, sorcerers, and false prophets not permitted in Israel?
- What is significant about the punishments in Israel in contrast to those in other parts of the ancient Near East?
- How should we understand the "eye for an eye" passages in the Old Testament? Is this as terrible as it appears to some readers? Again, how do Israel's punishments compare to other ancient Near Eastern legislation?
- What is your response to Walter Kaiser's position (pp. 95–96) on allowing most capital crimes to be commuted to "ransom" payments?
- Was infant sacrifice divinely permitted in ancient Israel? What about the examples of Mesha and Jephthah?
- Was unborn human life valued in ancient Israel? Give reasons for your answer.

10. Misogynistic? Women in Israel

- In what ways does the Old Testament appear misogynistic (woman hating)? Does Israel's patriarchal society prove this point? Why or why not?
- How does the Old Testament reveal the fundamental equality of male and female?
- How does Old Testament legislation actually reveal protective and caring concern for females?
- What are your impressions about the trial of jealousy in Numbers 5? Compare this with the ancient Near East's river ordeal. What is the point of Numbers 5? Is it anti-woman?
- Why was a woman considered impure longer after having given birth to a girl as opposed to a boy?
- Describe what takes place in a levirate marriage. Was this an anti-woman practice?
- Does "your neighbor's wife" in Exodus 20 indicate that a wife was the mere property of her husband in Israel?

- Was it sexist to prohibit women from Israel's priesthood? Why is it useful to compare Israel's religious practices to Canaanite practices in light of this question?

11. *Bride-Price? Polygamy, Concubinage, and Other Such Questions*

- Describe the practice of concubinage/polygamy in the ancient Near East and in Israel. What nuances and distinctions should be kept in mind?
- Does the Bible promote polygamy? Why is Leviticus 18:18 an important text to consider?
- Discuss the following texts, which allegedly support polygamy as legitimate: Exodus 21:7–11; 2 Samuel 12:8; Deuteronomy 21:15–17. Why are they inadequate supports for a pro-polygamy position?
- What is bride-price? Was this practice demeaning to women in Israel?
- Does the Old Testament treat rape lightly? Discuss Deuteronomy 22:23–29 and the three distinct situations to consider.
- Were women taken in warfare to be treated as sex objects? Did they have any protections? Discuss Deuteronomy 21:10–14 and 20:13–14.
- Discuss the "immodest lady wrestler" passage of Deuteronomy 25:11–12. Does the suggested interpretation make sense?

12. *Warrant for Trafficking in Humans as Farm Equipment? (I): Slavery in Israel*

- What was the status of (chattel) slaves in the antebellum South? How does this compare to servanthood in ancient Israel? Why is it unfair to lump together these two different historical scenarios?
- Describe Israel's debt-servanthood system. What features of this system are important to keep in mind in light of the critics' challenges?
- Was it a huge and difficult step to move from indentured service in Israel to acquiring freedom?
- What specific key texts should have been given more consideration in the proslavery appeals to the Bible in the antebellum South?
- Why is Deuteronomy 15:1–18 such an important text?
- In what ways did Israelite servants (slaves) have unprecedented rights in the ancient Near East?
- Why is it significant that kings like David and Ahab were called to account for their actions by prophets?
- Read Genesis 1:26–27 and Job 31:13–15. What is the importance of these texts in relation to the slavery question?

13. *Warrant for Trafficking in Humans as Farm Equipment? (II):*
    Challenging Texts on Slavery

- Read the challenging texts referenced in this chapter: Exodus 21:2–6;
  Leviticus 19:20–21; and 25:42–46. Which of these difficult passages
  stood out to you? Had you been aware of them before reading this
  book? Can you think of any others?
- Read through the explanation of Exodus 21:2–6. How does this
  compare to your impressions when you first read this text *without*
  the book's explanation?
- What are your thoughts on the engaged servant girl passage (Lev.
  19:20–21)? While not ideal, how does this situation compare to parallel scenarios in the ancient Near East?
- The passage from Leviticus 25:42–46 is perhaps the most jarring of
  the slave texts we've considered. What are some of the important
  background considerations as we approach this text?
- Go back to Deuteronomy 15:1–18. How does this text reveal some
  of the dynamics in the unfolding/developing Mosaic law? How does
  the incident involving the daughters of Zelophehad illustrate this
  (Num. 27)?
- How does the discussion of illegal immigration today shed light on
  the discussion of foreigners in Israel?

14. *Warrant for Trafficking in Humans as Farm Equipment? (III):*
    Slavery in the New Testament

- What is the point of comparing Lincoln's Gettysburg Address to the
  servanthood/slavery question in the law of Moses?
- In the New Testament, what are the implications of Galatians 3:28
  for slavery? For sexism? For racism?
- How was slavery in Rome during New Testament times different
  from the Old Testament picture of servanthood in Israel?
- How does the New Testament affirm the dignity and equality of
  slaves with their masters? What other interesting aspects of this topic
  emerge in the New Testament?
- What does it mean that the New Testament writers addressed
  deeper heart issues underlying slavery, just as Jesus did about
  money?
- Was the Onesimus-Philemon situation a throwback to Hammurabi's
  Code? Why or why not?
- Some charge that God's ultimate goal is to enslave all human beings,
  thus demeaning them and stripping them of their dignity. What is
  the problem with this picture?

15. *Indiscriminate Massacre and Ethnic Cleansing? The Killing of the Canaanites (I)*

- This book claims that the "Canaanite question" is the most difficult ethical challenge in the Old Testament. Do you agree? Why or why not?
- Some people claim that the Canaanites were the most wicked people ever or the most wicked in the ancient Near East. Does the believer *have to* insist on this?
- Was God just picking on the Canaanites by commanding this corporate capital punishment? What does the rest of Scripture tell us about matters of judgment, both outside and within Israel?
- Some people wonder who determines the moral point of no return for the Canaanites. How do you respond?
- Was Israel's act of killing the Canaanites the same thing as General Lin of a Chinese kingdom three thousand years ago wiping out a certain people group?
- The Israelites took the ark of the covenant into battle against the Philistines (1 Sam. 4) without divine approval. How is this a helpful illustration for our discussion on Israelite war?
- Shouldn't the Canaanites have known better so that they could turn from their ways?
- Why is the loaded term *ethnic cleansing* misleading and inaccurate?
- Is it fair to call the Israelites xenophobic? How was Israel's experience in Egypt supposed to shape their attitudes toward outsiders?
- Should God have been more efficient in destroying the Canaanites? Why not ensure that *no* Canaanites remained?
- What is the connection between Israel's destroying Canaan's idols and spiritual/cosmic warfare?

16. *Indiscriminate Massacre and Ethnic Cleansing? The Killing of the Canaanites (II)*

- Why is it important to understand that Israel's warfare with the Canaanites was a historically unique undertaking commanded by God?
- What did Israel's taking of Canaan involve? Why is the conquest model inadequate by itself?
- What are your impressions about the ancient Near Eastern bravado or exaggeration used in Joshua? Does this help shed light on Israel's conquest and the "utter destruction" of the Canaanites?
- Who were the Amalekites, and how do they fit into the discussion of Yahweh wars?

- Must we conclude that noncombatants were directly targeted by Israel's army? Does mention of "women and children" require this interpretation?
- What does the evidence show regarding Canaanite cities during the time of Joshua and Judges? What function did they serve? How is this helpful as we think through the Canaanite problem?
- Was the "ban" against Canaanite cities absolute and nonnegotiable?
- How do Israel's warfare methods compare with other nations in the ancient Near East?
- What is the significance of the predominant "driving out" language used in the Pentateuch?
- How does archaeology support a more gradual infiltration of Israel into Canaan rather than a sudden, dramatic conquest?

17. *Indiscriminate Massacre and Ethnic Cleansing? The Killing of the Canaanites (III)*

- What's the problem with the claim that fighting against the Canaanites would inevitably set a terrible war-making precedent for later generations of Israelites?
- How does God's concern for redeeming Canaanites and other enemies of Israel strike you? How does that help put the Canaanite warfare issue into clearer perspective?
- Compare the approaches to the Canaanite question in the previous chapter and this one. What is your view regarding these alternatives? What are the merits of each position?
- How do you respond to the question of Israelite soldiers being psychologically damaged by killing noncombatants? What if God calls us to endure what is extremely difficult or psychologically taxing? Would this necessarily be inappropriate or unjust? Does the analogy of Frodo and the ring offer any insight?
- Discuss this statement: If the Israelites hadn't done serious damage to the Canaanite religious infrastructure, then the result would have been incalculable damage to Israel's integrity and thus to God's entire plan to redeem humanity.
- Compare God's command to Abraham regarding Isaac to his command to Israel regarding the Canaanites. How is this comparison useful?
- What do you think of Miroslav Volf's comments on God's wrath? Does this help shed light on various Old Testament scenarios, including the Canaanite question?
- Why do we need to recover the concept of an untamable God?
- How may the story of Job give insight into the Canaanite issue?

• How do the incarnation and crucifixion of Christ provide us with resources for thinking through the Canaanite problem?

18. *The Root of All Evil? Does Religion Cause Violence?*

• What do you think of the claim that monotheism leads to violence? Are exclusivistic truth claims the problem? Why are Enlightenment values not the solution?

• Why is the term *religion* in this discussion often being used unfairly?

• What do you think about the claim that sociological, historical, ethnic, or economic factors commonly lurk behind religious hostilities? Can you give some examples?

• Regarding Regina Schwartz's critique, why is Cain not a good example of monotheistic exclusion? What about Esau?

• Must all gifts from God (e.g., intelligence, artistic abilities) be distributed equally to show that God is truly just? Why or why not?

• Why is absolute hospitality a picture of injustice? What do we mean by speaking of the right of self-exclusion?

• The Crusades are commonly mentioned as a critique of the Christian faith. How do you respond to this? How do the Crusades compare to Islamic jihad?

• Why are Old Testament Yahweh wars so unlike Islamic jihad?

Part 4: Sharpening the Moral Focus

19. *Morality without a Lawgiving God? The Divine Foundation of Goodness*

• Have you ever discussed the topic of morality with an atheist or skeptic? How have the conversations gone?

• What is the glaring inconsistency in Richard Dawkins's claim that God is a "moral monster"?

• Why is it important to distinguish between "knowing" and "being" when it comes to morality? Why is it so difficult to account for human dignity and worth if God doesn't exist?

• Atheists commonly claim that they are just as good as any religious believer. However, what are some moral obligations that atheists don't carry out?

• How do you respond to the claim that evolution explains morality? What is missing in purely naturalistic accounts of morality?

• How does the existence of a good God who makes human beings in his image offer a more likely context for objective moral values?

20. *We Have Moved beyond This God (Haven't We?): Jesus as the Fulfiller of the Old Testament*

- When Christopher Hitchens says that "religion poisons everything," what does he mean? What is the problem with his claim?
- Contrary to the New Atheists, what contributions have Jews made to civilization? This book lists some of them. Can you think of others?
- What have been some of the contributions Christians have made to the world? What Christ-inspired effects have brought light, help, and hope to the world? Can you think of any other contributions not mentioned in the book?
- Look at Jürgen Habermas's quotation on the influence of the Christian faith. What do you think of it, and why is this important in light of the New Atheists' critique?
- How does the coming of Jesus bring clarity to the Old Testament and some of its challenges?
- Overall, what have been some benefits you've taken away from reading and discussing this book? What have you learned about the character and activity of God across the two testaments? How have you been stretched and even strengthened in your faith?

Notes

Introduction

1. In order to keep the Hebrew simplified, I have primarily used the lexical form of these words in Scripture quotations in order to avoid complicating and cluttering the book with technicalities.

2. I should add that some of my arguments have been generated in response to critics such as Wes Morriston and Randal Rauser (in the November 1, 2009, issue of *Philosophia Christi*) as well as Hector Avalos (see his "Yahweh Is a Moral Monster," in *The Christian Delusion*, ed. John Loftus [Amherst, NY: Prometheus, 2010]).

Chapter 1: Who Are the New Atheists?

1. The conference presentations were published in Robert Stewart, ed., *The Future of Atheism* (Minneapolis: Fortress, 2009).

2. See David Kinnaman, *unChristian: What a New Generation Really Thinks about Christianity . . . and Why It Matters* (Grand Rapids: Baker, 2007).

3. See chapter 14 in Rodney Stark, *What Americans Really Believe* (Waco: Baylor University Press, 2008).

4. See Philip Jenkins, *The Next Christendom* (Oxford: Oxford University Press, 2002); and Philip Jenkins, *The New Faces of Christianity* (Oxford: Oxford University Press, 2008).

5. Michael Novak, "Remembering the Secular Age," *First Things* (June/July 2007), www .firstthings.com/article.php3?id_article=5922.

6. I was surprised at Dennett's casual dismissal of William Lane Craig's philosophical critique at the Future of Atheism conference (the recordings are available at www.greer-heard .com). A similar incident took place after process theologian Philip Clayton gave a presentation at a conference at Cambridge in 2009 (see Philip Clayton's blog "Dan Dennett as a Model for Philosophy," July 9, 2009, http://clayton.ctr4process.org/2009/07/09/dan-dennett-as-a-model-for-philosophy/).

Dennett selectively quotes David Hume's *The Natural History of Religion* (1779). In his *Breaking the Spell: Religion as a Natural Phenomenon* (New York: Viking, 2006), Dennett cites Hume: "As every enquiry which regards religion is of the utmost importance, there are two questions in particular which challenge our attention, to wit, that concerning its foundation in reason, and that concerning its origin in human nature" (24). Dennett wants to explore Hume's view that religion is a universal impulse that springs from an "original instinct." Yet Dennett glaringly ignores Hume's very next line, which affirms his own belief in a deistic god: "Happily, the first question, which is the most important, admits of the most obvious, at least, the clearest, solution. The whole frame of nature bespeaks an intelligent author; and no rational enquirer can, after serious reflection, suspend his belief a moment with regard to the primary principles of genuine Theism [i.e., deism] and Religion." Hume is "yet another of my heroes" (27), Dennett says, but why be so favorable toward one still under the "spell" of belief in God?

7. Katherine Swallow Prior, "New and Unimproved: Atheism's Brash but Ineffectual Makeover," *Salvo* 7 (2009), available online at http://www.salvomag.com/new/articles/salvo7/7prior.php.

8. Chris Hedges, *I Don't Believe in Atheists* (New York: Free Press, 2008), 2–3.

9. Stark, *What Americans Really Believe*, 120.

10. Michael Ruse's comment is found on the cover of Alister and Joanna McGrath's book *The Dawkins Delusion?* (Downers Grove, IL: InterVarsity, 2007).

11. Terry Eagleton, "Lunging, Flailing, Mispunching," *London Review of Books* (October 19, 2006), www.lrb.co.uk/v28/n20/print/eagl01_.html (accessed November 25, 2007). Eagleton gives a fuller critique in *Reason, Faith, and Revolution: Reflections on the God Debate* (New Haven: Yale University Press, 2009).

12. Quentin Smith, "The Wave Function of a Godless Universe," in *Theism, Atheism, and Big Bang Cosmology* (Oxford: Clarendon Press, 1993), 322.

13. William Lane Craig, "Dawkins's Delusion," in *Contending with Christianity's Critics: Answering New Atheist and Other Objectors*, ed. Paul Copan and William Lane Craig (Nashville: B & H Academic, 2009), 5.

14. Daniel Dennett said this in a debate with Dinesh D'Souza at Tufts University on November 20, 2007. Video available at http://ygod.web2.onlinenw.com/index.php?pr=Dinesh_vs_Dennett (accessed June 21, 2009).

15. Rev. Al Sharpton and Christopher Hitchens, "Can Morality Exist without God?" New York Public Library (May 7, 2007). Video available at http://fora.tv/2007/05/07/Al_Sharpton_and_Christopher_Hitchens.

16. In the words of Jeffrey Dahmer's father, Lionel, in the documentary *Jeffrey Dahmer: The Monster Within*, DVD, produced by Christine Shuler (A&E Biography, 1996).

17. Jeffrey Dahmer, interview by Stone Phillips, *Dateline NBC*, NBC, November 29, 1994.

Chapter 2: The New Atheists and the Old Testament God

1. See Paul Copan, "Is Yahweh a Moral Monster? The New Atheists and Old Testament Ethics," *Philosophia Christi* 10, no. 1 (2008): 7–37. Available at www.epsociety.org/library/printable/45.pdf/.

2. Richard Dawkins, *The God Delusion* (Boston: Houghton Mifflin, 2006), 248, 242, 243, 247.

3. Ibid., 241, 51.

4. Ibid., 31.

5. Daniel Dennett, *Breaking the Spell: Religion as a Natural Phenomenon* (New York: Viking, 2006), 206, 265, 267.

6. Christopher Hitchens, *God Is Not Great: How Religion Poisons Everything* (New York: Hachette Book Group, 2007), 99, 101–2.

7. Sam Harris, *Letter to a Christian Nation* (New York: Alfred A. Knopf, 2006), ix, 8.

8. Sam Harris, *The End of Faith* (New York: W. W. Norton, 2004), 18.

9. Harris, *Letter to a Christian Nation*, 18–19, 23–24.

10. Christopher J. H. Wright, *The God I Don't Understand: Reflections on Tough Questions of Faith* (Grand Rapids: Zondervan, 2008).

Chapter 3: Great Appetite for Praise and Sacrifices?

1. Richard Dawkins, *The God Delusion* (Boston: Houghton Mifflin, 2006), 37.

2. Lewis B. Smedes, *Love within Limits* (Grand Rapids: Eerdmans, 1978), 31. See also chapter 8, "The Great Sin," in C. S. Lewis, *Mere Christianity* (New York: Macmillan, 1952).

3. Gordon Slack, "The Atheist," *Salon*, April 30, 2005, http://dir.salon.com/story/news/feature/2005/04/30/dawkins/index.html. Also see Daniel Dennett, *Breaking the Spell: Religion as a Natural Phenomenon* (New York: Viking, 2006).

4. Christian Smith, *Moral, Believing Animals: Human Personhood and Culture* (New York: Oxford University Press, 2003), 110, 122.

5. Bob Dylan, "Gotta Serve Somebody," Special Rider Music, 1979.

6. Richard Bauckham, *Bible and Mission: Christian Witness in a Postmodern World* (Grand Rapids: Baker; Carlisle, UK: Paternoster, 2004), 37.

7. C. S. Lewis, *Reflections on the Psalms* (New York: Harcourt Brace Jovanovich, 1958), 94–95.

8. C. S. Lewis, "The Weight of Glory," in *The Weight of Glory and Other Addresses* (New York: Macmillan, 1965), 4–5.

9. Martin Hengel, *The Son of God: The Origin of Christology and the History of Jewish-Hellenistic Religion*, trans. John Bowden (Philadelphia: Fortress, 1976), 1.

10. Colin E. Gunton, *The Christian Faith: An Introduction to Christian Doctrine* (Oxford: Blackwell, 2002), 181.

11. John Goldingay, *Old Testament Theology: Israel's Life*, vol. 3 (Downer's Grove, IL: InterVarsity, 2009), 129.

Chapter 4: Monumental Rage and Kinglike Jealousy?

1. Richard Dawkins, *The God Delusion* (Boston: Houghton Mifflin, 2006), 243.

2. Thanks to my colleague Nathan Lane for this point. See his book *The Compassionate but Punishing God* (Eugene, OR: Wipf and Stock, 2010).

3. For example, see Exodus 20:5; 34:14; Deuteronomy 4:24; 6:15; 29:20; 32:16, 21; Joshua 24:19; 1 Kings 14:22; Ezekiel 8:3 (a graven "idol of jealousy"); 16:38, 42–43; 39:25; Joel 2:18; Nahum 1:2; Zephaniah 1:18; 3:8; Zechariah 1:14; 8:2; 1 Corinthians 10:22.

4. See the brief discussion on idolatry in Douglas K. Stuart, *Exodus*, New American Commentary 2 (Nashville: B & H Publishing, 2008), 450–54.

5. "Divine vulnerablity" comes from James Crenshaw, *Defending God* (Oxford: Oxford University Press, 2005), 82.

6. Gordon McConville and Stephen N. Williams, *Joshua* (Grand Rapids: Eerdmans, 2010), 134.

7. See J. B. Phillips's classic, *Your God Is Too Small* (New York: Touchstone, 1997), especially chapter 4 ("Meek-and-Mild").

8. See Frank G. Kirkpatrick, *A Moral Ontology for a Theistic Ethic: Gathering the Nations in Love and Justice* (Burlington, VT: Ashgate, 2004), 61–76.

9. Thomas Nagel, *The Last Word* (New York: Oxford University Press, 1997), 130–31.

10. Tim Keller, "The Gospel in All Its Forms," *Leadership Journal* 29, no. 2 (2008): 15. Available at www.christianitytoday.com/le/2008/002/9.74.html.

11. C. S. Lewis, "The Weight of Glory," in *The Weight of Glory and Other Addresses* (New York: HarperOne, 2001), 26.

Chapter 5: Child Abuse and Bullying?

1. See chapter 1 in James Crenshaw, *A Whirlpool of Torment* (Minneapolis: Fortress, 1984).

2. Bart D. Ehrman, *God's Problem: How the Bible Fails to Answer Our Most Important Question—Why We Suffer* (San Francisco: HarperOne, 2008), 70.

3. Søren Kierkegaard, *"Fear and Trembling" and "The Sickness unto Death,"* trans. Walter Lowrie (Garden City, NY: Doubleday, 1954), 41.

4. Some comments from this section are taken from John H. Sailhamer, *The Pentateuch as Narrative* (Grand Rapids: Zondervan, 1992), 33–79; and John H. Sailhamer, "The Mosaic Law and the Theology of the Pentateuch," *Westminster Theological Journal* 53 (1991): 24–61.

5. There is a relational component to the "fear of God" (e.g., Gen. 20:11; Deut. 10:12, 20; 13:4; 31:13). That is, to fear God means to be in relationship with him. See R. W. L. Moberly, *The Bible, Theology, and Faith: A Study of Abraham and Jesus* (Cambridge: Cambridge University Press, 2000), 81–84.

6. E. A. Speiser, *Genesis*, Anchor Bible Commentary 1 (Garden City, NY: Doubleday, 1964), 166.

7. Roland de Vaux, *Ancient Israel* (New York: McGraw-Hill, 1965), 443.

8. William L. Lane, *Hebrews 9–13*, Word Biblical Commentary 47B (Dallas: Word, 1991), 360.

9. Some of this is taken from Eleonore Stump's excellent discussion in her "Evil and the Nature of Faith," part of her Gifford Lectures. The anticipated title is *Wandering in Darkness: Narrative and the Problem of Evil* (Oxford: Oxford University Press, forthcoming).

10. Crenshaw, *Whirlpool of Torment*, 14.

11. The Hebrew word *n'* ("please") is in view. Gordon Wenham, *Genesis 16–50*, Word Biblical Commentary 2 (Dallas: Word, 1994), 104.

12. Nahum M. Sarna, *Genesis*, JPS Torah Commentary (Philadelphia: Jewish Publication Society, 1989), 151.

13. Wenham, 105. Of course, 2 Chronicles 3:1 informs us that Mount Moriah is the location of the Jerusalem temple.

14. I borrow from the insights of Matthew Flannagan in "Abraham and Isaac: Did God Command the Killing of an Innocent?" www.mandm.org.nz/2009/07/sunday-study-abraham-and-isaac-%E2%80%93-did-god-command-the-killing-of-an-innocent.html (accessed April 17, 2010).

15. John E. Hare, *God's Call: Moral Realism, God's Commands, and Human Autonomy* (Grand Rapids: Eerdmans, 2001), 68–69.

16. Ehrman, *God's Problem*, 169.

17. Jürgen Moltmann, *The Crucified God*, trans. R. A. Wilson (Minneapolis: Fortress, 1993), 273–74.

18. I have modified the NASB translation, since the same word used in Romans 8:32 ("spare" [*pheidomai*]) is used in the Septuagint (the Greek translation of the Old Testament).

19. James D. G. Dunn, *The Theology of the Apostle Paul* (Grand Rapids: Eerdmans, 1998), 225.

20. Thomas Torrance, *The Christian Doctrine of God: One Being, Three Persons* (Edinburgh: T & T Clark, 1996), 244.

Chapter 6: God's Timeless Wisdom?

1. One site with this letter is www.thehumorarchives.com/humor/0001065.html.

2. C. S. Lewis, *Surprised by Joy* (New York: Harcourt Brace Jovanovich, 1956), 207.

3. N. T. Wright, *The Climax of the Covenant* (Minneapolis: Fortress, 1991), 181.

4. Alden Thompson, *Who's Afraid of the Old Testament God?* (Grand Rapids: Zondervan, 1988), 33.

5. Ibid., 32.

6. Hittite Laws §167. See Martha T. Roth, *Law Collections from Mesopotamia and Asia Minor*, 2nd ed. (Atlanta: Scholars Press, 1997).

7. See Allen P. Ross, *Holiness to the Lord* (Grand Rapids: Baker Academic, 2006).

8. Bruce C. Birch, *Let Justice Roll Down: The Old Testament, Ethics, and Christian Life* (Louisville: Westminster John Knox, 1991), 43.

9. William J. Webb, *Slaves, Women, and Homosexuals* (Downers Grove, IL: InterVarsity, 2001).

10. Modified from chapter 2 in Webb, *Slaves, Women, and Homosexuals*. I am aware that not all evangelicals agree with Webb's approach. See, for example, Stanley N. Gundry and Gary Meadors, eds., *Four Views on Moving beyond the Bible to Theology* (Grand Rapids: Zondervan, 2009).

11. Paul Copan, *When God Goes to Starbucks: A Guide to Everyday Apologetics* (Grand Rapids: Baker, 2008), chaps. 8–10.

12. R. T. France, "From Romans to the Real World," in *Romans and the People of God*, ed. Sven K. Soderlund and N. T. Wright (Grand Rapids: Eerdmans, 1999), 245.

13. This section is slightly adapted from chapter 3 in John Goldingay, *Theological Diversity and the Authority of the Old Testament* (Grand Rapids: Eerdmans, 1987).

14. Hitchens, *God Is Not Great*, 101.

15. John Barton, *Understanding Old Testament Ethics: Approaches and Explorations* (Louisville: Westminster John Knox, 2003), 73.

16. See Daniel Block, "Will the Real Gideon Please Stand Up? Narrative Style and Intention in Judges 6–9," *Journal of the Evangelical Theological Society* 40 (1997): 353–66; and J. Daniel Hays, "Has the Narrator Come to Praise Solomon or to Bury Him? Narrative Subtlety in 1 Kings 1–11," *Journal for the Study of the Old Testament* 28, no. 2 (2003): 149–74.

17. John N. Oswalt, *The Bible among the Myths* (Grand Rapids: Zondervan, 2009).

18. See, for example, Paul Heger, "Source of Law in the Biblical and Mesopotamian Law Collections," *Biblica* 87 (2006): 325–29.

19. K. A. Kitchen, *On the Reliability of the Old Testament* (Grand Rapids: Eerdmans, 2003); James K. Hoffmeier, *Israel in Egypt: The Evidence for the Authenticity of the Exodus Tradition* (Oxford: Oxford University Press, 1999); James K. Hoffmeier, *Ancient Israel in Sinai: The Evidence for the Authenticity of the Wilderness Tradition* (Oxford: Oxford University Press, 2005); and the more popular James K. Hoffmeier, *The Archaeology of the Bible* (Grand Rapids: Kregel/Lion, 2008); and Iain Provain, V. Philips Long, and Tremper Longman III, *A Biblical History of Israel* (Louisville: Westminster John Knox, 2003).

Chapter 7: The Bible's Ubiquitous Weirdness? (I)

1. Christopher J. H. Wright emphasizes this threefold arrangement and notes these contrasting socioeconomic structures in *Old Testament Ethics for the People of God* (Downers Grove, IL: InterVarsity, 2004), 54–56.

2. He mentions this in passing in "Science and Ethics," in *Religion and Science* (Oxford: Oxford University Press, 1961), 223–24.

3. John Goldingay, *Old Testament Theology: Israel's Life*, vol. 3 (Downers Grove, IL: InterVarsity, 2009), 128.

4. Christopher J. H. Wright, *Eye for an Eye: The Place of Old Testament Ethics* (Downers Grove, IL: InterVarsity Press, 1983), 29.

5. Louise Antony, "Atheism as Perfect Piety," in *Is Goodness without God Good Enough?* ed. Robert K. Garcia and Nathan L. King (Lanham, MD: Rowman & Littlefield, 2009), 79; see also the final chapter in Erik Wielenberg, *Value and Virtue in a Godless Universe* (Cambridge: Cambridge University Press, 2005).

6. Paul Johnson, *A History of the American People* (New York: HarperCollins, 1997), 30–33.

7. That is, except when God's cosmic righteous and loving rule is ultimately established in the new heaven and earth (Rev. 21–22).

8. On the Scripture's authority, see N. T. Wright, *The Last Word* (San Francisco: HarperCollins, 2005).

9. For further discussion of national Israel's ending as the people of God, see Paul Copan, *When God Goes to Starbucks: A Guide to Everyday Apologetics* (Grand Rapids: Baker, 2008), chaps. 15–16.

10. Gordon J. Wenham, *Leviticus*, New International Commentary on the Old Testament (Grand Rapids: Eerdmans, 1979), 270.

11. Richard Bauckham, *The Bible in Politics: How to Read the Bible Politically* (Louisville: Westminster John Knox, 1989), 23.

12. Goldingay, *Israel's Life*, 131.

13. For example, demanding genealogical evidence to serve as a priest (Ezra 2:62; Neh. 7:64), observing the Feast of Unleavened Bread (Ezra 6:20–21), affirming that unclean food and carcasses are defiling (Hag. 3:11–13).

14. Maltbie D. Babcock, "This Is My Father's World" (1858–1901).

15. Goldingay, *Israel's Life*, 130.

16. Ibid., 609–15.

17. Jonathan Klawans, *Impurity and Sin in Ancient Judaism* (New York: Oxford University Press, 2000), 39.

18. Cyril S. Rodd, *Glimpses of a Strange Land: Studies in Old Testament Ethics* (Edinburgh: T & T Clark, 2001), 17.

19. See chapter 1 in Klawans, *Impurity and Sin in Ancient Judaism*.

20. Nobuyoshi Kiuchi, *Leviticus*, Apollos Old Testament Commentary 3 (Nottingham, UK: Apollos; Downers Grove, IL: InterVarsity, 2007), 212–13.

21. Ibid., 213.

22. Wenham, *Leviticus*, 23.

23. However, priestly clothing (cf. Exod. 39) was exempted from this, being made of both wool and linen. Wool didn't dye very well, so it was combined with linen.

24. Timothy A. Lenchak, "Clean and Unclean," in *Eerdmans Dictionary of the Bible*, ed. David Noel Freedman (Grand Rapids: Eerdmans, 2000), 263.

25. Wenham, *Leviticus*, 269.

26. David P. Wright, "Unclean and Clean (OT)," *Anchor Bible Dictionary*, vol. 6 (New York: Doubleday, 1992), 740.

Chapter 8: The Bible's Ubiquitous Weirdness? (II)

1. Gordon J. Wenham, *Leviticus*, New International Commentary on the Old Testament (Grand Rapids: Eerdmans, 1979), 167–68.

2. Ibid., 167; J. G. McConville, *Deuteronomy*, Apollos Old Testament Commentary (Downers Grove, IL: InterVarsity, 2002), 249; and Gordon J. Wenham, "The Theology of Unclean Food," *Evangelical Quarterly* 53 (1981): 7.

3. Mary Douglas, "The Forbidden Animals in Leviticus," *Journal for the Study of the Old Testament* 59 (1993): 3–23; and Mary Douglas, *Leviticus as Literature* (Oxford: Oxford University Press, 1999).

4. Wenham, "Theology of Unclean Food," 11; Wenham, *Leviticus*, 170.

5. Douglas, "Forbidden Animals in Leviticus," 3–23. I follow Douglas in the following paragraphs. Notice the very structure of Leviticus, which serves as a reminder for the themes she discusses (11).

6. Wenham, *Leviticus*, 174–75.

7. Douglas, "Forbidden Animals in Leviticus," 22.

8. Ibid., 23.

9. Timothy A. Lenchak, "Clean and Unclean," in *Eerdmans Dictionary of the Bible*, ed. David Noel Freedman (Grand Rapids: Eerdmans, 2000), 263.

10. Ephraim Radner, *Leviticus* (Grand Rapids: Brazos, 2008), 151.

11. John L. Hartley, *Leviticus*, Word Biblical Commentary 4 (Dallas: Word, 1992), 213–15.

12. Richard S. Hess, "Leviticus," in *The Expositor's Bible Commentary*, ed. Tremper Longman III and David E. Garland, rev. ed. (Grand Rapids: Zondervan, 2008), 713. Hess points out that in Israel, women married reasonably young, had many pregnancies, and didn't live as long as in modern societies; so they wouldn't have been unclean so frequently.

13. Thanks to John Hare for his paper "Animal Sacrifices" (September 2009), in which he uses this term.

14. Hess, "Leviticus," 573, 658.

15. John H. Sailhamer, *Pentateuch as Narrative* (Grand Rapids: Zondervan, 1992), 33–79.

Chapter 9: Barbarisms, Crude Laws, and Other Imaginary Crimes?

1. See chapter 3 in Joe M. Sprinkle, *Biblical Law and Its Relevance* (Lanham, MD: University Press of America, 2004).

2. Richard S. Hess, "Leviticus 10:1: Strange Fire and an Odd Name," *Bulletin for Biblical Research* 12, no. 2 (2008): 187–98.

3. Taken from Christopher J. H. Wright, *Deuteronomy*, New International Biblical Commentary 4 (Peabody, MA: Hendrickson, 1996), 235–36.

4. See Mary Douglas, *Leviticus as Literature* (Oxford: Oxford University Press, 1999), 98–104.

5. Harris, *End of Faith*, 18.

6. Wright, *Deuteronomy*, 264–65.

7. William H. C. Ropp, *Exodus 19–40*, Anchor Bible Commentary (New York: Doubleday, 2006), 218.

8. See Laws of Hammurabi §§192, 193, 194, 195, 205. References to ancient Near Eastern texts are taken from William W. Hallo, ed., *The Context of Scripture*, vol. 2, *Monumental Inscriptions from the Biblical World* (Leiden: Brill, 2003); Martha T. Roth, *Law Collections from Mesopotamia and Asia Minor*, 2nd ed. (Atlanta: Scholars Press, 1997); and Raymond Westbrook, ed., *A History of Ancient Near East Law*, 2 vols. (Leiden: Brill, 2003).

9. Laws of Hammurabi §§6–10.

10. David Lorton, "The Treatment of Criminals in Ancient Egypt," in *The Treatment of Criminals in the Ancient Near East*, ed. Jack M. Sasson (Leiden: Brill, 1977), 1–64 (see e.g., p. 25); and Andrea G. McDowell, s.v. "Crime and Punishment," *The Oxford Encyclopedia of Ancient Egypt*, ed. Donald B. Redford (Oxford: Oxford University Press, 2001), 1:318.

11. David L. Baker, *Tight Fists or Open Hands? Wealth and Poverty in Old Testament Law* (Grand Rapids: Eerdmans, 2009), 27. Baker notes that Hittite laws also utilized demands for restitution.

12. Johannes Renger, "Wrongdoing and Its Sanctions: On 'Criminal' and 'Civil' Law in the Old Babylonian Period," in *The Treatment of Criminals in the Ancient Near East*, ed. Jack M. Sasson (Leiden: Brill, 1977), 72; see also Christopher J. H. Wright, *Old Testament Ethics for the People of God* (Downers Grove, IL: InterVarsity, 2004), 310.

13. Hittite Laws §166.

14. Hittite Laws §167.

15. Ironically, Hector Avalos scoffs at the nonliteral "compensation" view, citing Raymond Westbrook for his backup. Yet Westbrook disagrees with Avalos! See Raymond Westbrook, *Studies in Biblical and Cuneiform Law* (Paris: J. Gabalda, 1988), 45, 47–55; also William Ian Miller, *Eye for an Eye* (Cambridge: Cambridge University Press, 2006), 207n. Other ancient Near Eastern cultures, however, still had brutal mutilation punishments, which I discuss in the present book.

16. Brevard S. Childs, *The Book of Exodus: A Critical, Theological Commentary* (Philadelphia: Westminster, 1974), 93.

17. Laws of Hammurabi §§197, 200.

18. Laws of Hammurabi §251. If he killed a slave, then a third of a mina would be paid to the master (§252; Eshnunna §54).

19. Laws of Hammurabi §§229–30.

20. Douglas K. Stuart, *Exodus*, New American Commentary 2 (Nashville: B & H Publishing, 2008), 485.

21. Paul Johnson, *Art: A New History* (New York: HarperCollins, 2003), 33.

22. Walter C. Kaiser, *Toward Old Testament Ethics* (Grand Rapids: Zondervan, 1983), 91–92.

23. Raymond Westbrook, "The Character of Ancient Near Eastern Law," in *A History of Ancient Near Eastern Law*, vol. 1, ed. Raymond Westbrook (Leiden: Brill, 2003), 71–78; J.J. Finkelstein, *The Ox That Gored* (Philadelphia: American Philosophical Society, 1981), esp. 34–35; Joseph M. Sprinkle, "The Interpretation of Exodus 21:22–25 (*Lex Talionis*) and Abortion," *Westminster Theological Journal* 55 (1993): 233–55 (esp. 237–43).

24. Susan Niditch, *War in the Hebrew Bible: A Study in the Ethics of Violence* (New York: Oxford University Press, 1993), 45–46. For a critique of some of Niditch's claims, see Ben C. Ollenburger, review of *War in the Hebrew Bible: A Study in the Ethics of Violence*, by Susan Niditch, *Interpretation* 48, no. 4 (1994): 436–37.

25. Iain W. Provan, *1 and 2 Kings*, New International Bible Commentary 7 (Peabody, MA: Hendrickson; Carlisle, UK: Paternoster, 1995), 186.

26. See Baruch Margalit, "Why King Mesha Sacrificed His Oldest Son," *Biblical Archaeology Review* 12 (November/December 1986): 62–63; John J. Bimson, "1 and 2 Kings," in *The New Bible Commentary*, 4th ed., ed. Gordon Wenham et al. (Downers Grove, IL: InterVarsity, 1994), 365; and Anson Rainey, *The Sacred Bridge: Carta's Atlas of the Biblical World*, ed. Anson Rainey and R. Steven Notley (Jerusalem: Carta, 2006), 205.

27. John Goldingay, *Old Testament Theology: Israel's Life*, vol. 3 (Downers Grove, IL: InterVarsity, 2009), 796. For a good discussion of the Ezekiel text, see Daniel I. Block, *The Book of Ezekiel: Chapters 1–24* (Grand Rapids: Eerdmans, 1997), 636–41.

Chapter 10: Misogynistic?

1. Much of the material in this chapter is taken from Richard M. Davidson, *Flame of Yahweh: Sexuality in the Old Testament* (Peabody, MA: Hendrickson, 2007).

2. Jonathan Klawans, *Impurity and Sin in Ancient Judaism* (New York: Oxford University Press, 2000), 39.

3. Daniel I. Block, "Marriage and Family in Ancient Israel," in *Marriage and Family in the Biblical World*, ed. Ken M. Campbell (Downers Grove, IL: InterVarsity, 2003), 63.

4. John Goldingay, *Old Testament Theology: Israel's Life*, vol. 3 (Downers Grove, IL: InterVarsity, 2009), 376.

5. D. Hollander and M. Schwartz, "Annealing, Distilling, Reheating, and Recycling: Bitumen Processing in the Ancient Near East," *Paléorient* 26, no. 2 (2000): 83–91; and Wolfgang Heimpel, ed., *Letters to the King of Mari: A New Translation, with Historical Introduction, Notes, and Commentary* (Winona Lake, IN: Eisenbrauns, 2003), 272–75.

6. Davidson, *Flame of Yahweh*, 327.

7. Hittite Laws §193. A fine summary about crimes and punishments related to women is Elisabeth Meier Tetlow, *Women, Crime, and Punishment in Ancient Law and Society*, vol. 1, *The Ancient Near East* (New York: Continuum, 2004).

8. J. G. McConville, *Deuteronomy*, Apollos Old Testament Commentary (Downers Grove, IL: InterVarsity, 2002), 369.

9. Robin Parry, *Old Testament Story and Christian Ethics: The Rape of Dinah as a Case Study* (Bletchley, UK: Paternoster, 2004), 68.

10. Gordon McConville, "Old Testament Laws and Canonical Intentionality," in *Canon and Biblical Interpretation*, ed. Craig Bartholomew et al. (Grand Rapids: Zondervan, 2006), 263.

11. Davidson, *Flame of Yahweh*, 250.

12. John Sailhamer, *The Pentateuch as Narrative* (Grand Rapids: Zondervan, 1992), 51–59.

13. Among the Hittites, bestiality with certain animals rendered a person merely ritually impure. See Westbrook, *History of Ancient Near Eastern Law*, 1:648–49.

14. See Douglas K. Stuart, *Exodus*, New American Commentary 2 (Nashville: B & H Publishing, 2008), 450–54; and Clay Jones, "Why We Don't Hate Sin so We Don't Understand What Happened to the Canaanites: An Addendum to 'Divine Genocide' Arguments," *Philosophia Christi* n.s. 11 (2009): 53–72.

15. Laws of Lipit-Ishtar §§27, 30.

16. Hittite Laws §194.

17. Hittite Laws §200a. Oddly, Hittite law didn't permit sexual relations with a cow or sheep or pig or dog (§§187–88, 199).

Chapter 11: Bride-Price?

1. See William G. Hyland Jr., *In Defense of Thomas Jefferson: The Sally Hemings Sex Scandal* (New York: St. Martin's, 2009).

2. Laws of Hammurabi §§170–71.

3. Werner Plautz, "Monogamie und Polygamie im Alten Testament," *Zeitschrift für die Altentestamentliche Wissenschaft* 65 (1963): 9–13; and A. A. Anderson, *2 Samuel*, Word Biblical Commentary 11 (Nashville: Thomas Nelson, 1989), 203.

4. See J. Daniel Hays, "Has the Narrator Come to Praise Solomon or to Bury Him? Narrative Subtlety in 1 Kings 1–11," *Journal for the Study of the Old Testament* 28, no. 2 (2003): 149–74.

5. Richard M. Davidson, *Flame of Yahweh: Sexuality in the Old Testament* (Peabody, MA: Hendrickson, 2007), 193–98; and Gordon P. Hugenberger, *Marriage as a Covenant* (Grand Rapids: Baker Academic, 1994), 115–18.

6. Davidson, *Flame of Yahweh*, 193–98.

7. This section borrows heavily from ibid., 191–93; and Douglas K. Stuart, *Exodus*, New American Commentary 2 (Nashville: B & H Publishing, 2008), 481–84. See Hugenberger, *Marriage as a Covenant*, 320–22. Thanks too for Richard Davidson's email correspondence on this passage (September 26, 2009).

8. Walter C. Kaiser, *Toward Old Testament Ethics* (Grand Rapids: Zondervan, 1983), 187.

9. Daniel I. Block, "Marriage and Family in Ancient Israel," in *Marriage and Family in the Biblical World*, ed. Ken M. Campbell (Downers Grove, IL: InterVarsity, 2003), 57, 63; Davidson, *Flame of Yahweh*, 249; Gordon Wenham, "Family in the Pentateuch," in *Family in the Bible*, ed. Richard S. Hess and Daniel Carrol (Grand Rapids: Baker Academic, 2003), 23–24; and Stuart, *Exodus*, 509–10.

10. The Greek Old Testament translation gets this wrong. It mistranslates this passage, "*he* is discovered," as though the man alone is guilty. The Hebrew indicates that *both* are culpable.

11. Davidson, *Flame of Yahweh*, 359, 519.

12. Duane L. Christensen, *Deuteronomy 21:10–34:12*, Word Biblical Commentary 6B (Nashville: Thomas Nelson, 2002), 474–75.

13. Derek Kidner, "Old Testament Perspectives on War," *Evangelical Quarterly* 57 (April 1985): 109.

14. See Davidson, *Flame of Yahweh*, 593.

15. See Jerome T. Walsh, "You Shall Cut Off Her . . . Palm? A Reexamination of Deuteronomy 25:11–12," *Journal of Semitic Studies* 49 (2004): 47–48; also, Davidson, *Flame of Yahweh*, 476–80. Unfortunately, the article by Marc Cortez advocating the amputation view fails to engage Walsh's textual arguments: "The Law on Violent Intervention: Deuteronomy 25.11–12 Revisited," *Journal for the Study of the Old Testament* 30:3 (2006): 431–47. I'm grateful for Walsh's correspondence on this topic (May 2010).

16. The Code of the Assyrians, I.8.

Chapter 12: Warrant for Trafficking in Humans as Farm Equipment? (I)

1. Frederick Douglass, *Narrative of the Life of Frederick Douglass, an American Slave* (New York: Spark Publishing, 2005), 20.

2. Harriet Beecher Stowe, *A Key to Uncle Tom's Cabin; presenting the Facts and Documents upon which the Story is Founded, together with Corroborative Statements verifying the Truth of the Work* (Boston: John P. Jewett, 1853), I.10, 139.

3. David W. Galenson, "Indentured Servitude," in *The Oxford Companion to American History* (New York: Oxford University Press, 2001), 368–69.

4. John Goldingay, *Old Testament Theology: Israel's Life*, vol. 3 (Downers Grove, IL: InterVarsity, 2009), 460.

5. Douglas K. Stuart, *Exodus*, New American Commentary 2 (Nashville: B & H Publishing, 2008), 474–75.

6. Goldingay, *Israel's Life,* 461.

7. On some of my comments on servitude in Israel, I borrow from Tikva Frymer-Kenski, "Anatolia and the Levant: Israel," in *A History of Ancient Near East Law*, vol. 2, ed. Raymond Westbrook (Leiden: Brill, 2003).

8. See Gregory C. Chirichigno, *Debt-Slavery in Israel and the Ancient Near East*, JSOT Supplement Series 141 (Sheffield: University of Sheffield Press, 1993), 351–54.

9. See Gordon Wenham, "Family in the Pentateuch," in *Family in the Bible*, ed. Richard S. Hess and Daniel Carrol (Grand Rapids: Baker Academic, 2003), 21.

10. J. A. Motyer, *The Message of Exodus* (Downers Grove, IL: InterVarsity, 2005), 239.

11. Peter Garnsey, *Ideas of Slavery from Aristotle to Augustine* (Cambridge: Cambridge University Press,1996), 1.

12. John I. Durham, *Exodus*, Word Biblical Commentary 3 (Waco: Word, 1987), 321.

13. John L. Hartley, *Leviticus*, Word Biblical Commentary 4 (Dallas: Word, 1992), 429. Hammurabi's Code made provision for release of debt slaves.

14. Gordon McConville, *Grace in the End: A Study in Deuteronomic Theology* (Grand Rapids: Zondervan, 1993), 148.

15. Christopher J. H. Wright, *Walking in the Ways of the Lord* (Downers Grove, IL: InterVarsity, 1995), 124.

16. Muhammad A. Dandamayev, s.v. "Slavery (Old Testament)," in *Anchor Bible Dictionary*, vol. 6, ed. David Noel Freedman (New York: Doubleday, 1992).

17. Ibid.

18. Frymer-Kenski, "Anatolia and the Levant: Israel," 1007.

19. Laws of Hammurabi §282. See also Elisabeth Meier Tetlow, *Women, Crime, and Punishment in Ancient Law and Society*, vol. 1, *The Ancient Near East* (New York: Continuum, 2004).

20. On this unique feature, see Christopher J. H. Wright, *Old Testament Ethics for the People of God* (Downers Grove, IL: InterVarsity, 2004), 292.

21. Laws of Hammurabi §§170–71.

22. I'm referring to Hector Avalos ("Yahweh Is a Moral Monster," in *The Christian Delusion*, ed. John Loftus [Amherst, NY: Prometheus, 2010]), who commonly engages in this type of evidence slanting. Despite his ad hominem accusations of my being a biased "religionist" or my "faith-based" approach, the issue is one of evidence and argumentation. As it turns out, Avalos's own tone and selectivity of his arguments certainly qualify him as truly "anti-religionist" and being "anti-faith-based."

23. Goldingay, *Israel's Life*, 470.

24. Laws of Hammurabi §16.

25. Laws of Lipit-Ishtar §12; Laws of Eshunna §49–50; Hittite Laws §24.

26. Joachim Oelsner, Bruce Wells, and Cornelia Wunsch, s.v. "Neo-Babylonian Period," in *A History of Ancient Near Eastern Law*, ed. Raymond Westbrook (Leiden: Brill, 2003), 2:932.

27. David L. Baker, *Tight Fists or Open Hands? Wealth and Poverty in Old Testament Law* (Grand Rapids: Eerdmans, 2009), 133–34.

28. This and other Lincoln speeches are available at http://www.lincolnbicentennial.gov.

29. Walther Eichrodt, *Theology of the Old Testament*, vol. 2, trans. J. A. Baker (London: SCM Press, 1967), 321.

30. Walther Eichrodt, *Theology of the Old Testament*, vol. 1, trans. J. A. Baker (London: SCM Press, 1961), 77–82.

31. Muhammed A. Dandamayev, s.v. "Slavery (ANE)," in *Anchor Bible Dictionary*, 6:61.

32. Bruce K. Waltke, *An Old Testament Theology* (Grand Rapids: Zondervan, 2007), 721.

33. Wright, *Old Testament Ethics*, 292.

34. Sam Harris, *Letter to a Christian Nation* (New York: Alfred A. Knopf, 2006), 14.

35. Goldingay, *Israel's Life*, 460–62.

Chapter 13: Warrant for Trafficking in Humans as Farm Equipment? (II)

1. Gregory C. Chirichigno, *Debt-Slavery in Israel and the Ancient Near East*, JSOT Supplement Series 141 (Sheffield: University of Sheffield Press, 1993), 155–63.

2. Laws of Hammurabi §§199–201.

3. Walter Kaiser, "Exodus," in *The Expositor's Bible Commentary*, vol. 2, ed. Tremper Longman III and Frank C. Gaebelein (Grand Rapids: Zondervan, 2008), 433–35.

4. Cf. (New) Hittite Laws §9. This paragraph is taken from Harry A. Hoffner, Jr., "Slavery and Slave Laws in Ancient Hatti and Israel," in *Israel: Ancient Kingdom or Late Invention?*, ed. Daniel I. Block (Nashville: B&H Academic, 2008).

5. Nahum M. Sarna, *Exodus* (Philadelphia: Jewish Publication Society, 1991), 124.

6. Much in this section is taken from Douglas K. Stuart, *Exodus*, New American Commentary 2 (Nashville: B & H Publishing, 2008), 476–81.

7. Chirichigno, *Debt-Slavery in Israel*, chap. 6.

8. Martin Noth, *Leviticus: A Commentary*, trans. J. E. Anderson (Philadelphia: Westminster, 1965), 143; see also Jacob Milgrom's lengthy discussion in *Leviticus 17–22*, Anchor Yale Bible 3A (New Haven: Yale University Press, 2000), 1665–77.

9. Richard M. Davidson, *Flame of Yahweh: Sexuality in the Old Testament* (Peabody, MA: Hendrickson, 2007), 361–62.

10. Tikva Frymer-Kenski, "Anatolia and the Levant: Israel," in *A History of Ancient Near East Law*, vol. 2, ed. Raymond Westbrook (Leiden: Brill, 2003), 1034.

11. Davidson, *Flame of Yahweh*, 250.

12. David L. Baker, *Tight Fists or Open Hands? Wealth and Poverty in Old Testament Law* (Grand Rapids: Eerdmans, 2009), 182.

13. J. Daniel Hays, *From Every People and Nation: A Biblical Theology of Race* (Downers Grove, IL: InterVarsity, 2003), 69–70; "gwr" in the *New International Dictionary of Old Testament Theology and Exegesis*, ed. Willem A. VanGemeren, 5 vols. (Grand Rapids: Zondervan, 1997), 1:836–38; 3:108–9; and Baker, *Tight Fists*, 180.

14. Of course, non-Israelite religious practices like child sacrifice were not to be tolerated in Israel, even if practiced by a foreigner (Lev. 20:2).

15. Jeffrey H. Tigay, *Deuteronomy*, Torah Commentary Series (Jerusalem: Jewish Publication Society, 2003), 146.

16. See Nehemiah 4, 6, and 13 as examples of foreigners who are hostile to Israel (for example, Sanballat and Tobiah); at the end of the book Tobiah is given a room in the temple by Eliashib the priest (Neh. 13:1–8).

17. Tigay, *Deuteronomy*, 189, 380nn28–29.

18. Richard Bauckham, *The Bible in Politics: How to Read the Bible Politically* (Louisville: Westminster John Knox, 1989), 108.

19. Roy Gane, *Leviticus, Numbers*, NIV Application Commentary (Grand Rapids: Zondervan, 2004), 441–42.

20. Walter C. Kaiser, "A Principalizing Model," *in Four Views of Moving beyond the Bible to Theology*, ed. Stanley N. Gundry and Gary T. Meadors (Grand Rapids: Zondervan, 2009), 40.

21. John Goldingay, *Old Testament Theology: Israel's Life*, vol. 3 (Downers Grove, IL: InterVarsity, 2009), 464 (and note).

22. Ibid., 465–66.

23. See James K. Hoffmeier, *The Immigration Crisis: Immigrants, Aliens, and the Bible* (Wheaton: Crossway, 2009).

24. See Robert L. Hubbard Jr., "The *Go'el* in Ancient Israel: Theological Reflections on an Israelite Institution," *Bulletin of Biblical Research* 1 (1991): 3–19.

25. Chirichigno, *Debt-Slavery in Israel*, 147–48.

26. Noth, *Leviticus*, 192.

27. Frymer-Kenski, "Anatolia and the Levant: Israel," 1008–9.

28. For example, see John H. Sailhamer, *Pentateuch as Narrative* (Grand Rapids: Zondervan, 1992).

29. Baker, *Tight Fists*, 166.

30. Christopher J. H. Wright, "Response to Gordon McConville," in *Canon and Biblical Interpretation*, ed. Craig Bartholomew et al. (Grand Rapids: Zondervan, 2006), 283. See Wright's fuller explanation in this chapter.

31. Ibid.

32. Ibid.

33. Douglas Stuart, *Hosea-Jonah*, Word Biblical Commentary 31 (Waco: Word, 1987), 316–17.

Chapter 14: Warrant for Trafficking in Humans as Farm Equipment? (III)

1. For example, in the debate at Knox College in Galesburg, Illinois (October 7, 1858), Lincoln defied Douglas (or anyone) to search the world's written records from 1776 to 1855 to find "one single affirmation, from one single man, that the negro was not included in the Declaration of Independence."

2. A. A. Ruprecht, s.v. "Slave, Slavery," in *Dictionary of Paul and His Letters*, ed. Gerald Hawthome et al. (Downers Grove, IL: InterVarsity, 1993), 881–83.

3. D. B. Martin, *Slavery as Salvation: The Metaphor of Slavery in Pauline Christianity* (New Haven: Yale University, 1990), 1–49.

4. Ben Witherington III, *Conflict and Community in Corinth: A Socio-Rhetorical Commentary on 1 and 2 Corinthians* (Grand Rapids: Eerdmans; Carlisle, UK: Eerdmans, 1995), 182. Some of my comments in this section are taken from pp. 181–85.

5. James Tunstead Burtchaell, *Philemon's Problem: A Theology of Grace* (Grand Rapids: Eerdmans, 1998), 16.

6. P. T. O'Brien, *The Letter to the Ephesians*, Pillar Commentary (Grand Rapids: Eerdmans, 1999), 454.

7. See Gordon D. Fee, *1 and 2 Timothy, Titus*, NIBC 13 (Peabody, MA: Hendrickson, 1988), 45–46n, 49.

8. O'Brien, *Ephesians*, 455.

9. I. Howard Marshall, *1 Peter*, IVP New Testament Commentary (Downers Grove, IL: InterVarsity, 1991), 89–90; and Karen H. Jobes, *1 Peter*, Baker Exegetical Commentary on the New Testament (Grand Rapids: Baker Academic, 2005), 180–87.

10. See Ronald C. White's *A. Lincoln: A Biography* (New York: Random House, 2009), which explores these themes in detail.

11. Jonathan Hill, *What Has Christianity Ever Done for Us?* (Downers Grove, IL: InterVarsity, 2005), 176.

12. For a fine general discussion, see David B. Capes, Rodney Reeves, and E. Randolph Richards, *Rediscovering Paul* (Downers Grove, IL: IVP Academic, 2007), 237–41. I also borrow insights from Allen Dwight Callahan, "Paul's Epistle to Philemon: Toward an Alternative Argumentum," *The Harvard Theological Review* 86, no. 4 (October 1993): 357–76; and Sarah Winter, "Paul's Letter to Philemon," *New Testament Studies* 33 (1987): 1–15.

13. See Callahan, "Paul's Epistle to Philemon."

14. Burtchaell, *Philemon's Problem*, 21.

15. Hector Avalos's argument here ("Yahweh Is a Moral Monster," in *The Christian Delusion*, ed. John Loftus [Amherst, NY: Prometheus, 2010]) is a remarkable example of brutally twisted exegesis.

16. This famous point is taken from Luther's *Concerning Christian Liberty*.

17. Gordon D. Fee, "The Cultural Context of Ephesians 5:18–6:9," *Priscilla Papers* 16/1 (2002): 7–8.

Chapter 15: Indiscriminate Massacre and Ethnic Cleansing? (I)

1. Some material in this chapter is adapted and expanded from Paul Copan, "Yahweh Wars," *Philosophia Christi* n.s. 11, no. 1 (2009): 73–90, in which I also interact with Randal Rauser and Wes Morriston, whose essays are also found in this issue. See also Paul Copan, "Is Yahweh a Moral Monster? The New Atheists and Old Testament Ethics," *Philosophia Christi* n.s. 10, no. 1 (2008): 7–37.

2. Gerd Lüdemann, *The Unholy in the Holy Scripture*, trans. John Bowden (Louisville: Westminster John Knox, 1997), 54.

3. See G. K. Beale, *We Become What We Worship: A Biblical Theology of Idolatry* (Downers Grove, IL: InterVarsity, 2008).

4. William F. Albright, *Archaeology and the Religion of Israel* (Baltimore: Johns Hopkins Press, 1968), 77. See also Richard M. Davidson, *Footsteps of Joshua* (Hagerstown, PA: Review and Herald, 1995), 95.

5. See Stephen J. Keillor's suggestive book, *God's Judgments: Interpreting History and the Christian Faith* (Downers Grove, IL: IVP Academic, 2007).

6. Mentioned in Michael Shermer, *The Science of Good and Evil* (New York: Henry Holt, 2004), 39–40.

7. Kai Nielsen, *Ethics without God*, rev. ed. (Buffalo: Prometheus Books, 1990), 10–11.

8. "Appendix" in C. S. Lewis, *The Abolition of Man* (San Francisco: Harper, 2001).

9. Patrick Miller, *The Religion of Ancient Israel* (Louisville: Westminster John Knox, 2000), 199–201.

10. Jeffrey H. Tigay, *Deuteronomy*, Torah Commentary Series (Jerusalem: Jewish Publication Society, 2003), 146.

11. David L. Baker, *Tight Fists or Open Hands? Wealth and Poverty in Old Testament Law* (Grand Rapids: Eerdmans, 2009), 185.

12. Douglas K. Stuart, *Exodus*, New American Commentary 2 (Nashville: B & H Publishing, 2008), 478n.

13. John Goldingay, *Old Testament Theology: Israel's Life*, vol. 3 (Downers Grove, IL: InterVarsity, 2009), 618.

14. Barna Magyarosi, "Holy War and Cosmic Conflict in the Old Testament: From the Exodus to Exile" (PhD dissertation, Romanian Adventist Theological Institute), 20–26.

15. God tells the Israelites that they will not quickly drive out the nations from their presence, which would leave the land empty (Deut. 7:22); on the other hand, Israel's disobedience and idolatry would *further* slow down the process and even prove to be a snare for Israel (Josh. 23:12–13; Judg. 2:1–3).

16. Magyarosi, "Holy War," 91.

17. Ibid., 79, 82.

18. Taken from Stuart, *Exodus*, 395–97.

Chapter 16: Indiscriminate Massacre and Ethnic Cleansing? (II)

1. For example, Walter Brueggemann, *An Introduction to the Old Testament: The Canon and Christian Imagination* (Louisville: Westminster John Knox, 2003), 109–13.

2. Gordon McConville, "Joshua," in *The Oxford Bible Commentary*, ed. J. Barton and J. Muddiman (Oxford: Oxford University Press, 2001), 159.

3. David M. Howard Jr., *Joshua 5*, New American Commentary (Nashville: Broadman & Holman, 1998), 39–40.

4. Christopher J. H. Wright, *Old Testament Ethics for the People of God* (Downers Grove, IL: InterVarsity, 2004), 474–75; and Iain Provan, V. Philips Long, and Tremper Longman III, *A Biblical History of Israel* (Louisville: Westminster John Knox, 2003), 149.

5. Taken from K. A. Kitchen, *On the Reliability of the Old Testament* (Grand Rapids: Eerdmans, 2003), 173–74; and K. Lawson Younger Jr., *Ancient Conquest Accounts: A Study in Ancient Near Eastern and Biblical History Writing* (Sheffield: Sheffield Academic Press, 1990), 227–28, 245. Thanks to Matt Flanagan for tipping me off to Younger's book. And though I disagree with the postmodern themes, see Lori K. Rowlett's documentation of this rhetoric in *Joshua and the Rhetoric of Violence: A New Historical Analysis* (New York: Continuum, 1996), especially chap. 5.

6. Gordon J. Wenham, *Exploring the Old Testament: A Guide to the Pentateuch* (Downers Grove, IL: InterVarsity, 2003), 137.

7. R. Gary Millar, *Now Choose Life: Theology and Ethics in Deuteronomy* (Downers Grove, IL: InterVarsity, 2001), 157.

8. David G. Firth, *1 and 2 Samuel* (Downers Grove, IL: InterVarsity; Nottingham, UK: Apollos, 2009), 173.

9. Barna Magyarosi, "Holy War and Cosmic Conflict in the Old Testament," 138–53. Even when David fights the Amalekites (e.g., 1 Sam. 30:26), *herem* language is not applied to this.

10. Richard S. Hess, "War in the Hebrew Bible: An Overview," in *War in the Bible and Terrorism in the Twenty-First Century*, ed. Richard S. Hess and Elmer A. Martens (Winona Lake, IN: Eisenbrauns, 2008); also Richard S. Hess, *Joshua*, Tyndale Old Testament Commentary 6 (Downers Grove, IL: InterVarsity, 1996). Thanks to John Goldingay for sending me chapter 5 ("City and Nation") from *Old Testament Theology: Israel's Life*, vol. 3 (Downers Grove, IL: InterVarsity, 2009). I utilize and summarize their insights in these chapters on warfare. I am grateful too for the extensive email correspondence with Rick Hess and Tremper Longman on these themes, which I also include in these warfare chapters.

11. Hess, "War in the Hebrew Bible," 25. Gordon Mitchell mentions a certain flexibility regarding how Joshua understands *herem* (e.g., Rahab, the Gibeonites, and others are spared). See Gordon Mitchell, *Together in the Land: A Reading of the Book of Joshua*, JSOT Supplement 134 (Sheffield: JSOT, 1993).

12. Richard S. Hess, "The Jericho and Ai of the Book of Joshua," in *Critical Issues in Early Israelite History*, ed. Richard S. Hess, Gerald A. Klingbeil, and Paul J. Ray Jr. (Winona Lake, IN: Eisenbrauns, 2008), 39.

13. On the exaggeration of numbers in the ancient Near East/Old Testament, see Daniel M. Fouts, "A Defense of the Hyperbolic Interpretation of Numbers in the Old Testament," *Journal of the Evangelical Theological Society* 40, no. 3 (1997): 377–87.

14. Hess, "Jericho and Ai," 46.

15. Ibid., 33–46; also, Hess, *Joshua*.

16. Hess, "Jericho and Ai," 29–30.

17. Ibid., 35, 42.

18. Similarly, the ages of those living before the flood may be symbolical—in keeping with the ancient Near Eastern use of numbers. See R. K. Harrison, "From Adam to Noah: A Reconsideration of the Antediluvian Patriarchs' Ages," *Journal of the Evangelical Theological Society* 37, no.

2 (1994): 161–68; and Carol A. Hill, "Making Sense of the Numbers of Genesis," *Perspectives on Science and the Christian Faith* 55, no. 4 (December 2003): 239–51.

19. Hess, "Jericho and Ai," 38–39.

20. Richard Hess, personal correspondence (January 28, 2009).

21. Hess, *Joshua*, 91–92. Note the laws of Eshnunna regarding the role of innkeepers (§15, §41). See D. J. Wiseman, "Rahab of Jericho," *Tyndale Bulletin* 14 (1964): 8–11.

22. Hess, *Joshua*, 91–92. I've inserted "female" since this is what Hammurabi's text indicates. A male is *not* in view here.

23. Moshe Weinfeld, *The Promise of the Land: The Inheritance of the Land of Canaan by the Israelites* (Berkeley: University of California Press, 1993), 141–43.

24. Hess, *Joshua*, 91–92.

25. Ibid., 142–43.

26. Hess, "War in the Hebrew Bible," 29.

27. Ibid.

28. Ian Morris and Walter Scheidel, *The Dynamics of Ancient Empires: State Power from Assyria to Byzantium* (Oxford: Oxford University Press, 2009), 62.

29. Hess, "War in the Hebrew Bible," 30.

30. Though Tigay takes the former view, see his discussion in Jeffrey H. Tigay, *Deuteronomy*, Torah Commentary Series (Jerusalem: Jewish Publication Society, 2003), 474.

31. Ibid., 470; and Magyarosi, "Holy War," 110–18.

32. Goldingay, *Old Testament Theology*, 570; also Hess, "War in the Hebrew Bible," 30.

33. Hess, "War in the Hebrew Bible," 30.

34. From Nicholas Wolterstorff, "Reading Joshua," presented at "My Ways Are Not Your Ways" conference, University of Notre Dame, September 2009.

35. This section is taken from Alan R. Millard, "Were the Israelites Really Canaanites?" in *Israel: Ancient Kingdom or Late Invention?*, ed. Daniel I. Block (Nashville: B&H Academic, 2008), 156–68.

36. James K. Hoffmeier, *Israel in Egypt: The Evidence for the Authenticity of the Exodus Tradition* (Oxford: Oxford University Press, 1999); James K. Hoffmeier, *Ancient Israel in Sinai: The Evidence for the Authenticity of the Wilderness Tradition* (Oxford: Oxford University Press, 2005).

Chapter 17: Indiscriminate Massacre and Ethnic Cleansing? (III)

1. For example, Karen Armstrong makes this Crusade-Canaanite connection in her book *Holy War: The Crusades and Their Impact on Today's World* (New York: Anchor, 2001).

2. John Goldingay, *Old Testament Theology: Israel's Life*, vol. 3 (Downers Grove, IL: InterVarsity, 2009), 572.

3. Christopher J. H. Wright, *The God I Don't Understand: Reflections on Tough Questions of Faith* (Grand Rapids: Zondervan, 2008), 102. Cf. Joshua 16:53; 2 Samuel 5:6–10. Wright says that the Jebusites moved from the "hit list" to the "home list," an indication that these enemy nations could be incorporated into God's people.

4. Richard S. Hess, "War in the Hebrew Bible: An Overview," in *War in the Bible and Terrorism in the Twenty-First Century*, ed. Richard S. Hess and Elmer A. Martens (Winona Lake, IN: Eisenbrauns, 2008), 29.

5. For a penetrating analysis of My Lai, see chapter 6 in M. Scott Peck, *People of the Lie* (New York: Simon & Schuster, 1983).

6. John Stott's response in David Edwards, *Evangelical Essentials: A Liberal-Evangelical Dialogue* (Downers Grove, IL: InterVarsity, 1988), 263.

7. Lee made this statement during the Battle of Fredericksburg in December 1862.

8. From *The Fellowship of the Ring*, directed by Peter Jackson (New Line Cinema, 2001), based on J. R .R. Tolkien's work by the same title.

9. Vernon Grounds, "Called to Be Saints—Not Well-Adjusted Sinners," *Christianity Today* (January 17, 1986), 28.

10. Paul K. Moser, *The Elusive God: Reorienting Religious Epistemology* (Cambridge: Cambridge University Press, 2008), 91–92.

11. Goldingay, *Israel's Life*, 569. I address the specific question of Abraham's sacrifice of Isaac in *"How Do You Know You're Not Wrong?"* (Grand Rapids: Baker, 2005).

12. Thanks to Alvin Plantinga for his insights in his "Response to Fales" paper presented at the "My Ways Are Not Your Ways" conference, University of Notre Dame, September 2009.

13. Miroslav Volf, *Free of Charge: Giving and Forgiving in a Culture Stripped of Grace* (Grand Rapids: Zondervan, 2006), 138–39; see also Volf's *Exclusion and Embrace: A Theological Exploration of Identity, Otherness, and Reconciliation* (Nashville: Abingdon, 1996).

14. Paul K. Moser, "Divine Hiddenness, Death, and Meaning," in *Philosophy of Religion: Classic and Contemporary Issues* (Oxford: Blackwell, 2008), 221–22.

15. C. S. Lewis, "Miracles," in *The Complete C. S. Lewis Signature Classics* (San Francisco: Harper, 2002), 383–84.

16. C. S. Lewis, *Surprised by Joy* (New York: Harcourt Brace & World, 1955), 166.

17. C. S. Lewis, "The Obstinacy of Belief," in *The World's Last Night* (New York: Harcourt Brace Jovanovich, 1960), 25–27.

18. From Mark Murphy, who kindly sent me his essay "God beyond Justice."

19. Murphy, "God beyond Justice," inspired these thoughts.

20. From *The Two Towers*, directed by Peter Jackson (New Line Cinema, 2002), based on J. R .R. Tolkien's work by the same title.

21. William Cowper, "God Moves in a Mysterious Way," 1774. This hymn can be found online at http://nethymnal.org/htm/g/m/gmovesmw.htm.

22. Michael Card, "This Must Be the Lamb," *Legacy*, compact disc, Benson Productions, B00004RC04, 1983.

Chapter 18: The Root of All Evil?

1. Mark Juergensmeyer, *Terror in the Mind of God* (Berkeley: University of California Press, 2000), 242, 159, 243.

2. Regina Schwartz, *The Curse of Cain* (Chicago: University of Chicago Press, 1997), 63.

3. Richard Dawkins, *The God Delusion* (Boston: Houghton Mifflin, 2006), 37.

4. In this chapter, I'll be following Mirsoslav Volf, "Christianity and Violence," in *War in the Bible and Violence in the Twenty-First Century*, ed. Richard S. Hess and Elmer A. Martens (Winona Lake, IN: Eisenbrauns, 2008); and R. W. L. Moberly, "Is Monotheism Bad for You? Some Reflections on God, the Bible, and Life in the Light of Regina Schwartz's *The Curse of Cain*," in *The God of Israel* (Cambridge: Cambridge University Press, 2007), 94–112.

5. Volf, "Christianity and Violence," 8.

6. This poem can be found online at ChristianHistory.net, "Fanny Crosby," August 8, 2008, http://www.christianitytoday.com/ch/131christians/poets/crosby.html.

7. Volf, "Christianity and Violence," 13.

8. C. S. Lewis, *The Problem of Pain* (New York: Macmillan, 1962), 118–19.

9. See my three chapters on Yahweh wars and Islamic jihad in Paul Copan, *When God Goes to Starbucks: A Guide to Everyday Apologetics* (Grand Rapids: Baker, 2008).

10. For documentation on Islam's track record, see Bat Ye'or, *The Decline of Eastern Christianity under Islam: From Jihad to Dhimmitude* (Teaneck, NJ: Farleigh Dickinson University Press, 1997); *The Dhimmi: Jews and Christians under Islam* (Teaneck, NJ: Farleigh Dickinson University Press, 1985); and *Islam and Dhimmitude: Where Civilizations Collide* (Teaneck, NJ: Farleigh Dickinson University Press, 2002).

11. Bernard Lewis, *The Crisis of Islam: Holy War and Unholy Terror* (New York: Modern Library, 2003), 37–38.

12. Again, see the chapters on Islamic jihad and Yahweh wars in Copan, *When God Goes to Starbucks*.

13. Norman Anderson, "Islam," in *The World's Religions*, 4th ed. (Downers Grove, IL: InterVarsity, 1975), 128.

14. From Michael Cromartie's interview with Ye'or, "The Myth of Islamic Tolerance," in *Books and Culture* 4, no. 5 (September–October 1998): 38, www.christianitytoday.com/bc/8b5/8b5038.html.

15. Ibid.

Chapter 19: Morality without a Lawgiving God?

1. Cited in Michael Novak, *No One Sees God* (New York: Doubleday, 2007), 76.

2. Sam Harris, "The Myth of Secular Moral Chaos," *Council for Secular Humanism*, www .secularhumanism.org/index.php?section=library&page=sharris_26_3 (accessed September 19, 2009).

3. Daniel Dennett, *Breaking the Spell: Religion as a Natural Phenomenon* (New York: Viking, 2006), 305.

4. Richard Dawkins, *The Root of All Evil?* directed by Russell Barnes (BBC, 2006).

5. Richard Dawkins, *River out of Eden: A Darwinian View of Life* (New York: Basic Books/HarperCollins, 1995), 132–33.

6. Richard Dawkins, *A Devil's Chaplain* (Boston: Houghton & Mifflin, 2003), 34.

7. Daniel Dennett, though he claims to believe in objective morality, oddly rejects intrinsic human rights, which would be the basis for the obligation to show respect to others. He calls such rights "nonsense upon stilts": Daniel Dennett, *Darwin's Dangerous Idea* (New York: Simon & Schuster, 1995), 507.

8. Dawkins, *River out of Eden*, 133.

9. Guenter Lewy, *Why America Needs Religion* (Grand Rapids: Eerdmans, 1996), 137.

10. Malcolm Muggeridge, "Me and Myself," in *Jesus Rediscovered* (New York: Pyramid Publications, 1969), 157.

11. Letter (July 3, 1881) to Wm. G. Down, *The Life and Letters of Charles Darwin*, ed. Francis Darwin (London: John Murray, Abermarle Street, 1887), 1:315–16.

12. Michael Ruse and E. O. Wilson, "The Evolution of Ethics," in *Religion and the Natural Sciences*, ed. J. E. Huchingson (Orlando: Harcourt Brace, 1993), 310–11.

13. Michael Shermer, *The Science of Good and Evil* (New York: Henry Holt, 2004), 57.

14. C. S. Lewis, *Miracles* (New York: Macmillan, 1960), 37.

15. Ibid., 38, 37.

16. Ruse and Wilson, "The Evolution of Ethics," 311.

17. Michael Ruse, *The Darwinian Paradigm* (London: Routledge, 1989), 262, 268.

18. Randy Thornhill and Craig T. Palmer, *A Natural History of Rape: Biological Bases of Sexual Coercion* (Cambridge, MA: MIT Press, 2000).

Chapter 20: We Have Moved beyond This God (Haven't We?)

1. John Adams, *The Works of John Adams, Second President of the United States: with a Life of the Author, Notes and Illustrations, by his Grandson Charles Francis Adams*, vol. 9 (Boston: Little, Brown, and Co., 1856). Available at http://oll.libertyfund.org/index.php?option=com_staticxt&staticfile=show.php&title=2107.

2. Thomas Cahill, *The Gifts of the Jews* (New York: Anchor, 1999).

3. Walter Sinnot-Armstrong, *Morality without God* (Oxford: Oxford University Press, 2009), 154.

4. Jonathan Hill, *What Has Christianity Ever Done for Us?* (Downers Grove, IL: InterVarsity, 2005), 176–77. For thorough documentation on these phenomena, see Alvin J. Schmidt, *How Christianity Changed the World* (Grand Rapids: Zondervan, 2004).

5. Jaroslav Pelikan, *Jesus through the Centuries* (New York: Harper & Row, 1985), 33.

6. Richard Dawkins, *The God Delusion* (Boston: Houghton Mifflin, 2006), 37.

7. Rodney Stark, *The Victory of Reason* (New York: Random House, 2005), xi.

8. Jürgen Habermas, *Time of Transitions*, ed. and trans. Ciaran Cronin and Max Pensky (Cambridge: Polity, 2006), 150–51.

9. Max Stackhouse, "A Christian Perspective on Human Rights," *Society* (January/February 2004): 25.

10. Ibid., 24. See also Max L. Stackhouse and Stephen E. Healey, "Religion and Human Rights: A Theological Apologetic," in *Religious Rights in Global Perspective*, ed. J. Witte Jr. and J. D. van der Vyer (Dordrecht: Kluwer, 1996), 486; and Mary Ann Glendon, *The World Made New: Eleanor Roosevelt and the Universal Declaration of Human Rights* (New York: Random House, 2001).

11. David Aikman, *Jesus in Beijing: How Christianity Is Transforming China and Changing the Global Balance of Power* (Washington, DC: Regnery, 2003), 5. This quotation serves as an exclamation point to round out Rodney Stark's study, *The Victory of Reason: How Christianity Led to Freedom, Capitalism and Western Success* (New York: Random House, 2005), 235.

12. Tim Keller, "Reason for God," *The Explorer* (Veritas Forum) (Fall 2008), www.veritas .org/explorer/fall2008.html#story1.

Paul Copan (PhD, Marquette University) is the Pledger Family Chair of Philosophy and Ethics at Palm Beach Atlantic University in Florida. He is the author or editor of over twenty apologetics and philosophy books and lives with his wife and five children in Florida.

Answers to Today's Faith Challenges

"TRUE FOR YOU BUT NOT FOR ME"

Overcoming Objections to Christian Faith

PAUL COPAN

"Here are incisive and insightful responses to many of the most common misconceptions about Christianity and faith. I'm thankful for Paul Copan's uncanny ability to see through popular opinion and focus on answers that make sense."

—Lee Strobel, author of *The Case for Christ*

BETHANYHOUSE
a division of Baker Publishing Group
www.BethanyHouse.com

Available wherever books and ebooks are sold.

Guidance for Coffeehouse Conversations about God

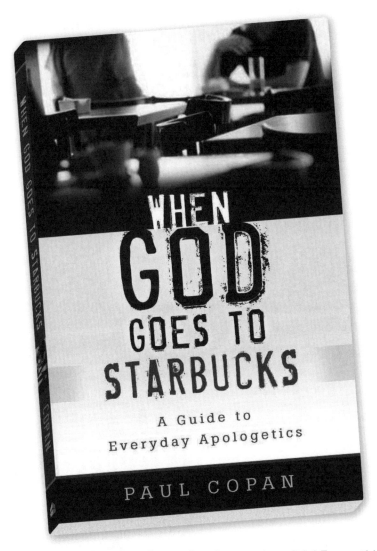

"If you want sound apologetics made relevant—here it is! From ethics to eschatology, Dr. Copan provides clear, orthodox, practical, accessible, and necessary answers to questions that stymie seekers and galvanize skeptics against historic Christianity."

—Hank Hanegraaff, president, Christian Research Institute; host, *Bible Answer Man* **broadcast**

Also by PAUL COPAN

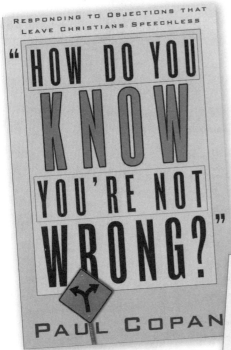